MW00534766

THE
HAMMER

THE HAMMER

POWER, INEQUALITY, AND THE STRUGGLE FOR THE SOUL OF LABOR

HAMILTON NOLAN

hachette
BOOKS

New York

Copyright © 2024 by Hamilton Nolan
Cover design by Amanda Hudson/Faceout Studio
Cover copyright © 2024 by Hachette Book Group, Inc.

Hachette Book Group supports the right to free expression and the value of copyright. The purpose of copyright is to encourage writers and artists to produce the creative works that enrich our culture.

The scanning, uploading, and distribution of this book without permission is a theft of the author's intellectual property. If you would like permission to use material from the book (other than for review purposes), please contact permissions@hbgusa.com. Thank you for your support of the author's rights.

Hachette Books
Hachette Book Group
1290 Avenue of the Americas
New York, NY 10104
HachetteBooks.com
Twitter.com/HachetteBooks
Instagram.com/HachetteBooks

First Edition: February 2024

Published by Hachette Books, an imprint of Hachette Book Group, Inc. The Hachette Books name and logo is a trademark of the Hachette Book Group.

The Hachette Speakers Bureau provides a wide range of authors for speaking events. To find out more, go to hachettespeakersbureau.com or email HachetteSpeakers@hbgusa.com.

Books by Hachette Books may be purchased in bulk for business, educational, or promotional use. For information, please contact your local bookseller or Hachette Book Group Special Markets Department at: special.markets@hbgusa.com.

The publisher is not responsible for websites (or their content) that are not owned by the publisher.

Print book interior design by Amy Quinn.

Library of Congress Cataloging-in-Publication Data

Names: Nolan, Hamilton, author.
Title: The hammer: power, inequality, and the struggle for the soul of
  labor / Hamilton Nolan.
Description: First edition. | New York: Hachette Books, 2024. | Includes index.
Identifiers: LCCN 2023037397 | ISBN 9780306830921 (hardcover) | ISBN
  9780306830945 (ebook)
Subjects: LCSH: Equality. | Labor movement. | Labor—Political aspects.
Classification: LCC HM821 .N65 2024 | DDC 331.8—dc23/eng/20230911
LC record available at https://lccn.loc.gov/2023037397

ISBNs: 978-0-306-83092-1 (hardcover), 978-0-306-83094-5 (ebook)

Printed in the United States of America

LSC-C

Printing 1, 2023

To my parents, who taught me about movements.

"I have seen
The old gods go
And the new gods come.

Day by day
And year by year
The idols fall
And the idols rise.

Today
I worship the hammer."

—*Carl Sandburg*

CONTENTS

THE
HAMMER

INTRODUCTION

My parents were sixties people. My dad, who grew up in Queens, went to the University of Virginia for a single year before dropping out to become a civil rights worker. He met my mom in Atlanta, where they both worked on an underground newspaper called the *Great Speckled Bird*. If you want to needle my mom, you can say she was a hippie. She'll get a stern look and reply, "We weren't hippies, we were *activists*."

In Atlanta, my dad was, among other things, a member of The October League, part of the wide universe of radical left-wing splinter groups that emerged when the idealism of the '60s exploded into the harder ideological shrapnel of the '70s. He talks about those days as a time when righteousness bled into farce. For example, because the group was monitored by the FBI, its meetings were held in secret locations. A car would come and pick people up and deliver them to the chosen, undisclosed spot. One day, the group rented a hotel meeting room for one of its secret assemblies. When the car delivering the members pulled up to the hotel, they looked up and saw a message on the hotel's large overhead sign: "WELCOME, OCTOBER LEAGUE!"

Still, the commitment necessary to be a true radical in 1970s Georgia was not inconsiderable. They were beaten up by rednecks while trying to sell them the Communist newspaper outside of factory gates, an example of the perils of overestimating your audience. The October League members were themselves required to get factory jobs, so as to be embedded in the proletariat and help them organize. (This tactic was in contrast to their counterparts who split off to form the Weather Underground, which was more inclined toward bombing than labor organizing.) My mom worked at a Sophie Mae peanut brittle factory. To this day, the smell of peanut brittle turns her stomach. My dad worked at a Nabisco factory. He has many happy memories of eating the world's freshest Ritz cracker right as it emerged from the oven, and of carting home free boxes of canned beef stew that had been "damaged" by coworkers purposely slamming the boxes on the ground. He was the type of guy who would read a book while on the line at the factory, but the work suited him.

The Nabisco factory had a union. Not unusual for the time, the union was racist. In August 1972, after a Black employee was unjustly fired from the plant, 250 of the Nabisco workers walked out in a wildcat strike. That group was made up of almost all the Black workers, along with a handful of white workers, including my dad. The union, long controlled by whites, refused to support the strike. But after three weeks of picketing, the company agreed to rehire all the striking workers and make at least some gestures toward addressing discrimination in the plant.

My dad ended up working at Nabisco for five years. "They would always say, 'Do what we want or we'll close the plant and move elsewhere,'" he remembers. In August 2021, almost a half century after that wildcat strike, Nabisco workers across the country went on strike again, trying desperately to hold on to a minimal middle-class lifestyle. But the Atlanta Nabisco factory was not among the strikers—it had closed for good just months earlier. Its parent company moved those jobs overseas. Some things never change.

=

I GREW UP HEARING STORIES OF THE *GREAT SPECKLED BIRD* AND THE CIVIL rights movement in the way that some kids grow up hearing about their dad's high school football games. It instilled in me a consciousness of the need to fight to make things better. Later, I fell into journalism, attracted more by its promise of a platform from which to yell about who society's villains are than by any sort of literary inclinations. Being a serviceable writer was also my only marketable skill. It was either journalism, or back to the kitchen at the pizza restaurant.

I moved to New York City and, in 2008, caught on with Gawker .com, which was very much my kind of publication. Gawker gave us, its wild-eyed and confrontational writers, a combo deal that was hard to find: it was widely read, and it offered near-total freedom to write whatever we wanted. It was great. Gawker became the devilish conscience of the New York media, vaguely disreputable but honest. It was the place that would publish what others wouldn't, and would say the things that others thought but felt constrained from saying by fear of professional fallout. It was anarchist journalism at its finest. For the type of writer who aspired not to work at the *New York Times*, but rather to gripe about why the *New York Times* was a bunch of dweebs, it was the best possible place to be.

While others at Gawker wrote most of the gossip and scoops that brought in big traffic, I coasted along indulging my passion for class war. I published letters from death row inmates and ran a forty-week-long series of first-person stories from unemployed people after the 2008 recession. I published letters from employees at Amazon, Target, and other big companies describing how terrible their workplaces were. And I became Gawker's de facto labor reporter, writing about union drives and union busting as part of the larger mission to promote the concept of Eating the Rich.

Gawker's parent company, Gawker Media, was one of several online media startups that had grown from shoestring operations into full-fledged profitable companies without ever stopping to build a lot of the workaday stuff that mature companies take for granted. We had a lavish roof deck at the office, but no system of getting regular raises; big parties with open bars, but no functional system of internal communication; a pancake machine in the kitchen, but no severance pay. All major company decisions were made inside the mysterious mind of the owner. He smoked a lot of weed. It was fun for a while, but it didn't give any of us a great sense of career stability.

I had written a story about how Vice Media, one of our competitors, was a bad place to work—employees there told me about its awful low pay and casual mistreatment. In April 2015, I met with Ursula Lawrence, a union organizer from the Writers Guild of America, East, at a bar in SoHo near my office. She wanted to know if I could give her any good contacts for people who worked at Vice. The union had decided to try to organize the online media industry, focusing on Vice, but they were having a hard time getting any traction. As we talked, the absurdity of the conversation crept up on me.

"Why don't you try organizing us?" I said at last. "We're better than Vice."

"Sure!" she said. So I went home and made a Facebook invite for a meeting at the union's office a couple of days later, and sent it randomly to fifty people I worked with. I had no idea if anyone would show up. On the appointed day, forty people came. We sat around a huge conference room table, and everyone vented about what they wanted to change about Gawker Media. This happened routinely in the form of private grumbling sent via instant message, but never had it taken place in a structured way, as a group. We decided to do it.

The next day, we had an all-hands meeting in the office to introduce the union effort. Because nothing could ever stay secret at Gawker for long, we also announced the whole thing to the world, with a blog post titled "Why We've Decided to Organize." Our owner, Nick Denton, said he would abide by whatever choice we made. We ran a union campaign that has been referred to as "non-traditional," but which was fully in line with the Gawker style of talking about everything openly. We even published a post and asked employees to use the comment section to weigh in, saying how they planned to vote on the union and why. I later learned that this tactic nearly gave the professional union organizers heart attacks. But to this day, other organizers still ask me to dig up that post and share it with them. It was one of the only times anyone had ever seen a union drive conducted publicly—laid out for readers to follow along with. There was a lot of arguing. That was, for us, very normal.

In early June, we voted "Yes" by a 3–1 margin, becoming the first major online media company to unionize. It was only six weeks after I sent that Facebook invite, and four months after the *Washington Post* had published an explainer story headlined "Why Internet journalists don't organize." Heh.

For a while, Gawker Media was the darling of the labor movement. We were seen as the "hip" and "young" and internet-savvy new generation of pro-union workers, though many of us were neither hip nor particularly young. I got invited to speak on stage at the AFL-CIO convention. I got invited to speak to various union groups. I got invited to speak on a panel at the White House, during a daylong event that the Obama administration threw for organized labor, as a consolation prize for not passing any laws that might help it. All was well, until it wasn't.

The workers at Gawker secured our first union contract just in time. Shortly after we signed it, the company was bankrupted by a lawsuit from professional wrestler Hulk Hogan—a lawsuit funded by right-wing tech billionaire Peter Thiel, who said he was mad that we had published the fact that he was gay (an open secret in Silicon Valley), but who was actually mad that we had relentlessly made fun of his failed hedge fund and insane political beliefs. Our company was sold to Univision, and Gawker.com itself, perceived as being politically radioactive, was shut down. But the employees were not laid off, and we all kept our salaries, thanks to that union contract.

The whole media industry watched Gawker unionize. And, as one, reporters everywhere said to themselves: "That is obviously a good idea." Other online media companies began joining us in the WGAE at a rapid clip. Salon unionized. So did HuffPost. So did Slate, and Vox, and Vice, the original target. Another long-standing media union, the News Guild, amped up its media organizing efforts too. Within a few years, media was considered one of the most active pro-union industries in the country. It all started with a bunch of people who realized that we needed more than a pancake machine to have a career.

=

MY IMMERSION INTO UNIONS FELT LIKE FINALLY GRASPING THE RIGHT TOOL after rummaging around in a toolbox for years. I did not start out as a writer interested in organized labor; I started out as a writer interested in why America was so fucked up. Why did we have such gargantuan levels of inequality? Why were thousands of homeless people living in the streets of cities where billionaires frolicked in penthouses? Why was it that certain classes of people worked hard their entire lives and stayed poor, just as their parents had been, and just as their children seemed doomed to be? Even while labor unions had fallen almost completely out of the public mind, it turned out that they were central to all our most fundamental problems.

I was born in 1979. Ronald Reagan took office when I was just a few months old. The biggest story of my lifetime is that the rich have gotten richer, and the rest of us haven't. Another way to say this is that, since 1980, the hourly compensation of the average American worker has stayed almost flat, even as their productivity has risen by 75 percent. During that same time, the share of national wealth held by the top 0.00001 percent of American earners—the richest of the rich—has increased by 1,000 percent.

The Occupy movement was widely derided for lacking any concrete goals, but it did have one very real accomplishment: it cemented the importance of inequality in the mainstream consciousness. The steady rise in inequality since the Reagan era has made the classic "American dream" of a single income supporting a middle-class lifestyle an impossible fantasy for most. And as everyone has had to work harder to try to earn the same amount, pensions have disappeared, education costs have skyrocketed, and the "gig economy" has gone a fair way toward its goal of eradicating the classic model of full-time employment. There are a lot of factors that conspired to give us the rise of Trumpism. The biggest one is the fact that inequality has grown so severe that it is destroying the fundamental belief that American society works.

In the broadest terms, there are only two ways to reverse our poisonous level of inequality. One way is for the government to do it—by aggressively taxing the rich, aggressively supplementing the incomes of the rest of us, and aggressively regulating capitalism. If you believe that will happen any time soon, you are far more optimistic than I am. (The government's tendency to do the opposite of all these things is how we got here in the first place.) The other way to fix inequality is for working people, who make up the vast majority of the population, to increase their own power so that they can reclaim their rightful share of the nation's wealth. The only mechanism for doing this is organized labor.

Once I grasped this, I realized that unions—neglected, decrepit, and forgotten though they were—are the single most important tool that exists to fix our single most important problem.

At the peak of organized labor's power in the 1950s, one in three American workers was a union member. Today, that number is one in ten. The decades-long decline in union membership is a mirror image of the decades-long rise in inequality. The primary reason for the decline of the union is that business interests understand very well the power unions create. They have engaged politicians for decades to undertake systematic legal and regulatory assaults that have made it impossible for many people to join unions, and extremely difficult for unions to sustain themselves in many parts of the country. The political battle to reinvent our broken and anti-worker labor law system is ongoing. It will be ongoing for a long time. If the labor movement ties its fate solely to that battle, it will die while it's waiting to win.

An additional reason for the decline of unions, however, is that many unions have more or less stopped trying. Rather than seeing the tens of millions of workers who could be organized as an urgent priority, the institutions of organized labor have, to a large degree, contented themselves with tending to the small and shrinking walled gardens of their existing membership. The urge to dedicate everything to organizing new members—the only thing that will extend the power of unions to enough people to bend the curve of inequality back toward sanity—remains a niche position in the union world. Instead of being the dominant guiding principle, it is confined to ideological pockets. Many labor leaders find it easy to preside over slow decline as long as that decline isn't severe enough to put them out of a job. If it stays that way, broad defeat is only a matter of time. The frogs in the pot may pretend the water isn't boiling, but it will get them eventually, sure as hell.

Here is the other thing to understand about organized labor: it should be at the center of American politics. Which is to say that politicians and political policies should exist as planets that revolve around a sun of a strong, mobilized, coherent labor movement. This is such a foreign notion to most Americans (and even to many union officials!) that they have never even considered it for a single second. In our country, politics is typically seen as a made-for-television contest between red and blue teams, a hopelessly corrupt feeding frenzy for the rich and powerful that provides little more than entertainment to the rest of us. More recently, it has become conventional wisdom that America suffers from an unbridgeable gap between red and blue states, two separate political cultures that can agree on nothing and have become entrenched and opposing armies. Unions, when they are thought of at all, are thought of as just one of a constellation of special interests. In fact, organizing people not as voters, but as workers, is the start of the path toward breaking out of this artificial political divide, and bringing elected officials to heel on behalf of the working class. It can be done. It is being done, in certain places. It just needs to be done much, much more.

This is a book about how, and whether, the labor movement can save America. It is about the dizzying potential of organized labor, as well as the heartbreaking flaws that hold it back. It is about one extraordinary person's frustrating quest to become a leader of this movement, and about many, many extraordinary people's unsung acts of courage in their own workplaces across the country. A strike; an ambitious campaign that took decades; a small group of workers in an uphill battle to organize; a union that has a successful formula to turn labor power into political power; the people desperately trying to keep unions alive in an anti-union state. These are the chapters in this book—the building blocks that, taken together, show what the labor movement is, and what it can be. This book is not a survey of every important union, or an encyclopedia of every worthy activist. Rather, it tells a small number of stories that illustrate a single point: the success or failure of the labor movement is absolutely central to the success or failure of the American experiment. If you have never given that proposition too much thought, I hope that this book will make you do so.

One of the greatest things about unions is that they are a tool that belongs to *you*. You! You may be an average person in an average place with an average job. You may not be rich or famous or influential or well-connected. But starting right at your unremarkable workplace, you can become part of something capable of exercising power beyond your wildest belief. You can do something historic. You can start a union. You can lead a strike. You can force enormous companies to listen; you can compel exalted politicians to bow to the demands of normal folks. Your labor is your weapon. It is your hammer. A better America is right there. It's waiting for you, and for all of us, to act.

CHAPTER ONE

SARA NELSON GOES TO WASHINGTON

"Labor unions offer a perfect arena for the use of all the arts in
the game of politics. Their struggles are the most bitter, skillful,
and cut-throat of any to be seen in this country. Civic politics reach
their peak only at intervals; labor politics continue incessantly."

—Communists Within the Labor Movement, *a pamphlet
by the United States Chamber of Commerce, 1947*

O n a sunny July day in 2021, Sara Nelson went for a run. As she made her way down a dirt road in Oregon, she tripped and fell. That stumble may have changed the history of the American labor movement.

At the time, it seemed like just another damn thing in a year of grinding health annoyances. In January, Nelson had gotten a nasty case of Covid and was sick in bed for weeks. The brain fog and trouble concentrating afterward persisted for months. During that time, she was also dealing with tooth problems that required several trips to the orthodontist for painful dental work. And now, under the blue skies and towering trees of her home state, where she had gone for a rare vacation, she lay sprawled on the ground, with scrapes and cuts on her hands and legs.

The cuts would heal, but as the days went on, Nelson felt a persistent pain where she had banged her right hip. It hurt to walk, and it hurt to sit. That was bad because she was always on the move. When she finally went and saw an orthopedist, tests revealed a degenerative condition in her hip, slowly eroding the strength of her bones. On August 31, she had surgery on her right hip. Then came a long and frustrating confinement. First, she couldn't move much at all; then, there were weeks in a wheelchair; then months more on crutches. There was physical therapy, and there was pain, and, through-out, pain meds that made it hard for her to concentrate and work. As fall 2021 turned to winter, Nelson was deep in a grueling recovery.

By December, she was beginning to feel whole again. When Christmas came, she and her family traveled from their Maryland home back to Ore-gon to see Nelson's mother. While she was there, an ominous pain began throbbing in her other hip.

Sara Nelson did not have a happy New Year's 2022. More trips to her doctors revealed that her left hip—left unexamined during all the work to fix her right hip—had the same degenerative condition, only worse. In early January, she had full hip replacement surgery on the left side. Back to the pain meds, and the physical therapy, and the constant discomfort. From the coldest depths of Feb-ruary, she could look backward at six months dominated by hip surgeries, which themselves followed six months dominated by other nagging health issues.

This does not mean that Nelson was not working the whole time.

She never really stopped working, from morning to night to weekend, on her phone and on Zoom and in TV interviews. But she was not work-ing the way she wanted to. Nelson was a career flight attendant who had become the head of the flight attendants' union, and she was used to flying around the country as casually as most people drive to the grocery store. Had she never stumbled and fallen on that trail on the first day of July, her hip condition might have remained hidden from her for years—hidden enough to ignore, at least. Instead, her bones threw up their red flags when they did, and her plans were harshly rearranged.

During those agonizing months of surgery and recovery, she still managed to do her job running her union. She had played an instrumental role in winning $40 billion in payroll support for airline workers in the 2020 Covid relief bills, and was constantly on the phone with elected officials. She still managed to do countless TV hits, propped in a chair in her home office, talking to cable news hosts about mask mandates and drunk airline passengers and the Biden administration's Build Back Better bill and everything else that fell in the broad, telegenic niche she had carved out as one of the media's go-to interviews on virtually anything pertaining to the airline industry or worker rights. She still talked to her board and her lawyers and her union members and her staff and all the reporters constantly asking her for quotes. But with all her unexpected burdens, she was not able to dedicate much time to the other project she had planned to be working on during those months: laying the groundwork to run for the presidency of the AFL-CIO, America's largest union coalition. That project was, in essence, to become the leader of the labor movement and save America. It was the biggest project of all.

You can imagine an alternate world in which Sara Nelson never tripped and fell during that jog. In that world, she came back from her run blissfully unaware of her slowly crumbling hip bones, which held on long enough to delay any surgeries for a couple of years. She spent the second half of 2021 and the first half of 2022 doing the delicate diplomatic dance of wooing the presidents of various major unions who ultimately cast the votes that decide who becomes the head of the AFL-CIO. She launched a simultaneous public campaign to harness the latent grassroots energy of millions of union members who were hungry for the sort of fiery, fighting leader that the labor movement has not had for decades. With this inside-outside strategy, a blitz of media coverage, nonstop barnstorming around the country, and some savvy backroom politicking, she secured just enough support to beat out the staid incumbent in a closely divided vote at the AFL-CIO convention in June 2022, instantly becoming the nation's most powerful and recognizable labor leader. Rallying the left wing of organized labor and the Democratic Party to her cause, she began ushering in a program of reforms that took advantage of America's post-pandemic spirit of activism and enabled new, large-scale organizing campaigns that halted the seventy-year decline of union membership once and for all. The tide had finally turned in the nation's long and brutal war against worker power. Huzzah!

That alternate world was not fanciful. In the shiny early summer of 2021, it was all so very plausible. But in the real world, things happened. By February 2022, Sara Nelson was four months away from the AFL-CIO convention, recovering from her second hip surgery and watching her window for building internal political support shrink by the day. She was forced to ask herself what her options really were. With fate being what it was, both she and the entire US labor movement set out on a different path.

NELSON HAS COIFFED BLOND HAIR, WHITE TEETH, AND EXPERTLY DONE makeup. She often wears silk scarves twisted around her neck in public appearances, in a visual nod to the uniform she wore when she worked flights for United. The *New York Times* once wrote that "she looks like a young Catherine Deneuve," which is true, but she really looks like something less obscure—the very image of the small-town all-American girl who grew up to become a flight attendant. That she has become much more than that is a testament to her ability to navigate the cruel bargain offered to attractive women in public life: doors are opened, but they lead into rooms where everyone will underestimate you.

The Association of Flight Attendants, which Nelson has led since 2014, has about fifty thousand members. That means it is on the smaller side of the AFL-CIO's sixty member unions, the largest of which have well over a million members. It is not intuitive that the head of a small and lesser-known union might aspire to vault directly into the biggest chair in the labor world. But Bernie Sanders came from Vermont, and Barack Obama was a little-known state senator a few years before he became president, and if American politics were mathematically rational, our nation would be a very different place. Union politics are no different. Whereas AFL-CIO presidents have historically been, for the most part, white male insiders, Nelson's ambition was to see if charisma and conviction could turn that around.

Nelson had been a union activist since the turn of the century, but she only shot to national prominence in 2019 during what became the longest federal government shutdown in history. Prompted by a typically deranged case of Trumpian brinkmanship over the border wall, the shutdown began on December 22, 2018, and dragged on into the new year. Eight hundred thousand federal workers were either furloughed or working for weeks with no pay. That burden fell heavily on air traffic controllers and TSA security workers, all of whom were expected to continue showing up on the job to keep air travel running smoothly, receiving no paychecks as the political spat continued. Those workers are legally prohibited from striking, and their unions were disinclined to do anything so radical as flout federal law.

On January 20, Nelson gave a speech at an AFL-CIO dinner, where she was accepting the MLK Drum Major for Justice Award. She took the opportunity to pound the table and tell the assembled crowd of union officials that they needed to do more: "Almost a million workers are locked out or being forced to work without pay. Others are going to work when our workspace is increasingly unsafe. What is the labor movement waiting for?" she asked. "Go back with the fierce urgency of *now* to talk with your locals and international unions about all workers joining together—to end this shutdown with a general strike."

A call for a general strike from a major labor leader who really appeared to mean it was the sort of thing not heard much since the middle of the twentieth century. Her demand went viral, and she was transformed almost immediately from the head of a medium-sized aviation industry union into a national political figure. Nelson's speech was not just some feel-good utopian wish, but a canny and calculated grenade tossed into an ongoing political battle. She was careful to absolve the powerful public sector unions themselves of the sole responsibility for escalating on behalf of their members, saying, "Federal sector unions have their hands full caring for the 800,000 federal workers who are at the tip of the spear. Some would say the answer is for them to walk off the job. I say, 'what are *you* willing to do?'" With that, the union world was able to receive the radical appeal for a general strike as a shared aspiration—freeing each individual union from the onus of actually having to prove itself by doing something.

Negotiations are a game of chicken. Vague threats that you never have to carry out, but that the other side believes you *might* carry out, are the essence of skillful negotiating. In late January 2019, the length of the government shutdown had already rendered the functioning of airports fragile, as workers grew more and more pissed off with their lack of pay. Republicans and business interests were nervous that severe cracks in America's aviation system could begin to show any day. In that environment, the mere possibility of a widespread labor action (along with Nelson's continued pointed remarks about "concern for our members' safety and security," barely coded threats that flight attendants could refuse to come to work) was a marvelously effective tool for instilling fear in those prolonging the shutdown.

On January 23, a coalition of airline unions including the AFA put out an ominous statement saying that "we cannot even calculate the level of risk currently at play, nor predict the point at which the entire system will break." Two days later, on the morning of January 25, LaGuardia Airport in New York was forced to briefly halt incoming flights due to staffing shortages after some air traffic controllers said they couldn't continue working safely. It was becoming clear that the breaking point was close. The same day, Donald Trump announced his support for a stopgap funding bill to reopen the government. It was the possibility of America's aviation system collapsing that caused the Republicans, at last, to blink.

In activist circles, Nelson was given credit for "ending the shutdown." It was an oversimplification, but a useful one, with more than a grain of truth. A month later, the *New York Times* published a splashy, admiring profile dubbing her "America's Most Powerful Flight Attendant" and referencing for the first time in print what was already being murmured about in the lefty union world: that she could be a candidate for AFL-CIO president in the election that was then scheduled for 2021. It was, at that time, the sort of self-fulfilling speculation that ambitious leaders often try to engineer for themselves, planting seeds of hope that might one day grow into reality. But the enthusiasm for Nelson among the long-suffering radicals in organized labor was already real enough. At long last, it seemed that there might be a credible candidate to make unions badass again.

I first interviewed Nelson around this time, in a bare-walled conference room at the Gawker Media offices near Union Square. It was an experience of hearing, for the first time ever, an actual union leader give voice to the very same set of beliefs that I was nurturing myself as a frustrated believer in the potential of organized labor: the urgent need to focus less on electoral politics and more on strikes and new organizing; the pressing importance of building union power in entirely new industries like tech; and most of all, the will to fight, and fight, and fight. "People think there's only a limited amount of power that you have, and if you exert some power, you're not gonna have enough for the next fight. That's just not how it works!" she told me, smacking her hand on the metal table. "Every time workers really grab their power and take action, it encourages the next group of workers to have that power and act more. Power expands, it doesn't contract."

I had wanted to pair my interview of Nelson with an interview of Liz Shuler, the then-secretary-treasurer of the AFL-CIO who was being groomed as the insider choice to succeed Richard Trumka as president. It would be a May Day package presenting what looked like the two likely candidates for leadership of the union world. Nelson quickly agreed and trekked to my office; the AFL-CIO's communications person denied my request to talk to Shuler, deriding the story's angle as "speculative." The piece ended up focusing solely on Nelson, who was riding a wave of media coverage that has never stopped since.

It is impossible to separate Sara Nelson's rise to prominence from her preternatural understanding of the importance of the media. She is the rare public figure who combines a deliberate strategic appreciation for the power of media coverage as a tool with the genuine desire to speak her mind. This combination manifests itself as her simply saying yes to everything. She will wake up early on a weekend or stay up late on a work night to do a one-minute cable news hit, and she will get on the phone with every reporter from an obscure website who wants to talk, and she will do preposterously long interviews with podcasters who have very few listeners. She hates to say no to anyone who asks for her time. In a single day, she might talk to airline industry reporters, political reporters, labor reporters, and TV hosts. (Even when appearing on TV to discuss straightforward aviation issues like unruly passengers, she poses in front of a bookcase festooned with union signs and left-wing labor history books.) Her determination to say yes to interviews and her particular career path has given her footholds in an unlikely assortment of worlds. She is almost certainly the only regular CNBC guest who has given a keynote speech to the Democratic Socialists of America convention.

Anyone so willing to accommodate the press triggers a natural and instinctive suspicion. Donald Trump, Anthony Scaramucci, and a long line of other grifters before them have used the tactic of being the world's easiest person for reporters to get on the phone to fuel their disastrous rises to power. Unlike them, though, Nelson's relentless drive to raise her voice in the public conversation is driven by a bona fide compulsion to change the world. It is the kind of emotionally rooted motivation that can get someone branded as a rube in Washington, DC. Her pairing of that emotional drive with a keen understanding of real-world hardball tactics is what sets her apart. She's as neck-deep in material battles as any union leader in the country. And she's better at talking about it than anyone else.

=

WHEN SHE TURNED THIRTEEN, SARA NELSON GOT A NEWSPAPER ROUTE IN her hometown of Corvallis, Oregon. Every single morning, 365 days a year, she would roll up the papers and stuff them into plastic bags and set out on her bike, tossing them at front steps, making it a game and awarding herself points based on how perfectly placed the paper was. For her first six months or so, she was delivering to a lower-income neighborhood of apartment buildings on the edge of town. Part of her job was collecting the money. She hated it. When the subscribers would make excuses—come back later, I lost my checkbook—she would often just let them slide. She had the sense they couldn't afford it, and it made her feel bad to press them on it. She ended up working several months for free, collecting just enough money to pay the newspaper for the copies that they fronted her.

Later, she landed a more desirable route closer to her own neighborhood, and kept on delivering papers until she graduated from high school. She never did get paid for those early months.

When Nelson was born in 1973, Corvallis was an idyllic small-but-not-too-small town, nestled in the Willamette Valley an hour from the Pacific coast. Oregon State University makes it a college town, but in Nelson's memory Corvallis was more of a farm town, surrounded by hills where her dad would take her running. From her house on Dixon Street, she could ride her bike anywhere she needed to be in ten minutes. Her elementary school was one block away from her house. Her middle school was two blocks away. And her high school was three blocks away. Kids ran from house to house playing in her neighborhood, and all the doors stayed unlocked; school field trips went to the sheep farms; her friends were in 4-H. When she snuck out of her bedroom window at night, it was to go climb a tree and read Judy Blume books by flashlight.

This unbearably wholesome upbringing was the end result of two parents who had come to Oregon by very different paths. Her mother's side of the family came from Minnesota; her grandmother earned a master's degree in chemistry there, but ran off to the wild west of Oregon with her grandfather, Charles, in the wake of the Great Depression. They lived for a time in a tiny house with an outhouse, a far cry from Minnesota's respectable society. Charles had tuberculosis as a child. He lived in Bend, and his parents traveled up and down the West Coast seeking help for his condition. A doctor in Los Angeles told them they should accept that Charles would die. Instead, they took him to a Christian Scientist practitioner in Portland. In a week, he was healed and regained his ability to walk. Thereafter the family became devout Christian Scientists. Sara's mother, Carol, grew up with the religion—leavened by Charles's irrepressible pioneering spirit, constantly out for adventure. In winter, he liked to charge up hills fast in a car with no tire chains, yelling, "Hang on to your left ear!"

Sara's father, Don, had a harder life. He grew up in Los Angeles. His father died when he was eighteen, and Don, the oldest child, had to grow up fast. He was drafted into the army, but narrowly escaped being sent to Vietnam when—according to family lore—an officer who noticed his athletic abilities pulled him out of line at the last minute and sent him off to Alaska to train with the army's biathlon unit, guarding against Russian invasion from the north. The job suited him perfectly, giving him a sense of purpose and catering to his love of physical activity. He also began studying Christian Science while he was in the army. After two years, he came back and reconnected with Carol, who he had been dating before his military stint. Conveniently, they had by then become religiously aligned as well.

Carol landed a teaching job in Corvallis and got pregnant with Sara shortly afterward. Don had gotten a master's degree in physical education, hoping to teach, but there were no jobs to be found. As a new family man, he was forced to sell his beloved sporty MG, get a more staid car, and go to work in a lumber mill. He lost part of his pinky finger to that mill before he was able to land a job in the company's sales office, away from the saw blades.

Always the athlete, Don would often run or bike the thirteen-mile round trip to work. He went to the Olympic biathlon trials one year, and didn't make the team, but kept in touch with friends who did. He even became a judge in the 1980 Olympic biathlon at Lake Placid. Sara was brought up running with her dad's local running club and idolizing Steve Prefontaine, the Oregon long-distance track star who died in an auto accident in 1975, leaving behind a slew of records. "Take the hill!" her dad would exhort her on their runs. "Don't let the hill take you!"

Growing up in a family of Christian Scientists—a rarity in Corvallis— helped to imbue Nelson's early life with its hale and innocent nature. Her parents were Republicans, though not particularly fiery ones. She did not drink or do drugs. (One foray into NoDoz pills to help her finish a school project left her throwing up all night.) She was a popular student, but refused invitations to be a cheerleader because she wanted to actually watch the games instead. When she was a senior in high school, she would use her paper route money to buy spray paint in her school's colors, then sneak out at night, go to the rival high school across town, and paint a ceremonial rock in front of it in the colors of her own high school. Her most rebellious act of all, though, came when she and a group of friends broke into their high school at night, through the roof, to sing Broadway songs on the stage of the school auditorium.

Christian Science's most basic beliefs are captured by an overarching "Statement of Being," written by its founder, Mary Baker Eddy, in the late 1800s: "There is no life, truth, intelligence, nor substance in matter. All is infinite Mind and its infinite manifestation, for God is All-in-all. Spirit is immortal Truth; matter is mortal error. Spirit is the real and eternal; matter is the unreal and temporal. Spirit is God, and man is His image and likeness. Therefore man is not material; he is spiritual." When Nelson was a child, this idea was explained to her like so: Imagine the sun, and the rays of the sun. The rays have all the qualities of the sun, but they are not the sun. They are a reflection of the sun. Likewise, we are a reflection of god.

Rather than saying "god," Nelson was raised to always say, "Father, mother, god." She now sees those religious teachings as one of the first things that introduced her to the tenets of feminism, albeit in a nontraditional way. Both male and female qualities, she learned, are equally important expressions of god. What some churches call the work of the devil, Christian Science simply brands as "error." It is something wrong with the world that demands correction.

"When you see someone doing something that's not God-like, that's not actually them; that's error at work. I can equate that now to, 'that's the union buster at work,'" Nelson says. "I think that even though my church is seen as very, very conservative, for me, I got my greatest lesson in equality. I didn't grow up thinking that there were any hurdles for me because I was a woman."

When high school was over, Nelson went to Principia College, a tiny Christian Science–driven school in Elsah, Illinois, about thirty miles up the Mississippi from St. Louis. The decision of where to go did not feel particularly profound to her: she chose the school because a girl she went to church with who she thought was cool went there. She also considered the process of applying to many different colleges to be a hassle on par with homework, which she didn't like.

Principia was a socially conservative institution. Its campus was dry. Men and women lived separately, and visiting hours were enforced. If there was a member of the opposite sex in your room, you were supposed to keep a shoe wedged in the door. But for Nelson, soaked in small-town purity, it felt like what she imagined college should be. She did not miss the booze-soaked frat parties (though she admits to leading some streaking episodes on campus). It is hard to disbelieve her when she recalls, "I was high on life!"

If you get Sara Nelson talking about anything for any meaningful length of time, it is likely that she will tear up at least once. This happens most frequently when she is relating a story about someone else's pain, or an injustice that persists in the world. It happens in press interviews, on TV, and when she gives speeches. It happens just as often in private conversations. It is a sort of automatic reaction to her own heartstrings being plucked by a memory. This sentimental tic could be a potent weapon if deployed for cynical purposes. In her case, though, it is a real involuntary response. As such, it is a good gauge for which experiences truly moved her the most. She doesn't pick and choose the moments to cry, so much as they pick her.

She became an English and education major at Principia, planning to be a teacher like her mom. As part of one of her classes, a professor took groups of students to St. Louis to have dinner with Black families and hear about their lives and experiences of racism firsthand. At one of these dinners, a Black teenage girl told a story of being accused of stealing from The Limited—a clothing store where Nelson shopped regularly—and being humiliated by having her bags searched in front of everyone. Listening to this tale was a pivotal experience for innocent young Sara from Corvallis.

"That particular story pushed it all together for me. I remember just having a real, all night cry, realizing that other people had not had this idyllic childhood growing up," she says. She cries now, almost thirty years later, remembering it. "I was so injured by that. And so angry. And disgusted."

It seems unimaginable, looking back after everything that came later, that Sara Nelson was once so naive about America's sins. A long process of awakening had begun. She graduated from college and moved to St. Louis. It was early in the cold winter of 1996. Her student loan payments were soaking up her meager income, and her diet for a while shrank to bread and butter and apples filched from hotel lobbies. She was juggling four jobs. The best of those was waitressing at California Pizza Kitchen, a gig she landed after walking in and announcing to the manager that she was going to work for them, and then returning several days in a row with the same message until she was finally hired.

Nelson was broke. She couldn't afford to travel to see her great aunt, who was sick, or her younger brother, who was a senior in high school. She was planning to get a full-time teaching job, but had no idea how she was going to afford to buy the various things she would need to set up her classroom and make it presentable. On a snowy, miserable day in February, her friend Chloe called her from Miami Beach—where she was sitting with her feet in the sand—to gloat.

Chloe was a flight attendant. The more she described the job to Nelson, the better it sounded: a pension, a higher salary than she would make as a teacher, and all that travel. It held a powerful allure on a gray and freezing Missouri afternoon. The next day, since she didn't have a shift at the restaurant, Nelson got in her car and drove to Chicago, where United was holding a "cattle call" for potential flight attendants. They called her back for a second interview, and then again for a physical. By the end of August, she was in training as a flight attendant, setting her life on a much different path than she planned.

United assigned her to Boston. Nelson and six other new flight attendants from her training class rented a three-bedroom apartment in the North End, on two floors connected by a ladder that went through a hole in the floor because the landlord refused to install a staircase. Three weeks after she started, she was getting anxious. She hadn't received her first paycheck yet. Rent would be due soon. Her bank account had dwindled to twelve dollars. She tried to gorge herself on airplane food and went on dates just to get free dinners. Days later, she was forced to tip a driver with her last quarter. Now she was really broke. There was no food in the apartment. The next morning, she sat in the jump seat on a round-trip flight to Chicago just so she could eat two airline meals.

When she got back to Boston, her check still had not hit her bank account. She went into the United office and demanded help. They blew her off—be patient, it's coming, you're still on probation. The feeling of being treated as nothing more than a number descended upon her. This was her breaking point. How would she pay her rent? Her student loans? How would she even buy a sandwich?

Right then, someone tapped her on the shoulder. It was a flight attendant she had never met before, holding a checkbook. "How do you spell your name?" the woman asked her. Then she handed her a check for $800. "Take care of yourself," she said. "And call our union."

This incident is one that Nelson has recounted in dozens of speeches, choking up almost every time. She had thought little about the union until that moment. The main thing she knew about the union, in fact, was that they had chartered a sightseeing bus to drive all the new hires around Boston when they first got to town, which was fun. After she had her first check in hand, the Association of Flight Attendants local asked her if she wanted to get involved. She began giving union presentations to new hires while she was still working on her probation period at United. At the same time, contract negotiations were heating up. As soon as Nelson left her exit interview to get off probation and become a full-time flight attendant, she went directly to the picket line to lead chants.

Though she did not fully grasp it then, her life had gained a new animating cause. It didn't take long for her to morph into a type familiar in all unions: the super-involved true believer. She became communications chair of the Boston local. She began attending every meeting and agitated against a controversial new contract that eventually got approved. "People kept giving me jobs," she says, "hoping it would shut me up." It didn't work. Nelson became the national strike chair when AFA was taking a strike authorization vote pegged to a potential United–US Airways merger in 2000. Her work with the union grew.

Late at night on September 10, 2001, Nelson took a flight into Chicago from the West Coast. There was a Hilton hotel at the airport where she knew the staff, and they let her go down and sleep on a massage table in the fitness center for a few hours, so she didn't have to spring for a room. Early in the morning, someone shook her awake and told her that they thought she would want to know that a plane had hit the World Trade Center. She clicked on the television in the fitness center and watched a nightmare unfold.

United Flight 175 was a Boston-to-LA flight that Nelson worked regularly. That morning, it was hijacked and struck the south tower of the World Trade Center at 9:03 a.m. Nelson rushed into the union office and started to help checking crew lists and updating hotline messages for members. Information was spotty. Eventually, there was a briefing that confirmed that the plane had, in fact, been United 175. Nelson felt herself start to fade out, to drop down. She had a very clear vision of a young woman with blonde hair and blue eyes cocking her head to the side and saying, "We're okay, Sara. We're all okay." The woman was her friend Amy King, a flight attendant who had died on United 175 along with her boyfriend and fellow flight attendant, Michael Tarrou. In the hectic early hours, before it was fully established who was on board, Nelson thought (mistakenly, as it turned out) that her friend Chloe—the one who had lured her into the job in the first place—might have died on the flight as well.

Beyond the human toll, the 2001 terrorist attacks were devastating for the airline industry and, by extension, its unions. United struggled mightily in the year after 9/11, losing billions of dollars and laying off nearly twenty thousand employees. One in five United AFA flight attendants were furloughed, including half of those based in Boston, where many workers had less seniority. In December 2002, days after the federal government decided not to guarantee a $2 billion loan the airline was seeking to stay alive, United filed for Chapter 11 bankruptcy. Its operations continued, but creditors circled, and everything its unions had won over the course of decades now had the potential to be lost.

This was the environment in which Sara Nelson took her first full-time union job. She was elected as the AFA's national communication chairperson for the United chapter, and she found herself plunged directly into this atmosphere of crisis in July 2002. "I remember during that time that there was a big sign on our union door that said, 'Never forget,'" she says. "I remember thinking, 'Who the *fuck* is ever gonna forget this?'"

Life was frenetic. During the three-year-long bankruptcy battle with United, Nelson routinely worked eighteen-hour days, collapsing at night to watch and rewatch a box set of *Friends*, her only entertainment at home. Flight attendants took massive cuts to their salaries and health care and waged enormous battles to try to protect the last vestiges of their pensions and health care for retirees. There were lessons in those years. At one point, AFA bought a series of newspaper ads in major papers across the country,

including *USA Today*, to enlist the public in the campaign to save their retirees' benefits. Those ads elicited a single email from the public in support. At
the same time, a tiny, ragtag group of retired flight attendants picketing in
front of O'Hare International Airport earned a front-page story. The power
was not in being able to outspend the corporations, but rather in having
people who cared enough about something to do it for free.

"We fought them on everything. On absolutely everything," Nelson says.
That was the biggest lesson of all. When she gives speeches to labor groups
today, she always tells them that power is not a limited resource—that using
power builds power. It is something to be exercised, not conserved. It is better to fight and get your ass kicked, she learned during those endless bankruptcy days, than not to fight at all. That single insight made her a radical.

The next decade brought an endless parade of opportunities to wage more
fights against more airlines. In April 2010, Nelson was elected international
vice president of the AFA. Four years later, she was elected as the union's
president. Now she had a seat at the big table.

=

OFFICIALLY, THE AFL-CIO IS AMERICA'S LARGEST ORGANIZED LABOR
group, a coalition of sixty unions representing nearly thirteen million members. Unofficially, the AFL-CIO is the Grey Gardens of the labor movement, a once-grand mansion whose owners sometimes seem to carry on
oblivious to their crumbling surroundings. People employed at the grassroots level of unions often scoff and dismiss the AFL-CIO as a remote,
out of touch, meaningless bureaucracy, far removed from the actual work
of organizing workers. Its history is marked by racism, self-destructive
red-baiting, and an elitist streak that undermined the real potential for a
truly unified labor movement spanning all classes of workers in the twentieth century. Today, its primary function is as a mediocre in-house lobbying
firm and traffic cop for America's unions. By any reasonable analysis, it has
for the past fifty years failed to accomplish its most important goal: building
(or even maintaining) power for the working class.

The people most attracted to the proposition of working at or leading
the AFL-CIO, therefore, tend to be either visionaries or rote bureaucrats.

It is an organization that subsists on dues money from its member unions, but which lacks any real mechanism for telling those unions what to do; it is a house divided, and many of those in the house like that just fine. There is a scene in *Goodfellas* where Ray Liotta explains in a voiceover the simple nature of the Mafia: "That's all it is—they're like the police department for wise guys." This is the same thing that many union leaders want the AFL-CIO to be: a voluntary association that adjudicates jurisdictional disputes among unions, puts in a word with the right politicians, and otherwise leaves everyone alone. This attitude—which prevails among the more conservative building trade unions and, if we're being honest, also prevails among the majority of other unions—is what creates the overwhelming sense of inertia that seems to grip everything that the AFL-CIO does. Despite its millions of notional members, it is functionally controlled by a small handful of leaders of major unions. And they don't want it to do anything that would step on their toes.

This state of play is enough to cause many in the radical wing of labor to write off the AFL-CIO entirely. But it is possible, also, to look at this crumbling mansion and imagine what it could be. If there is to be a labor movement in America, it must have a center. The AFL-CIO, like it or not, is that center. To give up on it completely is to forswear the umbrella organization that most of the nation's union members belong to. In this sense, debates over the AFL-CIO resemble the broader political left's constant hand-wringing over the Democratic Party: sure, it is a hopelessly sprawling group of natural enemies riven by factionalism and prone to sickening compromise with villains . . . but it is the army we have, and the people on the other side want to destroy us. Any labor movement big and strong enough to compete with the power of modern corporations, which is what progressives and socialists and anyone with a valid reading of American capitalism wants, will necessarily have some central organization through which broad national decisions can be coordinated. If you wiped the AFL-CIO off the map due to its shortcomings, you would just have to rebuild it.

Indeed, that has been tried. Twice in the past century there have been major splits in the union world prompted by the collective disgust of those who wanted to organize the masses with the collective disinterest of the existing union power structure to do that. The first came in 1935, when John Lewis, the crusading head of the United Mine Workers, took all the unions that wanted to do large-scale industrial organizing and formed the Congress of Industrial Organizations (CIO). They split bitterly from the American Federation of Labor (AFL) in 1937 and lasted until 1954 before they reunited again into today's AFL-CIO after years of cutthroat competition, personal rivalries, and mutual distaste for one another's philosophies.

The second time was in 2005, when a coalition of big unions including the Service Employees International Union (SEIU) and the Teamsters, frustrated with the AFL-CIO's failure to support organizing, broke off to form a rival federation called Change to Win. To keep this story brief, it didn't work. By 2009, Change to Win unions started trickling back into the AFL-CIO; the new federation was unable to effectively organize on a large scale, though there were some valiant attempts. Today, Change to Win as a brand name no longer exists. The Teamsters and SEIU still have not bothered to rejoin the AFL-CIO, secure in their belief that to do so would be a waste of time and dues money.

There has basically been one single dispute running through the entire history of the American labor movement. On one side are the people who believe that the most urgent task is to organize everyone who doesn't have a union, because unions are the only tool that can maintain the critical balance of power between labor and capital. On the other side are the people who already have unions, and who believe that the important thing is to protect what they have. Organizing millions of unorganized workers seems to them to be at best a pleasantly idealistic, faraway goal, and at worst a fundamental threat to the style of power that they have cultivated—power that comes from organizing key pockets of skilled labor rather than from organizing everyone. This dispute is sometimes referred to as "industrial unionism" versus "craft unionism," but it is really the divide between those who feel a moral responsibility to help *all* workers and those who don't. There is nothing wrong with organizing highly skilled workers into their own unions, as long as you also have a plan to organize everyone else as well. The second part of that equation, in practice, usually gets left out.

When Nelson became AFA president in 2014, her attention was still firmly focused on the aviation industry. Her union was dealing with the merger of American and US Airways, a muddled mix of several different unions representing different parts of the workforce, all of which the companies wanted to pit against one another. Sitting at bargaining tables during corporate mega-mergers, though, began hammering home to her that the problems her members faced were bigger than any single union, no matter how energetic, could solve. "Here I was thinking I was going to build power by bringing all these flight attendants into one union," she says. "But immediately what I was seeing was big, systemic problems in capitalism. And that the only way that we were going to fight back on those things was if we built a strong labor movement."

In 2013, the AFL-CIO had elected Richard Trumka as its president for his second term. Trumka, a mustachioed teddy bear of a man who nonetheless had an appetite for combat, had become the head of the United Mine Workers in 1982, when he was in his early thirties and had the reputation of a reformer. He was elevated to the number two job at the AFL-CIO in 1995, on the ticket of President John Sweeney, who came in with genuine—but ultimately unsuccessful—plans to reinvigorate new union organizing. Trumka succeeded Sweeney as president in 2009. He was reelected on a ticket meant to evoke the diversity of the labor movement. His second-in-command was Secretary-Treasurer Liz Shuler, an Oregon native who had spent her entire working career as a union staffer at the International Brotherhood of Electrical Workers, where her father was a member. Filling out the ticket in the executive vice president spot was Tefere Gebre, a native of Ethiopia who had come to America as a refugee at the age of fifteen and had previously been the head of the Orange County Labor Federation in California.

Despite its progressive appearance, this group of AFL leaders was unable to make any substantive gains for the labor movement. For the next four years, union density—the percentage of American workers who are union members—continued its inexorable slide, ticking down from 11.3 percent in 2013 to 10.7 percent in 2017. The Obama administration never ended up passing any transformative pro-union legislation. In 2016, Trump was elected despite the AFL's big spending on Democrats. Nelson had joined the AFL's fifty-five-member executive council, which functions as the federation's board. She began meeting leaders of other unions and started advocating for some of their issues, like the long struggle to rescue the pensions of coal miners. As the AFL's 2017 convention approached, a handful of other union leaders who had taken notice of her fire privately urged her to run for AFL president.

She didn't take the idea very seriously at the time. But a few days before the convention was scheduled to begin in St. Louis, Richard Trumka called and invited her out to dinner for the first time ever. At the end of a banal evening, he said to Nelson something along the lines of: "You know, if someone has an issue with me, I prefer if they just come out and say it to me straight." She agreed, "Absolutely! Me too!" She didn't understand the context of what he said, until she got to St. Louis and a reporter told her that there was an (untrue) rumor that she was thinking about waging a fight for the presidency from the floor of the convention.

What Nelson remembers most from that dinner with Trumka, though, was his answer to one particular question. He had been telling her how much he'd loved being president of the United Mine Workers after growing up in a family of coal miners. "So what do you love about being president of the AFL-CIO?" Nelson asked him.

"Nothing," Trumka replied. Leading an unwieldy collection of affiliates, he said, was far less fulfilling than just running a union. Later that week, Trumka, along with Shuler and Gebre, was reelected to lead the AFL-CIO for four more years.

As time went on, Nelson's profile slowly began to grow in the wider world of organized labor. When the government shutdown began on December 22, 2018, she plunged into the work of pulling together the aviation industry—unions and companies alike—to help end it. On January 10, 2019, the AFA, along with unions representing airline pilots and air traffic controllers, held a rally outside the US Capitol, raising dire warnings about the deterioration of aviation safety standards. On the same day, the American Federation of Government Employees (AFGE) held its own rally outside of the AFL-CIO's headquarters near the White House, with federal employees decrying the fact that nobody was being paid.

Publicly, the line on these overlapping rallies was that "labor is everywhere." But privately, Nelson found the episode embarrassing—neither the

AFL-CIO nor anyone else was coordinating the actions of all the disparate unions alarmed by the shutdown. The chaotic, disorganized nature of the crisis response got her thinking more about all the things that the AFL should be doing, but wasn't. Ten days later, she gave the "general strike" speech that vaulted her into mainstream public conversation. Within weeks, she was perhaps America's most-quoted labor leader. That title is less impressive than it might sound because few American labor leaders were considered relevant enough to be quoted very much in the national press.

As with all political positions, there is a chicken-and-egg quality to becoming a candidate to lead the labor movement: you become a legitimate candidate by having people believe you're a legitimate candidate. Impression and curiosity fuel reality, and vice versa. For the rest of 2019, people whispered about the possibility of Nelson running for president of the AFL-CIO; she coyly declined to come out and say that she was considering it, but she also never quite denied it. Thus, it became conventional wisdom that the 2021 AFL-CIO presidential election would be a race between her and Liz Shuler. Richard Trumka, it was assumed, was going to resign when his term was up, and Shuler was perceived as his handpicked successor. Not a single element of this entire supposition was known for sure, or confirmed by the principals publicly, but it was more or less taken as a given within the union world.

Then a few things happened. The Covid pandemic hit. The 2021 AFL-CIO convention was postponed until 2022 so that it could be held in person, which extended Trumka's term for another year. On August 4, 2021, I went to a rally in rural Brookwood, Alabama, for the 1,100 United Mine Workers members at Warrior Met Coal, who had by then been on strike for more than five months. It was one of the toughest and most high-profile strikes in the country during a strike-laden year, and union leaders from around the country, including Sara Nelson, had shown up to speak. Thousands of UMWA members had ridden buses from far-flung states to be there. But Richard Trumka only appeared via video with a recorded message of support. I remember thinking that was seriously disappointing, considering the fact that the UMWA had been Trumka's own union. The next day, news broke that Trumka had died of a heart attack the previous night while on a camping trip with his family. He was seventy-two.

Liz Shuler was elevated to the AFL-CIO presidency, at least until the convention happened in 2022. Sara Nelson's health problems dragged on for the next six months, through two major surgeries. That, along with the pandemic wiping out virtually all in-person meetings, laid waste to her plans to campaign and network and build support both inside and outside the federation to position her for a possible run for the presidency. Hers were just another set of plans that the pandemic years made a mockery of.

Nelson, though, is animated by an internal energy that sometimes seems too strong for her to consciously control. She could not stop thinking about the gap between where the labor movement could be and where it actually was. In 2021, unions' public approval rating hit its highest point in more than fifty years—68 percent—yet less than 7 percent of workers in the private sector actually had unions. The seeming inability of the nation's largest labor organization to do anything to quench the public thirst for unions was maddening. Major unions largely failed to reap the benefits of the outpouring of money and activism on the left after Trump was elected in 2016. There was no effective mechanism for channeling the burst of mainstream political panic into the cause of labor. And even while the pandemic radicalized a new generation of working people, who were hungry for protections on the job, union density continued to fall. Everyone said that we must be entering a bright new day for union organizing, but nobody at the top had a plausible plan to make that happen. There were speeches, but no strategy. That an opportunity for big things existed was beyond question. But no one inside the AFL-CIO appeared to be prepared to take advantage of a moment that could, at any time, begin slipping away.

Between the time that the AFL was founded in 1886 and when it merged with the CIO in 1955, it routinely issued "direct charters" to small local unions—twenty thousand in total, according to the historian Dorothy Sue Cobble—as a way to immediately connect new unions with the backing of the national federation. These charters were a quick and easy way of spreading union organizing nationwide, and of drawing the newly organized back into a central organization. Nelson dreamed of reviving this strategy, throwing open the resources of the AFL-CIO as a way to spark large-scale organizing once again. She envisioned a team of organizers, attorneys, and communications based at the AFL-CIO itself to serve as a base to help the countless workers whose aspirations to organize die on the vine because they don't have access to existing unions. These ideas had danced in her mind for years as crises came and went, chances arose and winked out, and the biggest union organization in America seemed to remain perpetually afloat in its own cultural isolation tank.

"This labor movement has become sort of enamored with its own irrelevance," she said. "When you're irrelevant, people don't ask questions of you. What you're doing. You don't have to answer to anyone. You don't have to show your work. It can become very comfortable. It can become a little world where you have some control."

The gray days of February 2022 faded into March. The AFL-CIO convention was three and a half months away. And Sara Nelson was still not sure what she was going to do.

CHAPTER TWO

THE PLACE WHERE UNIONS GO TO DIE

SOUTH CAROLINA, THE MOST
ANTI-UNION STATE IN AMERICA

The most famous event in the labor history of South Carolina is a massacre. In 1934, beaten down by the Depression and the insistence of mill owners for more work for less pay, textile workers across the South walked off the job in a general strike. "Flying squadrons" of workers from one mill would rush to the next mill to inform their counterparts that the strike was on. It spread with breathtaking speed. By the first week in September, some 400,000 workers all the way up the East Coast were on strike, a wave of radicalism that was not so radical in light of the brutal working conditions at the time.

That wave broke in tiny Honea Path, South Carolina. On September 6, a group of strikers there began scuffling with scabs who were trying to enter the mill. Dan Beacham, the mill owner, had hired a team of armed men, and they opened fire, killing six strikers. Because Honea Path was a company town in total thrall to the mill, the local churches would not even allow themselves to be used for funeral services for those killed. Instead, thousands gathered outside in the open air to mourn the dead. None of the

33

shooters were convicted of crimes. Within two weeks, the general strike was over. Despite a set of tepid guarantees from the federal government, thousands of strikers found themselves blacklisted. Families living in company housing were evicted and made homeless. It was a flinty demonstration of just how far Southern bosses were willing to go to maintain their absolute power over employees.

Today, it is somewhat more difficult for employers in South Carolina to order mass shootings of picketers. In the general sense, though, not a lot has changed. In the United States of America, it is difficult to build and maintain labor unions even in the best of circumstances. Even in the bluest and most union-friendly states in the country, less than a quarter of working people are union members. If you trace your finger down a list of all fifty states, at the very bottom you will find South Carolina, where in 2022 only 1.7 percent of working people were union members—the lowest union density in the entire nation. That is, for perspective, less than one-third of the union density that Mississippi has. There are more students at the University of South Carolina's Columbia campus than there are union members in the state of South Carolina. Corporate hostility to unions is everywhere; in the South, state governments are implacably hostile as well. But nowhere in this country are unions weaker or more marginalized than they are in South Carolina.

Every single Southern state has "right to work" laws. These laws technically mean that no one can be compelled to be a union member and pay dues as a condition of employment, and they are presented as a stand for freedom of speech and association. In reality, they exist simply because they make it harder for unions to organize, maintain membership, and achieve financial stability. They make it possible for employees to get all the benefits of a union contract without ever paying dues if they don't want to—giving any free rider in the workplace a chance to experience the selfish joy that rich people must feel when they evade taxes. They are effective bureaucratic barriers to union power and therefore are the legal tool of choice for every state government that despises unions and wants to erode their existence on behalf of business. Thus, the South as a region has America's lowest union density, along with the worst education and highest rates of poverty.

The labor movement is forever discussing the urgent need to "Organize the South." As soon as World War II ended, the CIO, the more radical labor federation of its day, launched "Operation Dixie," an ambitious plan to flood the South with union organizers. It scored many isolated successes but failed in its goal of Organizing the South, due mostly to eye-watering racism and oppressive red-baiting that ate away at union solidarity from within and without. Its aspirations could not be sustained. Still, Operation Dixie is regularly evoked in a dreamy way as the example of what could be done if we really wanted to Organize the South. Today, the South is still racist and decidedly not organized. Union power in America peaked shortly after Operation Dixie petered out around 1950 and has been slipping away ever since.

Rebuilding organized labor's power in blue states will be hard. And those are the easy places. To really understand what it would mean to change the country through labor power, it is necessary to reckon with a state like South Carolina. Nowhere, after all, needs the labor movement's help more than the place where it has had the shit beaten out of it the most.

=

FROM THE TOP OF THE ARTHUR RAVENEL JR. BRIDGE, WITH ENORMOUS overhead steel support wires arcing down all around you, Charleston looks like the playroom for god's erector set. Down below, on the edge of the Cooper River, you can see the huge cranes that never stop loading and unloading containers, an endless conveyor belt of commerce. Charleston is a port city—along with nearby Georgetown, one of the ten biggest ports in America. Each year, tens of billions of dollars of merchandise from around the globe flow through the port. Charleston looks like a tourist town, with its frantic historic downtown of T-shirts and cookie stores. But the real money is in the ports. The biggest piece of organized labor's power in South Carolina lives at those ports as well.

The airy, campus-like headquarters building of the International Longshoremen's Association (ILA) Local 1422 sits on a spacious lot near the river. Its conference room has a photo of the Obamas on one wall and a painting of Barack Obama on another wall, interspersed with historic photos of longshoremen and a copy of the local's initial charter from the American Federation of Labor. At a polished oval table sits Charles Brave, with a neatly trimmed gray goatee and a gold pinky ring on long, elegant fingers. He is the president of the ILA local. For the past two terms, he has been the president of the state chapter of the AFL-CIO, making him the only Black state federation president in the country at the time. He is also, perhaps more importantly, still a full-time longshoreman. He began working on the docks in 1968 at the age of fourteen. Now he's a crane operator. Only twenty-six people in the union are ahead of him on the seniority list. In 2021, he says proudly, he made $290,000 working on the docks.

As long as there is a globalized economy, American companies will be importing and exporting vast amounts of merchandise. The shipping companies control the goods coming in and out of the ports, but the ILA controls the workers. No matter how poor or backward the rest of the state of South Carolina may be beyond the Charleston waterfront, the port itself is a vital node in the global economy. Its workers are not hemmed in by purely local economic conditions. That simple fact has enabled the ILA to become the strongest union in the state, and to make longshore jobs into a model of well-paid blue-collar work that could not be more different from the standards outside of the docks.

Each day, the shipping companies will tell the union how many fifteen-man gangs they need to handle the day's cargo. The union then assigns people to the gangs, according to seniority and who wants to work that day, and makes sure everyone is getting paid according to the contract. There are generous rules governing overtime and staffing. Certain contract provisions guarantee that existing jobs won't disappear even if the company automates the tasks that those workers do. The work is hard, but lucrative. It's a pretty sweet gig.

The benefits that come with seniority on the docks mean that people will hang on to their jobs as long as possible. The union does its best to make that possible. "We got guys on the waterfront now in their eighties. All they do is water person. All they do is fix water for us," Brave says with satisfaction. "We won't allow the companies to go to bottled waters. They still fix them, and bring the ice, and we fix it in the cooler. Drinking water. We still do that. Every single ship we got. Right now, we got seven water persons. That's all they do. They don't do nothing else." The youngest water person now is seventy-five, but Brave recalls two men who worked into their nineties. Water person is a job that pays well into six figures, thanks to the seniority that those men have.

The contracts that the ILA has won over the course of many decades are a wonderful Rorschach test for people's inherent attitudes toward unions. Some will look at the longshoremen and say they are obstacles to efficiency. They fight tooth and nail against technological change. They force companies to pay human beings to do jobs that could be automated. They require staffing levels that are higher than optimal. They hobble companies' ability to make business decisions based purely on profit and efficiency and lowering prices. They are, a technocrat would say, making more money than this sort of blue-collar work deserves. They are squeezing cash out of their privileged position in the global economy's supply chain, and that ultimately raises prices for consumers down the line.

But that is the wrong way to look at what the ILA has built. It is better to understand the union as one tiny oasis of power for working people that is able to secure for its members the slice of business proceeds that would, in a just world, be flowing to everyone who works everywhere. They are one small bulwark against the overwhelming ability of global capitalism to extract money that should accrue to workers and redirect that money toward investors. They are a de facto replacement for South Carolina's utter lack of an adequate social safety net. They are also a rare source of accessible, stable, good-paying careers for Black working-class people in a state where that sort of thing barely exists. The era of free trade and outsourcing has vaporized most of those jobs in America, moving them overseas. But all the stuff that gets manufactured overseas for the American market has to be shipped back in, and someone has to unload it. That has allowed the ILA's power to persist while so many other once-strong blue-collar unions have been sucked dry.

And let's not forget that the higher-paid, (relatively) easier jobs that go to the most senior members of the union were earned by many long decades of hard work. The fight against, for example, replacing water men with bottled water is really a fight to ensure that a long-due bill gets paid. "That's why we tried to keep it the way it is. Because we come from a long way," says Brave. "Man, I remember the time when we had to load cowhide. I mean, the flesh of a cow. We had to literally stack them in the hold of a ship, with maggots on them. Work was real hard back then. Nobody wanted it." That is also the reason why the ILA's "deep water" locals—the people who do the actual loading on the docks—are overwhelmingly Black. They were difficult, unappealing jobs that only became attractive after a long, organized struggle.

Kenny Riley has a round head, a swoop of gray stubble, and the thickness of limbs, even in his late sixties, that indicates a lifetime of lifting heavy things. He grew up in North Charleston. His father worked as a longshoreman part of the year and spent the other part making his way up the East Coast as a migrant farm worker, picking cucumbers, tomatoes, beans, and potatoes. Kenny and his brother would accompany their father to do the picking, then return to Charleston in time for the school year. They spent time at the county dump, searching for scrap metal and rags to sell and keeping the decent clothes they found to wear.

When he was in the eleventh grade, in 1969, the city of Charleston integrated its schools. Riley was sent to a new and mostly white high school, where racist abuse was rife. He began working on the docks as a senior in high school and continued off and on as he attended the College of Charleston. To him, being a longshoreman was an unbeatable job: you got paid, you got a good workout, and you didn't have to work when you didn't want to. He and his older brother Leonard both went full-time on the waterfront when they graduated from college.

His first month as a full-time longshoreman, he stopped by his first Friday night union meeting. He assumed it would be a sedate affair, considering how great the job was. Instead, he was horrified to find a group of huge men, as big as any football lineman, yelling and cussing at one another over various grievances. At one point, a reverend who had come to the meeting to say the opening prayer jumped up to tell everyone to calm down; when he did, a gun fell out of his pocket and clattered on the floor. When Kenny got home that night, he told his brother that if they were planning to stay on the docks, they needed to get involved in the union to help straighten things out.

Within a year, Kenny was on the board. By 1997, he was the president of the ILA local in Charleston, a position he kept until he lost it to Charles Brave in 2021. Riley is the sort of up-from-the-ranks radical who makes the labor movement great, the kind who possesses an idealism married to a relentless practicality. He knows that his union's power is directly tied to the success of the Charleston port itself. The ILA is far from a leech on productivity. Until the late 2000s, Charleston was the nation's fourth busiest port—due in large part to the efficiency of its workforce—before it was overtaken by Savannah, which offered more space for distribution centers for big-box retailers. Riley's aim with the ILA is not to sit around and suck the companies dry, but rather to use the leverage that longshoremen have as a tool for progressive change. That has meant everything from working to improve the conditions of far more exploited dock workers in the Caribbean and Africa, to temporarily shutting down the Charleston port to protest a fire that killed factory workers in Bangladesh.

"One of the most difficult challenges for me over the past twenty-five years is getting dock workers prepared for the real struggle. The strength and power that we have should not be squandered. With that comes, I believe, a responsibility, a social responsibility to weigh in on unjust causes," Riley says. "This is a struggle. You know, one guy will say, 'Do you think there's gonna be fines and discipline?' Who cares? It's the cause that's more important than the person. This is what we do. This is solidarity."

It is an irony of circumstance that a state like South Carolina finds itself home to a union like the ILA. As much power as the longshoremen have in the context of the global economy, their ability to use that power to make it easier for other workers in their backyard to build strong unions of their own is limited. It is in some ways easier for them to exert influence on Amsterdam, Dhaka, or Liberia than on the statehouse down the road in Columbia. While the entire South is inherently anti-union, no state has built its entire economic reputation around aggressive hostility toward organized labor with as much zeal as South Carolina.

"When you think about the deep South—Mississippi, Alabama, Louisiana—it don't get any deeper South than South Carolina. You're like a black hole on the East Coast," Riley says. "We're one of the smallest and poorest states on the Eastern Seaboard. And yet the amount of anti-union forces and pressures that come to bear is unbelievable. That's our ticket to attracting foreign investment: that we have some of the most productive workers in the world, yet they're paid 23 percent less than the national average."

There has long been a sick competition among poor Southern states to offer themselves up as the place most willing to debase themselves for businesses willing to relocate there. It is an approach that harkens back to the nineteenth century, when the North was industrializing, but the South remained stubbornly wedded to free labor as its panacea. "We may be bad, but we're cheap," the theory goes. Though the South was grudgingly forced (at gunpoint) to accept that workers must be paid, its social and political order still centers around a determination to keep that pay as low as possible. States see themselves as beggars at the altar of business, and their citizens not as people to be cultivated, but as troublesome little units of labor costs whose interests must be minimized, lest the businessmen get scared away.

A key part of this is assuring employers that they will not be troubled by unions. South Carolina has succeeded in this metric more than anywhere else. That is a primary reason why the state is now used as a destination of choice for companies looking to escape their own unions. Boeing, a company with a long-unionized workforce in Washington, built a factory in South Carolina for this purpose. Automakers like BMW, Volvo, and Mercedes, which have long histories of union labor overseas, have flocked to the state for decades. So, too, have tire manufacturers like Michelin, Bridgestone, and Giti, making South Carolina the nation's top exporter of tires. South Carolina does not just hurt South Carolinians by depriving almost all of them of any reasonable chance to unionize; it poses a serious threat to unions across the country by serving as a friendly acid bath that companies can dive into to dissolve any remnants of organized labor that may be clinging to them elsewhere.

Unions understand this, but they have never been able to overcome it. The International Association of Machinists (IAM) lost a major, years-long drive to unionize three thousand employees of the South Carolina Boeing factory in 2017, when 74 percent of the workers voted against unionizing after an all-encompassing anti-union campaign from the company and the state's politicians. A year later, the IAM succeeded in unionizing a smaller group of 178 technicians at the plant, only to have the Trump administration's National Labor Relations Board rule that such a "micro-unit" was not legal.

The United Steelworkers, who represent thousands of workers in the tire industry—including at many companies with union-free plants in South Carolina—began trying to organize the Giti Tires factory in Chester County in 2021. It appeared to be (though no one could tell me for sure) the largest union campaign in the state that was happening as the pandemic waned into 2022. Yet the company felt bold enough to spread manure on sidewalks near the plant when a union rally was scheduled. By the spring of 2022, the Steelworkers told me that Giti workers still felt too intimidated to speak to the press.

Any large union organizing campaign in a Southern state is also, by necessity, a political and community organizing campaign. This adds an entire extra layer of work for the union. That work can be expensive, painstaking, and time-consuming, but there is no way around it. Whenever a union undertakes organizing a big, industrial workplace in the South these days, here is what happens: the company insinuates to workers that unionizing will cause them to lose their jobs; state and local politicians holler about how unions are poison that will scare away these real nice jobs you got; and the company spreads money around town in order to get a halo of approval from any charity, preacher, or local institution whose affinity is for sale to lend themselves an air of civic responsibility as they go about trying to keep local wages as low as possible. Companies locate their Southern plants in isolated regions with few other comparable job opportunities in order to make these threats carry more weight. The drearily familiar union-busting playbook is a shotgun pointed at poor people, concealed by the thinnest veneer of paternalistic goodwill. It works very well. It is why, for example, the Mississippi Civil Rights Museum in Jackson has a "Nissan Cafe" and free weekend admission sponsored by Nissan, and the Nissan plant down the road in Canton still does not have a union, thanks to Nissan's union busting. All these things are of a piece.

The South is an existential problem for organized labor. As long as the region exists as a haven for companies to flee from unions, companies will keep doing so. This will continue until just about every industrial or manufacturing company in America that was once heavily unionized migrates to the South, and the unions in those industries find their membership base completely eaten away. So unions have no choice but to keep launching big, years-long campaigns to organize hundreds or thousands of workers in big Southern factories. Most of these types of union drives in recent decades have failed. The approach of unions needs to keep evolving, but giving up is not an option.

Brandon Upson is a clean-cut military veteran in his mid-thirties, a native of Aiken, South Carolina, who fell in love with politics in college and made it a career, working as a strategist for progressive groups and helping run billionaire Tom Steyer's unsuccessful 2020 presidential campaign. Today he's the chairman of the South Carolina Democratic Black Caucus and a close ally of organized labor, perhaps because both groups are equally beleaguered in the state. He's been rallying press and community support for the Giti Tires union campaign. "These workers are working in an abusive relationship, right? Think about a person who's in an abusive relationship: They're afraid to leave. They think this is their fault. They're afraid to say something because of the retribution. And that's how Giti Tires has conditioned their workers."

It is hard not to notice that reviving the labor movement in South Carolina and reviving the Democratic Party in South Carolina would require the exact same things: outside investment, effort, and an actual long-term strategy. A state in which 98 percent of workers aren't union members has, by definition, a whole lot of targets waiting to be unionized. What is missing are the unions, their organizers, and their resources. Charleston is a tourist hub, but nobody has unionized any of its hotels; there are lots of service workers, but few organizers trying to rally them together; the United Auto Workers has decades of work ahead of it to try to organize the state's growing auto industry. Any South Carolina worker who is interested in unionizing would have a damn hard time finding someone to help them out. The traditional blue-collar unions that do still have a presence in the state—the Longshoremen, the Machinists, the Steelworkers, the Operating Engineers—are doing their best to maintain the members they have, but the new organizing is meager in their industries, not to mention all the other industries that don't have anyone paying attention to them. It's hard to see how the state's nonunion workers can ever climb up into the labor movement if no one offers them a ladder.

Likewise, when Brandon Upson contemplates why neighboring North Carolina is a perpetual purple swing state while South Carolina is still deep red, he sees the same dynamic at play. When he was working for MoveOn.org in 2016 in North Carolina, he counted one hundred groups that were working to turn the state blue. In South Carolina, he counted only twenty, most of which planned to pick up and leave after the election was over. The difference was a lack of belief among outside forces that change was possible.

"The reason why North Carolina is always on the purple bubble, and now we have Georgia moving heavily towards being that true purple state, is that people have dug in roots and said, 'We're gonna be here, we're committed to it,'" he says. "Even Texas. Have mercy! Hundreds of millions of dollars are invested in Texas every cycle. Not from the DNC, but from these individual organizations that are committed to it. We have the numbers [in South Carolina]. We don't have the investment." Upson, a local who has worked all over the country, is brutally clear-sighted about what his state's future will look like if no one is willing to make a long-term commitment to alter its course. "Our state, we need a twenty-year strategic plan. You can't get to Disney World if you've never been there before without a map. And right now, there's no map for how we get to where we want to be. So unless we get that, in the next ten years, we're going to be a poster child for the worst this nation can see—from employment, labor, education, environment, health care, you name it."

Stronger unions in South Carolina would benefit the Democratic Party, and a stronger Democratic Party would benefit unions. In theory, each of those institutions could build one another up in a virtuous cycle. In reality, the lack of resources and lack of a plan leaves both groups unsuccessfully trying to tread water. Nowhere does this dynamic show up more clearly than in the woeful condition of public sector workers.

Nationally, public sector workers—those employed by the government—are far more widely unionized than private sector workers. In 2022, 34 percent of America's public sector workers were union members, versus only 6 percent of private sector workers. This gap means that major public sector unions like the American Federation of State, County and Municipal Employees (or AFSCME, which represents all types of state, county, and city employees) and the American Federation of Teachers (or AFT, which represents teachers) are some of the strongest members of the nation's union establishment, and their decline has been slower than that of unions that represent private sector workers. (In 2018, the Supreme Court's ruling in *Janus v. AFSCME* made the entire public sector "right to work," exposing all those strong public unions to the same forces that have long eroded private sector unions. But that erosion has only proceeded slowly so far, and the public sector will remain the bastion of America's union density for the foreseeable future.)

There is no federal law that requires states to collectively bargain with their public employees, so the policy on that question is set by each individual state. Union-friendly states make such collective bargaining mandatory; more moderate states make it legal, but not mandatory. South Carolina has the most hostile version of this state law that exists, flat-out prohibiting public sector collective bargaining. Unlike many Republican states, they don't even have an exception for police officers and firefighters. Hostility toward organized labor outweighs even the usual Republican need to worship at the altar of law enforcement.

Unionized teachers constitute the single biggest group fueling the political power of the labor movement in many states. Knowing this fact makes the conditions for teachers in South Carolina all the more heartbreaking. The South Carolina Education Association (SCEA) headquarters sit in a spacious but cluttered building on a low hill just off a highway cloverleaf outside of Columbia. When I visited, they were in the process of packing up to move to a smaller office because their building was going to be demolished for roadwork. The state AFL-CIO has office space in the same building. It was quiet inside, with the morose atmosphere of an army that knows it is losing the war. Two walls were covered with maps surrounded by taped-up, color-coded notecards indicating the party affiliation of each member of the state legislature. They were mostly red, with a few blue flecks for variety.

With her matter-of-fact speaking style and sensible black and blue sweater, Sherry East looks for all the world like the high school science teacher that she has been for decades. She grew up in West Virginia, in a family of coal miners who were all members of the United Mine Workers of America. When she moved to South Carolina in 1991 for a teaching job, she innocently asked a coworker how she could sign up for the teacher's union. "We don't have unions here," she was told. "You must treat people really nice, if you don't need unions!" she replied brightly.

After a couple of years on the job, she joined the SCEA and started taking on ever greater responsibilities in the group. In 2018, she was elected to her first term as president, a position where she remains. She also coached cheerleading at her school for ten years, and, for twenty-three of the years that she has been teaching, worked a second job at Advance Auto Parts on nights and weekends, in order to make ends meet on a South Carolina teacher's salary. She got better dental insurance there than she did from her job at school.

Although the SCEA is the state affiliate of the National Education Association (NEA), America's single largest union, it refers to itself as an "association" rather than a "union." This is a gentle attempt to avoid sparking a knee-jerk negative reaction when trying to recruit new members. South Carolina has been something of a culture shock for East, who spent her youth steeped in the West Virginia coal miners' proud pro-unionism. Her recruiting conversations in South Carolina often run into deeply held stereotypes that have never been examined: unions only want your money, unions want to make you go on strike when you don't want to, unions are all mobbed up. She finds people who have learned these things from their parents, and others who have learned them at church. It's clear that South Carolina needs a statewide public education campaign to start chipping away at this wall of resistance, but that is not the sort of thing that the state AFL-CIO has ever spent the money to undertake. Instead, these educational battles are fought one person at a time, by people like Sherry East.

A few years back, a man who East knew from work called her. His wife, a teacher, was being mistreated at work. East told him to convince his wife to join the SCEA so they could help her. "He called me back and he's like, 'Sherry, I can't get my wife to join.' And I said, 'Why?' I said, 'Jim, what's the problem?' And he said, 'Well, she's been told that you all are in the mob.'" You can see the strain of keeping it together start to pull at the corners of East's face, as if she were talking to a recalcitrant student. "I said, 'Jim, *I'm the leader.* I'm the leader of this association. I work two jobs. You know me. I'm not in the mob.'" Nevertheless, Jim's wife could not be convinced to join.

When the wave of teacher strikes swept America in 2018, East looked on in admiration and helplessness. She watched as friends and family who were teachers back in West Virginia rallied for a daring strike, shut down schools across the state, took over the state capitol, won improvements including five percent salary increases, and became national working-class heroes. There, she says, the deep culture of unionism that has permeated the state for decades meant that the members of the teachers' union understood what the potential of a strike was, and how to pull it off. Even though the strike was illegal, the teachers won the implicit support of many administrators and superintendents, who had come from union families and did not want to be enlisted as strikebreakers by state politicians. In South Carolina, where the culture of unionism is almost completely absent, such a thing was too audacious to materialize. Thousands of teachers rallied at the South Carolina statehouse in two big protests in 2019, but it did not translate into any meaningful material wins. There is a direct relationship between labor power and how unrewarding teachers' jobs are. According to NEA research, states that allow teachers to collectively bargain have starting pay that is $2,000 higher, and top pay that is $13,000 higher, than states that prohibit such bargaining.

On top of everything else, the SCEA has a competitor, called the Palmetto State Teachers Association (PSTA), that exists to thwart them. It functions as a sort of anti–teachers' union. The PSTA—formed in 1976 by conservative teachers upset with the SCEA's ties with the civil rights movement and its desire to become an actual union—keeps its dues slightly cheaper than the SCEA and ostentatiously notes that it does not endorse political candidates. It lists as one of its selling points that it is "Respected in the Legislature," which says it all.

The contrast between the formidable power of other states' teachers' unions and the enforced meekness of the SCEA is grim. In a state like, say, New York, the typical teachers' union contract runs fifty or even one hundred pages, with scrupulously detailed enforceable provisions covering everything from salaries to sabbaticals to school supplies. In South Carolina, thanks to the legal prohibition on public collective bargaining, a typical teacher's contract is a single-page Contract for Employment, similar to what you might sign to accept a job at McDonald's. It guarantees teachers nothing except the salary that the school board decides on—which, it is careful to note, may be reduced at any time due to loss of funding or furlough or decline in enrollment.

The difference between a one-page teaching contract and a fifty-page teaching contract is that one of them has forty-nine extra pages of things that are good for teachers. Keeping this simple truth forever obscured is a bedrock goal of the South Carolina political establishment. Despite being almost as politically tormented as it is possible for any organization to be, the SCEA will not even reveal how many members it has, or which schools they work in, for fear of exposing them to further political intimidation.

From her office chair, Sherry East gestures toward all the color-coded notecards hanging up in the next room, each one representing a state legislator. "You see that wall in there? On that wall in there are some very vengeful people. They hold a grudge." She sighs. "We don't bargain. We beg."

=

In February 1968, a group of Black nurses at Charleston's Medical College Hospital walked off the job to protest discrimination at work. They were fired. Though they were later rehired, their small uprising had planted the seeds of what would become the famous Charleston hospital strike of 1969. A year of internal organizing among Black workers and local activists turned into a union-organizing campaign among hospital workers. The hospital's president, William McCord, rejected the idea, offering workers, instead of a union, an additional holiday—for Robert E. Lee's birthday.

On March 19, 1969, hospital workers again walked off the job. The strike was on. It drew the attention of the entire civil rights movement. Coretta Scott King, Andrew Young, Ralph Abernathy, and other civil rights leaders came to Charleston to support the strike, which became a landmark part of civil rights history in the wake of Martin Luther King Jr.'s 1968 assassination. He had been killed supporting the cause of organized labor, the Memphis sanitation workers. In Charleston, the movement saw another chance to champion the ties between civil rights and labor rights.

By late April 1969, South Carolina's governor had ordered a thousand state troopers to Charleston and imposed a citywide curfew. The strike ended in an uneasy truce in June, with strikers rehired and the hospital agreeing to modest reforms—but without any union recognition.

In March 2022, I got the chance to see one of the original strikers, Louise Brown, speak to a college class about her experiences. She sat at the front of the classroom in a rakish orange scarf and stylish eyeglasses, holding court about the very human details that often get obscured in the march to beatify stirring labor actions: who was weak, who was a rotten scab, who was whose boyfriend, how hard it was to maintain unity under such duress. Brown, like many, spent time in jail during the strike. She still possesses the ability to keep the big picture in mind. "You can like who you like, and don't like who you don't like," she says. "But treat people right that's on the job. If they want a union—they doing work. Why don't you give them what they want?"

After class was over, I stepped out onto the classroom's third-floor patio with Kerry Taylor, the genial, bearded Citadel history professor who had brought Brown in to speak. Taylor is a labor activist himself. Since moving to Charleston in 2008, he has worked with the Carolina Alliance for Fair Employment (CAFE), a nonprofit that tries to support organizing efforts in the state. From the patio table, he gestured out to the surrounding neighborhoods—the same neighborhoods where many of the 1969 strikers lived. Today, there are pricey new condo towers being built, and million-dollar homes are common on nearby blocks. For all the glory and nobility that the strike earned in history books, it is even more impossible to be a poor person in Charleston today than it was then.

One of the state government's responses to the 1969 strike, Taylor notes, was a hasty declaration from the state attorney general that collective bargaining with state employees was simply not done, which subsequently hardened into accepted doctrine and hobbles worker power to this day. There are few straight lines or neatly predictable narratives in labor battles; as in all battles, the long-term outcome depends on more moving pieces than anyone could possibly account for.

When the Machinists were trying to unionize the South Carolina Boeing workers in the 2010s, CAFE helped them build support in the community and its churches. Taylor had an up-close view of the work that went into that campaign, which the union lost by a huge margin. No amount of organizing was able to overcome Boeing's economic might and the influence it wielded with state politicians, things that combined to convince workers that sticking with what they had was safer than doing anything to anger their out-of-town employer/benefactors. "You can do everything right and still get your ass kicked," Taylor says in a resigned tone. "With Boeing, the resistance was unbelievable. They had everything sewed up."

The May 26, 1969, issue of *The Nation* carried a story with a South Carolina dateline and the headline "THE 'MOVEMENT' FINALLY ARRIVES." It was a chronicle of the protests surrounding the Charleston hospital strike, and of Black student protests in a nearby town in the wake of the 1968 Orangeburg Massacre, where state troopers murdered three student protesters on the campus of South Carolina State College. The story was written by David Nolan—my father—then twenty-four years old, in his first paid byline. At the time, my dad was living in Frogmore, South Carolina, working at Penn Center, once a school for freed slaves, serving his alternative service as a conscientious objector to the Vietnam War draft. He was writing pieces for various radical publications about the happenings in South Carolina. Unlike most of them, *The Nation* gave him a fifty-dollar check.

"South Carolina, like other Southern states, has been engaged in a frantic scramble over the past twenty years to convince Northern industries to move down, offering generous tax incentives and the promise of a cheap, unorganized labor force," he wrote in that 1969 story. "To keep the industry that arrives it must hold the unions out, and at the same time provide an ample force of skilled labor. It must keep its white people docile: in many cases despite hungry bellies and slim pay checks." His story concluded with a confident declaration that "the winds are rising" that would change South Carolina for the better. He would have been surprised to learn that half a century later, his son would be writing about the exact same problems in the exact same place.

=

ERIN McKEE STILL HAS A NEW YORKER'S BLUNTNESS. AND ACCENT. A quarter century in South Carolina has not eroded her New York voice, though it has ground down her spirit a bit. She grew up in Long Island and became a flight attendant in 1984. In 1989, she and her coworkers unionized Tower Air, and McKee became a member of the Association of Flight Attendants. She spent the next four years helping her union local negotiate its first contract. Her son was born in 1993. By 1996, she was a single mother who traveled constantly for work, and who had just lost her regular babysitter. It was unsustainable. Somewhat reluctantly, she quit her job as a flight attendant and moved down to South Carolina, just outside of Charleston, where her mother lived.

When she went out in search of a new job, she listed all her union activism on her resume. For some reason, her phone never rang. At last, she landed a job with a union life insurance company, which told her she needed to attend local Central Labor Council meetings. That was where she first heard the term "right to work."

"I remember raising my hand and I said, 'Excuse me, what does that mean?'" McKee, who had grown up amid an entire constellation of New York relatives who were members of the Teamsters and Laborers and police and teachers' unions, was flabbergasted. "When they told me, I said, 'This is the United States of America, what do you mean?' And they're like, 'No, this is South Carolina.'"

McKee stayed active, becoming the head of the Charleston Central Labor Council, and, in 2013, she took over as president of the state AFL-CIO. It was not a job that was in high demand. It came with a modest salary and no health insurance, so McKee kept her other job at the local branch of the International Brotherhood of Electrical Workers. She led the AFL until 2019, when Charles Brave took over.

Her six years as the notional highest labor official in the state were an unrelenting lesson on how small the power of unions there really is. The state AFL-CIO has no budget to hire union organizers itself, so it could contribute little material support to new organizing. The biggest union drive that happened in South Carolina during those years was at Boeing, which ended in a lopsided loss. McKee had a lobbyist keeping tabs on the state legislature, but that amounted to monitoring more than lobbying itself. All the actual legislative movement was in the opposite direction. Nikki Haley, the state's governor at the time, declared in 2014 that "We discourage any companies that have unions from wanting to come to South Carolina, because we don't want to taint the water"—a fair articulation of the apocalyptic Republican governing philosophy that has successfully kept the state mostly poor and union-free. (Haley's Democratic opponent in the election that year was also a "right to work" supporter.)

The incident that burns most brightly in McKee's mind as a demonstration of South Carolina's attitude toward unions is the story of Gary McClain. He was a longtime employee of Tenneco, a plastic manufacturing company in Beech Island, a tiny community in western South Carolina near the Georgia border. In July 1999, the Operating Engineers began a drive to organize the plant. McClain was an active supporter, wearing a union hat and passing out fliers. As recounted in court documents, at an internal anti-union meeting led by the plant manager, McClain spoke up to argue; other employees later testified that they perceived this as "very rude" and were alarmed by his behavior at the meeting, such as "rubbing both hands on his legs, the top of his thighs." Company managers, who believed that McClain was an unstable and dangerous individual whose condition might be exacerbated by the "stressful" situation of a union drive, called McClain's doctor, as well as the local sheriff's department. The next day, sheriff's deputies—who had found that McClain had a four-year-old warrant for a nonviolent offense—pulled him over on his way to work, cuffed

him, and took him to the local hospital, where he was involuntarily committed as a mental health risk. He remained committed for the next six months.
The company refused to allow him to return to work until he was approved
by a psychiatrist of their choice, an offer that McClain rejected. The union
filed unfair labor practice charges against the company for calling the sheriff
on McClain. They were denied.

Tenneco successfully avoided the unionization of its South Carolina plant.
The company did have another facility in Kettering, Ohio, with a unionized
workforce. That plant received millions of dollars of subsidies from state and
local governments. In 2021, the company announced that it planned to close
that facility and move five hundred jobs to Mexico and China.

Unions in South Carolina are looking up from the bottom of a deep,
daunting hole. The boss can call the sheriff if you speak too rudely at an
anti-union meeting. The governor and the legislature are proud to tell
the world that they want to obliterate you. And the basic staff necessary
to even give working people in all but a few industries access to unions is
nonexistent. There are true believers to be found in the deep South's labor
movement, but without outside investment, they are something closer to a
volunteer activist group than a formidable opponent for the power of capital.
"When you're in a state where the only full-time [union] presidents or business managers are the building trades or the longshoremen, how much can
you accomplish?" McKee says.

No matter how hostile South Carolina is politically, simple math tells you
that the state's worker standards will never be pulled out of the gutter without new union organizing. Yet new organizing campaigns are sparse, due in
large part to the fact that few unions spend any real resources trying to organize there. It's a downward cycle. One of the paths to escaping it is hinted at
by something that happened in March 2022: two South Carolina Starbucks
stores filed for union elections.

One of those was the Millwood store in Columbia, near the University
of South Carolina. Sophie Ryan, a USC student with short hair, tattoos,
and an affinity for stuffed animals, had been a barista at the store for a year
when she began reading stories on Reddit about the series of Starbucks
union drives that had been popping up across the country since late 2021.

Her interest was piqued. She found out that a store in Greenville, South Carolina, was organizing and reached out to a staffer there, who connected her to Workers United, the union that was running the Starbucks campaign nationwide. After learning the process and talking to her coworkers, she got a batch of union cards. Within a week, three-quarters of the store's twenty-eight workers had signed a union card—more than enough to file for an election. The entire process, from Ryan's initial interest in the union to the public announcement of the union election filing, took only four weeks.

When she first saw the news of Starbucks stores unionizing in New York, Ryan says, she thought, "Oh, that's cool. I didn't know that was a thing we could do." She did, after all, grow up in South Carolina. But only a matter of weeks later, she was officially part of the labor movement. "I was telling my dad about it. He was like, 'Oh, in South Carolina, you're gonna do that?'" she says. "Yeah. I mean, why not?"

It is far trickier to organize thousands of workers in a Boeing factory than a few dozen workers at a Starbucks store. Still, there is a valuable lesson here. Why was a group of young Starbucks workers with no union experience able to successfully organize and file for union elections in a month in a state where most union campaigns struggle to reach that stage after hard-fought years? Because they were part of a *national movement*. They were not playing in the local sandbox ruled over by local tyrants; they were plugged into a nationwide campaign targeting an employer who is everywhere. In less than six months, the Starbucks Workers United (SBWU) campaign filed for union elections not just in labor-friendly blue state bastions, but in hostile "right to work" states from the Carolinas to Texas to Georgia. By operating from a national playbook, they ascended away from the parochial, localized animus that seems to pose such a barrier to organizing in the South.

I was interviewing labor leaders across South Carolina not long after the state's first Starbucks union drives were announced. I asked them if they were excited, or if they were offering to help out. None of them had heard about them yet. But by the end of 2022, workers at three separate Starbucks in the state had won union elections, by a combined vote of 38–1.

=

UNTIL THE AMERICAN LABOR MOVEMENT AS A WHOLE IS ABLE TO CONCEIVE of itself as a national movement responsible for reinforcing its own weak spots, the grinding fight to tread water in America's most anti-union state will be sustained primarily by the scattered work of true believers. Often, it will be carried on the backs of longshoremen. And not an insignificant part of the time, one of those longshoremen will be a Riley.

Like his younger brother Kenny, Leonard Riley sports neat gray stubble peppering his dark skin. He talks in a hoarse, throaty voice and wears a fresh new blue "ILA" baseball cap and a chain with a silver anchor pendant. He and Kenny both lived through the turbulent and traumatic racial integration of Charleston's high schools, then went to work on the docks as teenagers, and carried on as longshoremen after college. At the age of seventy, Leonard is still full-time on the docks, though he will tell you dismissively that he sometimes works as few as sixty hours a week these days. He has not been quite as aggressive as Kenny in running for leadership positions, but he spent many years on the executive board of the local, and his life has been defined by union activism rooted in the basic belief that working people should be treated fairly.

When Leonard came to the docks in the 1970s, joining the union was taken for granted; you got a good job, and part of the expectation was paying your hundred bucks to be an ILA member. Over time, the longshoremen were squeezed by the twin forces of automation, which shrank the size of the workforce, and by stricter enforcement of "right to work" laws, which made the process of recruiting members for the union more of a chore. Yet the ILA has been able to maintain its foothold—in large part by being good enough at their jobs to keep Charleston's port an attractive option to shippers—and Riley has used his perch on the docks as a launching pad to try to push progressive change.

He is closely attuned to the weak points in the South Carolina labor movement. His wife is a teacher, a financially tolerable job only because her low pay is offset by his own good pay. But the weakness of the state's teachers' union has locked the entire state in an unsustainable cycle: lack of political power drives down wages for teachers, hurting public schools; state politicians throw tax credits at out-of-state companies to attract jobs;

the taxes that those companies don't pay further erode public school funding; and the poor schools make South Carolina an unattractive place for companies, necessitating ever greater tax incentives to lure employers in. The idea of building a robust local economy that pays people who already live in the state good, livable wages is never seriously considered by the state's Republican power structure. The ILA represents one of the few places where working people can actually try to put the brakes on the whole rotten process. "We know that [longshoremen] are in a decent position, because we leverage our power, right? But we also know it's so necessary, because if we don't work, you don't have that nice T-shirt on, or those nice tennis shoes," Riley says. "So if we stop working, and we are together, we can demand a lot of things. That's what we want to see for workers around the city."

Indeed, the ILA has a long history of lending its weight to less strategically powerful workers—from supporting the nurses during the 1969 Charleston strike, all the way to the brief shutdown of the docks in support of workers in Bangladesh (which Leonard Riley helped to engineer, in the sort of righteous-but-maybe-not-totally-legal labor action that brings a twinkle to the eye of any true union partisan). Yet all attempts to organize workers in a poor state run up against the hard fact that many of the people most in need of a union also feel, often correctly, that the job they have is the best one they can get where they live, and trying to improve it also puts them at risk of losing it altogether. The fact that this sort of desperation is the product of careful and purposeful engineering does not make it any less real.

Charleston was the biggest slave port in the United States. More enslaved Africans landed there than in any other city. The Black longshoremen who have made the Port of Charleston the home of their state's strongest union have seized back a measure of justice from the claws of the past. But hundreds of years have not been enough to escape the tendrils of history. Leonard Riley does not hesitate when asked why South Carolina has so aggressively made unions weaker than anywhere else. "They are addicted to free labor. Or cheap labor." It was that way when his father was hauling paper rolls and picking produce and scouring the dump to keep his family afloat. It was that way when ILA protesters were getting thrown in jail for protesting to protect their contracts. It is that way now. Riley loves Charleston. He could have moved away, but he chose to spend his life where he grew up. That love is part of what has driven him to spend his life trying to change it. "Church on every corner, and all that good stuff . . . The water seems calm on the surface," he smiles wryly. "But there are undercurrents."

CHAPTER THREE

THE BIG DEAL
THE CHILD CARE WORKERS OF CALIFORNIA

et's say that—due to a deep love of children and a boundless appetite for exhaustion—you decided to open a business providing child care out of your home in California. You would join tens of thousands of other providers in a state-licensed field with extremely high customer demand. A typical day for you in your new profession would go like this: Wake up at 4:30 or 5 a.m. Start cooking food, cleaning, and preparing your space for the day. At 5:30 or 6 a.m., the first child shows up, dropped off by a parent on the way to an early job. More come at 6:30, and at 7, and at 7:30. The fact that many providers take care of kids ranging in age from infants to tweens makes the timing trickier—a young child who arrived early may need to be put down for a nap at the same time you're rounding up the school-age kids for their morning ride to school.

Make breakfast. Wash hands. Serve breakfast. Wash hands. Clean up. Change diapers. Now it's 9 a.m. Activities! Dancing! Social circle! Singing songs! Snacks! Go outside. Come back inside. It's 11:30. Wash hands. Prepare lunch. Serve lunch. Wash hands. Clean up. Change diapers. Then quiet time. Naps, if you're lucky. By 2 or 2:30 p.m., the kids are up again. Wash hands. Gather around. Read a book. Some more quiet time, if you're lucky. Get your assistant to supervise the youngest kids while you drive to school to pick up the school-age children. Around 3, some parents begin to arrive and pick up their kids. Others, who work later shifts, begin to arrive and drop off their kids. Activities! Play time! Go outside! Sing songs! Come inside. Wash hands. Prepare dinner. Serve dinner. Clean up. Wash hands. Change diapers. Some kids will be picked up after dinner, at 7. Some will be picked up at 8. Sometimes, when a parent is working late, you may keep a child until 10 or 11 or 11:30 at night. Say goodbye to the last kid. Wash the dishes. Wash the clothes. Put everything away. Clean up the space. Disinfect everything. Get everything ready for the next day. And are you done? No. You are a small business owner. You have administrative work. You have payment forms for your assistant. You have forms you must fill out to get reimbursed by the state government for the care of low-income children. You have assessment forms where you must write observations of certain children who are under the supervision of social agencies. You must do all this, after all the other things. And then—and then—you can try to get some sleep.

Sleep well. The alarm goes off really early.

It is hard to be a parent. It is hard to take care of one or two children at home. Taking care of ten or twelve children at your home is infinitely more intense. When those children are poor, have single mothers who are working two jobs just to get by, or have emotional problems or learning disabilities, it is harder still. To spend time talking to child care providers is to come to a fervent belief that, if the world is going to have millionaires, it should be them. But in reality these providers—who embody more than just about anyone the American valorization of hard work, entrepreneurialism, and family values—can end up making less than minimum wage when you compute the hours they actually work and all the expenses they are responsible for. They are an unseen but vital part of America's infrastructure, providing a service that enables working parents to go to work. But for generations, their work has been taken for granted, and they have been taken advantage of.

It is unsurprising that these women (and they are almost all women) pulled off the biggest union drive this nation had seen in a decade. It was one that was at one time considered unlikely to succeed, was completed in spectacular fashion, and was then widely ignored—just like the child care providers themselves.

Miren Algorri, an elegant woman with long, dark hair and a bright yellow polo shirt, sits in a child-size chair at a child-size table in the day care room attached to her neat brown suburban house in Chula Vista, just outside of San Diego. The children have been ushered out into the backyard, which she has transformed into a playground, so we can talk. Algorri was born in Mexico and moved to California in 1991 when she was seventeen. Her mother was already there, running her own in-home child care business, and Algorri was immediately enlisted as an (unpaid) assistant.

Her mother was a visionary. By the late '90s, she had begun organizing other child care providers with the intent of forming a union. There were a number of obstacles to this dream. For one thing, these workers—each independent, but earning much of their income from the state in the form of subsidies paid to take care of poor children—were not legally allowed to collectively bargain. Earning that right would require a change in state law, and the state was not interested in the change. Apart from that little matter, the workforce itself consisted of tens of thousands of individuals with no common work sites or formal networks, many of whom were immigrant women (not only from Mexico and Latin America, but also from Africa, eastern Europe, and elsewhere) with language barriers. They were, as a group, positioned firmly at the bottom of America's social and economic pyramid. The job was characterized by isolation and fatigue, two enemies of labor organizing. Almost every single factor was an argument *against* the practical possibility of shaping this disparate group into a real, functioning union.

Nevertheless, Algorri's mother believed. She began attending organizing meetings with other providers, using their own informal social networks to build membership lists. The things that made the idea of a child care providers' union difficult were the same things that made it feel necessary: the utter lack of power; the lack of a way to resist exploitation; the lack of any *centrality* in the sprawling, unaccountable industry. It was a field rife with middlemen—not only the state itself, which paid the bills, but social service agencies that referred needy children to providers and controlled the ability to disperse funding. Algorri witnessed a representative from one of those agencies literally shut a door in her mother's face when her mother went to complain about not being paid correctly. Such treatment only made her mother more determined to change things.

As a teenager, Algorri was already being enlisted to hold down the child care duties while her mother went to talk union issues with other providers, or traveled to Sacramento to rally for a change to the state law that would allow them to unionize. When Algorri got married and had a child of her own, she decided to open her own child care facility in her own home, both because she loved the work and in order to spend more time with her daughter. Compelled by what she had seen, she followed her mother into the movement to build a union.

"As a child, these experiences that you live through with your parents really scar you for life," Algorri says. "I remember my mom crying herself to sleep because she was not paid. At times, months without receiving pay. Imagine you are the sole breadwinner, and you have four children. And you're thinking, 'How am I going to continue to run my facility so I can provide for my own children? How can I continue to support these families that are relying on me for child care services, so they can get to work?'" Her mother worked until the age of seventy-two because she couldn't afford to retire. Algorri made it her mission to prevent the same fate from befalling generation after generation of child care workers to come.

In order to truly understand where child care providers in California are coming from, you must understand the institutionalized insanity of the way they are paid. We are speaking here of child care providers who work out of their own homes, taking care of the kids of people who have to go to work every day at not particularly glamorous jobs. How does a working parent who is barely earning enough to pay the rent and buy food also afford child care? They get a subsidy from the state. In California, thousands of child care providers earn virtually all their money from standard reimbursements paid by the state. (Those providers can also watch the children of parents who can afford to pay, but in practice most are paying the subsidized rate.) That state reimbursement, known as the "Regional Market Rate," is set periodically for each geographic area of the state. And how does the state determine what that rate is? Well, they do a survey of providers to determine how much it costs to actually provide child care in that area. These baseline surveys may be years out of date—in 2021, for example, the state had to be pressured into using a survey it had done in 2018, which was an improvement on the 2016 survey it had been using prior to that. None of the Covid-era inflation was included in the 2018 survey, of course, so the cost figures were already too low.

Then, once the state has ostensibly determined how much it costs providers to provide child care, it sets the reimbursement rate at *less than 100 percent* of that figure. As of 2022, family child care providers were paid 85 percent of the 2018 survey rate to take care of kids. Consider what this means: not only does the state fail to keep its cost estimates current, but it boldly and without reservation declares, "We have determined how much it costs you to take care of kids, and we will pay you less than that. Deal with it." It is an unambiguous example of state-enforced poverty imposed on an entire class of workers. The providers could, in theory, charge parents a copay to make up for the gap in what the state pays, but that wouldn't really work in practice—the parents are, by definition, already unable to afford the cost of child care. Miren Algorri, for example, has never charged a copay in her twenty-five years in business. It's just not practical. But the upshot is that the entire system is built on forcing family child care providers to take a financial hit on every customer. "The state is making me subsidize the subsidized system," Algorri says. "The state is able to quote-unquote 'pay' by underpaying us. We're actually covering the cost of the services we're rendering."

Even in a fantasy world in which the state did reimburse 100 percent of the surveyed costs, it would not reflect the full amount of work that providers do. Many of them watch kids six days a week but spend the seventh day—their "day off"—cleaning and prepping and getting groceries and doing paperwork and otherwise getting ready for the week to come. In other words, working. Also not included in official figures is the fact that these family businesses often involve unpaid work by the provider's family members. Daughters help their mothers, husbands help wives, and all of that is generally considered just pitching in for the family. Were all these working hours to be properly tallied, the already low hourly rate earned by providers would drop considerably.

According to an analysis from the Center for American Progress, the true cost of taking care of one kid at a home-based family child care provider in California was $1,269 per month in 2022; if you were to pay providers the same amount that kindergarten teachers made, and give them retirement benefits, the cost would rise to more than $2,000 per month per child. At the same time, the Regional Market Rate paid to family child care providers in San Diego County for full-time monthly care was $1,051 for infants, $988 for two-to-five-year-olds, and $744 for school-age children. The financial hole in the system is big enough to leave child care providers with nothing after a lifetime of hard work.

So they worked harder. By 2003, SEIU and AFSCME—the two big unions that had each been trying to organize California's child care workers separately—struck an agreement to work together. They divided the state into three regions. The United Domestic Workers (UDW), which is part of AFSCME, got thirty-nine counties anchored in San Diego; SEIU Local 99, based in Los Angeles, and SEIU Local 521, in northern California, divided nineteen counties between themselves. Each one of those unions had an existing membership base that complemented the new campaign: the UDW had domestic work, Local 99 had support staff workers in schools, and Local 521 had in-home service workers. Family child care is a bit of all those things, and more. Each union handled organizing duties in its own part of the state, and they all came together to form a new organization called CCPU: Child Care Providers United. It would eventually encompass forty thousand members, representing the entire family child care industry in California. But it wouldn't come easily.

When a little more than one hundred of my colleagues and I unionized at Gawker Media, it took six weeks. To unionize a big factory or warehouse or office might take six months or a year, and challenging campaigns across multiple work sites can take several years. Successfully unionizing the child care workers of California took two decades of nonstop work, leading up to one of the largest American union elections of the twenty-first century.

Generations of providers came and went in the movement, as with Algorri and her mother. The most concrete political task that CCPU had to achieve in order to become a real union was to get California's state law changed to allow them to collectively bargain with the state—which is, in essence, their employer since it sets the reimbursement rates. Bills to this effect were passed through the state legislature over and over again only to be vetoed: three times by Republican governor Arnold Schwarzenegger in the years from 2004 to 2008, and again, more disappointingly, by Democratic governor Jerry Brown, who vetoed the bill in 2011, saying it would cost too much. It was not until October 2019 that newly elected Democratic governor Gavin Newsom signed Assembly Bill 378 into law, giving child care providers the right to negotiate as a group.

That legal success was the culmination of close to twenty years of lobbying, organizing, and rallies at the Sacramento statehouse. When Newsom was running for governor in 2018 and courting union support, he got an extra nudge when he appeared at a rally at SEIU Local 521's union hall in San Jose. Newsom was onstage surrounded by child care providers when he was asked whether he would commit to sign the collective bargaining bill if it got to his desk. As hundreds of the very people whose livelihoods were at stake stared him down, he publicly vowed to support the bill. Every little bit of pressure helps.

It is impossible to sustain a campaign for as long as the child care providers did based solely on the *aspiration* of being a union; for most of those years, CCPU was acting like it already was a union. Long before the collective bargaining law passed, the group got thousands of workers to pay voluntary dues of ten dollars a month. It stayed involved in state politics and won a series of concessions from legislators in the years leading up to 2019: annual increases in the Regional Market Rate paid by the state, funding for apprenticeship training for child care workers, and a bill that guaranteed access to direct deposit. As significant as the legislative victories were, though, it would be a mistake to view CCPU as some sort of lobbying campaign. All the political work was in service of—and the product of—the more meaningful work of grassroots labor organizing by marginalized and ignored working people, at a staggering scale.

=

Touched by an Angel Child Care operates out of Jackie Jackson's neat, tan two-story house in the stucco expanse of South Central Los Angeles, just off the towering and tangled interchange of the 110 and 105 freeways. Jackson, whose unlined face is framed by prim black glasses, is voluble, almost manic, the sort of person who is kept young by her own overflowing energy. The only hint that she is a fifty-eight-year-old grandmother is the narrow band of gray on the edges of her pulled-back curly hair. Her four kids are all grown and gone. Now her home is occupied by four dogs—one chihuahua, one Belgian Malinois, one poodle, one English bulldog—and a day care center with a dozen kids in it each day. The first-floor living room of her home is lined with cubbies, cabinets, folded-up mats, and a two-foot-high sink for handwashing; the kitchen, barred by a child safety gate, is crammed with big plastic boxes of dishes and toys and Tupperware that must be washed and sanitized daily. Over the past quarter century, she has taken care of two thousand children right here, in the same community she grew up in. She is the image of health and zeal. Which is good because she hasn't been to the doctor in all those years. She can't afford it.

Jackson was once a preschool teacher, but she gave that up in favor of working from her home, where her liveliness can find infinite outlets. "I'm like a teacher. I'm a custodian. I'm a driver. I'm everything that I'm getting underpaid for," she says. "I got a special needs mother [of one of the children she cares for]. I gotta address that. You got parents that are coming here that need housing. You got to address that. You got parents coming in here that are going through abusive relationships. You have to address that. You got children coming in here with delays. Children coming in here where you're watching the baby walk on their tippy toes, and you understand that's not normal. You're investigating. So you turn into everything. Everything you could possibly name, and what you can't name, is what I am."

Growing up, Jackson had ADHD, which forced her to teach herself coping skills. Now she has an intuitive understanding of what struggling kids need and how to reach them. When kids come to her, she likes to watch them closely for a month to determine what their special talent is, and then set about nurturing that. The child who loves building with blocks could grow up to be an architect; the one who memorized all the body's organs could be a future doctor. Jackson considers this to be her own gift, and she is not stingy with it. Because there is far more demand for home child care than she can provide herself, she has taught the business to several other women in her neighborhood, who have opened their own businesses. Her customers are working parents, parents with mental health issues, homeless parents, foster care parents, the whole range. She has one assistant, and together they are paid fifty-two dollars a day per child, although she gives scholarships when parents don't have enough money. It is a life lived, at all times, right on the edge of insolvency.

Jackson has been working to get child care providers a union for twenty years, beginning when the effort was being led by the community organizing group ACORN. She helped organize a bus convoy of providers to go lobby in Sacramento way back when Schwarzenegger was governor. For years, the union didn't win anything politically tangible, but she kept on with the effort because it felt like a lifeline against resigning herself to a system that seemed impossible to live with. Her voluble, gregarious nature made it easy for her to talk to other providers, to pull them into the union's orbit. She would first sit and listen to their complaints, which tended to be the same set of complaints that all their peers had. Then she would dive into the meat of the conversation. "Well, how do you think that we're gonna make this change?" she would say. "If you feel like you're being treated unfairly, if you feel like you're not getting the money that you're supposed to get? You feel like you want to be compensated for this sick time? You feel like you want retirement, you want medical? Okay, how do you think we're gonna resolve it? Now let them answer it. It doesn't take a mad scientist to realize. Now that you expressed all of that, are you willing to walk with me on this walk? If you're willing to walk with me on this walk, we're getting ready to make a change. I ain't say tomorrow! But we're getting ready to make a change."

Not everyone is blessed with the sort of unswerving fortitude of a Jackie Jackson. For many years, providers were being recruited into the movement, and their efforts to win collective bargaining were failing over and over at the statehouse. What prevented everyone from throwing up their hands and drifting away during that long stretch in the California political wilderness? It was the basic determination of CCPU to act like a union, well before it received the official blessing of lawmakers.

So if providers were having trouble being paid correctly, the union could help them complain to the state. The union could help them navigate the interminable system and slash through the force fields of inertia that bureaucracies erect to insulate themselves. Above all, it was necessary for CCPU to demonstrate to all the workers that they were not just being used as fodder for a long-term lobbying campaign with uncertain prospects of success. In order to keep all these busy, underpaid, and mistreated people engaged for so long, it was necessary to demonstrate *power*.

When Max Arias was hired as the executive director of SEIU Local 99 in 2015, the CCPU campaign had already been underway for more than a decade. Arias, a burly man whose salt-and-pepper ponytail and long goatee lend him a resemblance to the '80s pro wrestler Captain Lou Albano, grew up in a politically active family in El Salvador and had spent most of his career with SEIU organizing health care and nursing home workers across the country. Arias saw the CCPU drive to get California's state law changed as a tool to pull workers into direct labor organizing, not a way to use labor organizing for state politics. SEIU, which has 700,000 members in California, is one of the state's most potent Democratic political forces. It was able to help trace the complaints of local child care providers who weren't being paid properly up to their root causes in state agencies and budgets.

At Local 99, the push to integrate child care providers into the structure of the union was formalized in 2011, when the bylaws were changed to allow child care workers to serve on the union's board and win elected positions. With thousands of (technically nonunion) workers voluntarily paying monthly dues, participating in the Local 99 elections, and running a public political pressure campaign, "We were properly acting like a union," Arias says with satisfaction. Acting like a union got the law changed—and when it was, it was not really an act of creating a union, but rather one of bestowing formal rights on a union that already existed. All the group's decisions, including its contract negotiations, are driven by a statewide committee of workers.

"When we bargained with the state over Covid money, we could have just had a group of researchers, right? But if it had just been researchers, we would not have had a hundred providers show up on the Zoom with the state. And then they're not making decisions, so they're not gonna go out and activate in the same way," says Arias. With a union as geographically dispersed and unwieldy as CCPU, a top-down approach would lead to a hollow administrative shell with little actual member enthusiasm. That is often a tempting path for union bureaucrats, but it is how true labor power suffocates and dies. Arias is determined not to let that happen. "You have to have as many [people] as possible. They actually told me I was crazy. 'A committee of thirty? Are you sure?' Yes, I'm sure. It's a big state! It's a lot of counties."

The legislative win for CCPU in 2019 seemed like the culmination of a long and dramatic struggle. Little did they know that the real drama was only beginning. As the unions were preparing for the statewide member vote that would officially bring the union into existence, Covid hit. The particular qualities of that crisis threw a brighter spotlight on the importance of the family child care industry than anything ever had before.

Recall the fraught early weeks of the pandemic: Schools closed. Businesses closed. Infection levels soared, hospitals filled, and a panicky confusion gripped the nation. It quickly became clear that America's entire ability to function would, for some period of time, rest on the shoulders of those who were hastily dubbed "essential workers," who would be tasked with keeping food and water and energy and other necessities flowing for the millions of people who were huddled at home during the shutdowns. If all those grocery store workers and transit workers and delivery drivers and nurses and pharmacists and gas station attendants and other "essential workers" did not continue showing up for work, society would collapse. And what was one inescapable necessity for all those essential workers, without which they, in turn, would stop coming to work?

Child care.

And since the schools were closed, who the hell was going to be taking care of the children of these suddenly vital but still poor essential workers? The answer, for countless working families across the country, was family child care providers.

It is no exaggeration to say that the providers who made up CCPU had without warning become one of the critical support beams keeping this entire country from falling into the abyss. If all those providers had stopped taking care of children during the pandemic, all those other essential workers would have had to stay home with their kids, and all those essential services would have ceased to function. What would have happened then is almost too horrific to contemplate. All these people who cared for children in their own homes were *infrastructure*, every bit as important as roads and bridges and farms and power lines. Their personal willingness to risk their health in order to keep taking those kids in every day allowed America to stave off a level of chaos that would have been much, much worse than what we experienced. No matter what you did during the pandemic—whether or not you stayed home, whether or not you have children—you and I and everyone else directly benefited from the work of child care providers during those unnerving times.

The union was able to win some immediate things for California's providers in the pandemic. It got them to the front of the line for access to cleaning products and PPE, and got the state to partly reimburse the workers for the financial hit they were taking from the combination of increased costs for cleaning supplies and lost revenue from reduced capacity. But nothing could fully mitigate Covid's enormous burden on child care workers. Hours had to be spent each day sanitizing every last surface; screaming toddlers had to be prodded to wear masks; backyards had to be quickly transformed into classroom spaces to minimize time spent indoors. Many providers lost their livelihoods when they got sick. Others died.

Patricia Moran, who runs a family child care in San Jose and is an active organizer for CCPU, saw providers she had recruited into the union pass away, and others get stricken with long Covid that still afflicts them today. The sudden state of crisis was a validation of the years of work she and others had invested in the union project—without it, there would have been no way for these thousands of workers who carried the economy on their backs to tell the government what they needed. It would have been pure guesswork. "There was no table for providers to discuss the issues with the state before CCPU," says Riko Mendez, who runs SEIU Local 521. "It wasn't until the providers like Patricia were at the bargaining table with the state sharing their own needs that we were able to advocate and convince the power brokers in Sacramento to do things that they never would have even thought of before."

Moran moved to America from Bolivia. She had a law degree there. But she couldn't use it here, so she went back to school and remade herself as a child care provider. For her and many women like her, building the union is just one more thing that is necessary in order to achieve a minimally decent life. It is a measure of toil imposed on women and immigrants and the poor that they must fulfill if they want that American dream that comes more easily to others. When you talk to child care workers, a common refrain from them is "We're not babysitters." They can feel society's dismissal of their work, and they resent it. They know that they are nurturers, analysts, psychologists, and more. Moran is a proud and accomplished woman. When she began talking to her fellow providers in California, she was shocked that the conditions they described could exist here in America, the nation she had come to expressly because it was supposed to be better than this. "We were invisible," she says, shaking her head. "We were working hard, but we were invisible."

=

IN A HILLY RESIDENTIAL NEIGHBORHOOD NORTHEAST OF DOWNTOWN SAN Diego, the United Domestic Workers have taken over a sprawling gray and white former church as their headquarters. What were once Sunday school classrooms and the pastor's house are now offices; the steeple is still crowned by a cross, but now the main building is a union hall. A Shrine to Our Holy Lady of Domestic Work. The UDW is massive, with more than 175,000 members in California, nearly 100,000 of whom voluntarily pay dues. Most of them are women of color, concentrated in in-home support service workers, who are paid by the state to care for low-income senior citizens and people with disabilities. The UDW is also home to thousands of family child care providers, who were working with the union for years before they gained the right to collectively bargain in July 2020. It was a natural fit. Just like home care workers, they are a widespread but isolated quasi-independent, quasi-public, underpaid, largely female workforce that underpins the hidden "care economy."

The deputy director of the UDW (and vice chair of CCPU) is Johanna Hester, who moved to California from the Philippines as a teenager to join her father, a labor leader with a hotel union. She grew up going to picket lines as a weekend family activity. As one of the triumvirate of union leaders overseeing the newly formed child care workers' union, she knows that getting California's collective bargaining law changed was only the beginning of a much longer fight to wrest concessions from the state government. Just because the sitting governor had signed their law did not mean that the contract negotiations, which began in 2020, were easy. CCPU had to navigate the political tightrope of butting heads at the bargaining table with an administration that had just granted it a grand policy wish.

"The state was hardcore. Adamant, and digging in their heels," Hester recalls. Eventually, the two sides handled some of the knottiest long-term issues by agreeing to form nine separate "joint labor-management committees," each tasked with meeting further to chew over things like retirement, health care, and how much to raise the reimbursement rate for providers. There was an element of kicking the can down the road in this approach, yes. But CCPU was dealing with the added wrinkle, familiar to many public sector unions, of the fact that the state has an annual budgeting process, and they needed to get a deal signed on time to be included in the budget. Their first contract, which members voted to ratify in June 2021, did not magically resolve all the persistent problems facing child care workers, but it did, for the first time in state history, create a formal structure for those workers to force the state to address them.

That first contract included money to fund a study about how to provide retirement to child care workers, 15 percent pay increases, and a $40 million fund for job training. A year later, workers received thousands of dollars each in supplemental pay from the state to cover some of their extra pandemic costs. In September 2022, members voted to approve a dues structure, as well as a health care agreement that puts $100 million per year into a health care trust that the union can use to help providers defray their expenses. The labor-management committees met with an eye toward the second contract, which they won and ratified in 2023. Discussions were underway about how to change the regulations that say that providers who accept state-subsidized kids can't charge higher prices to parents who can afford to pay, which traps providers in poverty and tends to segregate young children by class. After twenty years, the negotiating table had been built. The next generation of providers will sit at that table and engage in the grinding business of improving their own lives.

It is mind-boggling to consider the vast amount of work that lies ahead for CCPU, given the amount of work that has already been done. Now that the legal structure exists, all of the tens of thousands of providers in the state must be pulled into it by time-intensive outreach from the various unions. When Johanna Hester speaks about organizing the providers in the nearly forty counties she is responsible for, she lists the different communities that must be reached: Armenians, Bengalis, Bangladeshis, Vietnamese, Chinese, Somali . . . just for starters. Members from each of these groups of providers must be recruited to become organizers for the union themselves. In this way, the painstaking process of drawing many people into a coherent group proceeds. In this way, as time passes, a union is made.

Hester scoffs at outmoded views of what "diversity" means for organized labor—Black, white, maybe some Mexicans, if you're in California. She sees CCPU as a part of the "cosmopolitan" future of unions, an everyone-in group embodying the ideal of solidarity in a world that seems to be everywhere teetering on the edge of socialism or fascism. This is the idea of unions as a tool for political change: a power center that sits outside of political parties, changing people themselves through democratic participation, forming a bulwark against the far right's temptations for the working class.

"What's happening globally affects us. The fact that there's a rise of right-wing leaders coming up that are anti-immigrant, anti-refugees, anti-abortion. Suppressing people's rights is happening globally," she says. None of this is sloganeering. If you want to find an organization that is by its very nature dedicated to women's rights and immigrant rights and economic and social and political equality, look no further than CCPU. The urgency of those rights is not an academic issue for them, but an existential one. Hester knows that there is a lesson for the entire labor movement here about the benefits of organizing at scale—as they have done in California— and the consequences of failing to do so. "Status quo has dwindled our numbers. It has dwindled our power. Shooting our numbers up equates to power. We stay the same? We protect only us? There won't be anybody else," she says. "And then they're coming for us."

=

CCPU IS A GREAT EXAMPLE OF THE ILLUSORY NATURE OF LIMITS TO ORGA-nized labor. A union does not need to arise out of a single group of workers who come to the same building every day and get paid by the same company. A union can be made from any coherent group of working people with a common interest—even if they are spread across a thousand miles of distance and work individually out of their homes and are not allowed to *be* a union, according to the current law. It may take twenty years, but it can be done. Contemplating this fact, you begin to understand that America is a vast, virgin landscape for labor organizing, an enormous array of potentially powerful groups just waiting for someone to invest the time in pulling them together.

Typically, the power of a union is rooted in its ability to strike. Even if they have no other leverage, workers have the ability to withhold their own labor. For child care providers, though, this is not so simple. Set aside for a moment the legal challenges from the state, and set aside also the logistical challenges of pulling together such drastic collective action from a widely dispersed pool of independent businesspeople with little financial cushion to carry them through. Any child care strike would have to wrestle with the fact that it would impose its harshest burden on the working parents who would be deprived of a place to deposit their children so they could work, and on the children whose routines would be disrupted. The power of the strike, in other words, would have to be delivered by exacting pain on society's most vulnerable groups. The employer who would be the actual target of a strike—the state of California—would only feel its pressure indirectly, through the cries of citizens whose lives were being upended. (A group of citizens that does not have much pull with lawmakers anyhow.) CCPU's own leaders will muse on the theoretical possibility, one day, of a tightly planned strike with strict geographic limits and a set timeline. But to the extent that winning strikes depends on public support for the strikers, child care workers find themselves in a tenuous position. A strike would be possible, but would require an extraordinary amount of coalition-building in order to ensure it didn't backfire.

In fact, the support and sympathy of parents for the providers has been a cornerstone of their union drive since the very beginning. Decades ago, when Miren Algorri was watching kids while her mother took an overnight bus to Sacramento to rally for the union, they were very open with the parents about what they were fighting for and why. As you might imagine, parents who are fond of their child care provider will naturally want to support that provider's right to dignity and economic security. As with teachers' unions who use their labor power to win things like smaller class sizes and better resources for students, CCPU wants to bargain for the common good.

Because of this, parents have been cultivated as natural allies of the campaign. "Parents know how involved I am. Parents from my child care have been part of the [CCPU] actions. Parents who are essential workers have been interviewed, and they're very adamant about, 'Respect my child care provider. I wouldn't be able to be a part of the workforce if it wasn't for my provider,'" Algorri says. "And of course, when they see that we're fighting for, let's say, family fees to be eradicated—why wouldn't they support the providers, when they see that the providers are advocating for them as well?"

Child care is a tattered-to-nonexistent piece of America's paltry social safety net. That is maddening since it is a universal need, and studies show that public investment in it pays off down the road in a variety of social and educational benefits. A 2018 report from the UC Berkeley Labor Center found that the number of licensed family child care facilities in California had fallen by 30 percent over the preceding decade, leading to desperate shortages of capacity. Providers and their assistants frequently left the industry because they didn't make enough money, a problem that is under the direct control of the state. The result is that hundreds of thousands of women don't participate in the labor force because they don't have reliable child care. The report estimated that every dollar the state spent on the industry would generate $1.88 in increased economic activity, and would help women in the state save and earn billions of dollars. Still, we are nowhere close to a national political consensus that child care should be a priority, even in the arena of social spending.

The most obvious institutions with the will and expertise to forge that consensus are the child care unions like CCPU. Though they may not know it, the sanity of millions of working parents is tied to the ability of these unions to translate labor organizing into political power into state spending. In private industries, businesses like to wail about unions as entities that raise costs. But in a quasi-public industry like subsidized child care, that argument is turned on its head. An organized workforce will ultimately extract more subsidies from the state that are desperately needed to make the lives of "consumers" (parents, in this case) easier, not harder.

What could be more wholesome, more admirable, more *American* than a group of hardworking, self-motivated entrepreneurs banding together to work in a nonviolent collective manner for years on end to shake a government bureaucracy out of its shameful paralysis and create a better life for everyone? How could even the most conservative observer not celebrate these paragons of family values, these women who sacrifice to improve the lives not only of their own families, but of *your* family? These are true public servants, who sacrifice sleep and money and health care and retirement to nurture and care for the children of those who do the jobs that make society function. In a rational world, a union of child care providers would be considered as mainstream and uncontroversial as the Rotary Club or Sunday school. We're talking about a group dedicated to work and love and family and humanity. That CCPU is only at the beginning of its journey after twenty years of struggle is a testament to how hostile American politics is to organized labor. It is as good an explanation for the failure of neoliberalism as anything you are likely to find.

As the shrieks of children at play echo from Jackie Jackson's backyard in South Central LA, she perches on a chair designed for a toddler and reflects on her sacrifices. Can't afford retirement savings. Can't afford to buy health insurance. Can't afford a vacation, and couldn't get the time off even if she could. Can't even take a sick day. How could she? Wake up at 4 a.m. and desperately call a dozen different parents to tell them their only child care option was closed that day because she didn't feel good? Instead, she exercises and takes vitamins and prays.

"I've filled up everybody's cup in this community. I've cared for over two thousand children in that blue van, right across the street," she says, nodding at the battered blue van with "WE LOVE THE KIDS" lettered on the back window, which she uses to shuttle kids to and from school. That vehicle is now recognized everywhere in this part of town. "They've been taken care of. Who's gonna take care of you, when it's all said and done?"

One of her sons is a promising college basketball player at New Mexico State University; he might make the NBA, and then she would be set. If not, the union is her only safety net.

This is the reward that generations of people have earned who have decided to take the initiative to dedicate their lives to caring for needy children: no health care, no retirement, low pay, and endless toil. This job is hard and materially thankless. Nobody would do it if they did not have a deep well of care in their hearts. That is the same well that the union has drawn its sustenance from.

When Miren Algorri thinks back on what she's gone through—being an immigrant, shouldering the load of her mother's business, seven long years spent without a single day off when she herself was a young mother with her own new child care practice—she is not bitter. Her pain is tempered by her knowledge of the pain that others have gone through alongside her. She thinks of the providers she knows who are afflicted with fibromyalgia or neuropathic illness, bodies broken from a lifetime of work. She thinks of the child she cares for whose mother wakes him up at three o'clock in the morning to commute to San Diego from their home in Tijuana because the family can't afford to live on the American side of the border. She knows that she is part of a vast web of mutual support that is fueled by love. It sure ain't fueled by money. To have the state of California put its stamp of legal approval on this invisible network of love is not an act of creation, but instead of bestowing a name on something that was always there.

"Be relentless. Be relentless," Algorri says. When she sits at the little children's table, she looks like the giant that she is to all of those she has cared for. "It's not like, 'Oh, we're planning on forming a union.' Act like you're a union. Get up every day, and be like: 'My union. It's mine.'"

CHAPTER FOUR

SARA NELSON HAS A DREAM

On the next to last day of March 2022, when the snow had sub-
sided but the chill had not, Chicago leaned into its Gotham quality,
dark and urban and foreboding. The crowds on the streets of the Loop hus-
tled to get into the warm indoors. Low gray clouds dusted the top of the
Willis Tower, and dropped fat raindrops that soaked you through in just a
few seconds. A dozen bike cops leaned unnecessarily against the skyscraper's
entrance, and a line of Chicago PD vans were parked around the corner on
Wacker Drive.

Across the street from the tower's impassive glass face, huddled under
umbrellas that the wind kept flipping inside out, were a couple of hundred
union members. Most of them were with SEIU Local One, a fifty-thousand-
strong Midwestern working-class powerhouse, and they came covered in the
purple swag that the SEIU does so well: purple, union-branded rain slickers,
purple windbreakers, purple T-shirts and sweatshirts and skullcaps and ball-
caps and facemasks and yellow and purple bandannas. There was a PA system, and a purple tent had been set up to shelter the speakers. Several union
staffers had assigned themselves the job of reaching up to grab the metal
struts of the tent when the wind gusted to keep it from flying away.

The event was one of more than twenty happening across the country that day to promote the SEIU's campaign on behalf of airport workers. The union represents thousands of people who clean airplane cabins, push wheelchairs through terminals, move baggage, and do other tasks that make airports function. They were trying to pressure CEOs of all the major airlines to sign a "Good Airports Pledge" to give living wage jobs and union rights to the many subcontracted airport workers who receive less of everything than their counterparts with a union do. Inside the gleaming Willis Tower are the offices of United Airlines—so outside, across the street, in the rain, and surrounded by bored police officers, was the union rally. This afforded the assembled workers the opportunity to raise their twenty-watt electronic bullhorns up at the impassive skyscraper windows and unleash the siren's "WOOP" sound, which was cathartic.

In addition to Mary Kay Henry, the thin woman with short brown hair and transition lenses who has been the president of the two-million-member SEIU for more than a decade, the headline speaker of the Chicago rally was Sara Nelson. She stood out there in the rain, in impeccable makeup, and raised her fist up at the tower and yelled for United CEO Scott Kirby to sign the pledge. This was at least a tad bit more meaningful than the average union demand shouted up at an office tower, since Nelson knows Kirby well from contract negotiations, and she is a United flight attendant herself. (The same day, former United CEO Oscar Munoz, who retired in 2019, published a gushing LinkedIn essay about Nelson declaring her "formidable" and calling her the future of American labor. It was a weird compliment coming from a former CEO, but it's a reflection of how often airline unions and companies found themselves on the same side during various crises, both with the basic common interest of keeping the airlines alive and their employees employed in the face of various catastrophes.)

Nelson hollered to the crowd of airport workers that she was there representing fifty thousand flight attendants who were, at that very moment, flying overhead, raining down solidarity—a standard line from her, but an appropriate one in the context of the sodden day. People cheered. Throughout the entire rally, one man in a rain slicker stood calmly behind the speakers, holding up a little blue inflatable airplane to lend a sense of aviation to the whole affair. Over an hour in the gusting drizzle, the mood on the sidewalk remained boisterous to the very end.

Though the flight attendants and their union were not technically part of the SEIU's airport campaign, a quick jaunt to Chicago to speak at the rally was typical for Sara Nelson. She went everywhere, all the time. There were several reasons for her constant whirlwind of speeches: of all union leaders in America, she gives the most rousing speech; she is one of the few union leaders recognizable to at least some people who are not in her union, which makes her a popular guest; and, as previously mentioned, she is generally disposed to say yes to every incoming event invite and interview request. Also, her passion for the labor movement propels her like a nuclear reactor does a submarine. This mix of aggressive media savvy and legitimate ideology makes her something of a polarizing figure in the small and clubby world of union leadership. Her style can be interpreted either as that of someone who stays visible to further the cause, or, less generously, as someone whose cause is staying visible. That small and clubby world of union leadership consists of the same people who decide who will become the president of the AFL-CIO, an ambition that Nelson was still chewing over. She needed more allies. So she needed to schmooze.

Due to the nagging grind of recovery from her surgeries and everyone's slow emergence from Covid's activity freeze that characterized early 2022, much of that necessary schmoozing had not happened yet. Nelson remained torn on what to do. Her ambition to lead the labor movement burned, but she felt, more than ever before, hemmed in by the unavoidable limitations of time and space.

In February, as Nelson was grappling with her future, she'd had dinner with Randi Weingarten. Weingarten, a blunt New Yorker, is the longtime president of the 1.7 million–member American Federation of Teachers, one of the AFL-CIO's biggest unions. She is the public face of teachers' unions in America, making her a seasoned political operator and a power broker within the Democratic Party—and, to an even greater extent, within the union coalition. Her support would be critical for anyone hoping to become AFL-CIO president.

Weingarten is, broadly speaking, on the progressive end of the union spectrum, though that tendency is constrained by the reality of leading such a huge organization. She was not as freewheeling, nor as fiery, as Sara Nelson, but any campaign strategist seeking to build a group of unions to support a Nelson run for AFL president would probably start with Weingarten. You would expect her to be more sympathetic to Nelson's larger vision than some of the other leaders of the biggest unions. For Nelson to win the AFL's presidency without the support of AFT would be like a Democrat winning the White House without winning California: mathematically possible, but practically unthinkable.

At dinner, Weingarten was frank. She said nice things about Nelson's talents, but she also said that she did not think Nelson would win in a race against Liz Shuler, the incumbent whose predictable style most of the big unions felt comfortable with. Weingarten told Nelson that she would not get the votes of the big unions—including Weingarten's own union, AFT. Weingarten counseled her that she might be better off just using her political capital to get on a committee she was interested in inside the AFL-CIO, or getting some resolutions passed at the convention. The conversation was not a definitive closed door, but it was a flashing sign that the inside game at the labor coalition was unlikely to pan out.

The physical constraints on her ability to exercise her personal charm rankled Nelson. "Union leaders haven't been together in over two years. People like me, when they work with me. It's easy to just read what's in the papers, or see what's on TV, or hear what people are saying about someone. But it's different when you can have those one-on-one connections," she reflected. "I'm saying all of that because I had always envisioned running a campaign that didn't look like anything that had ever happened in the lead up to the election of AFL president . . . I think one of the problems is that the people that are closest to it can't imagine what that position could actually be."

She kept thinking about her 2017 dinner with Richard Trumka, on the eve of his reelection as AFL-CIO president, when he told her that nothing about the job excited him. Did it have to be so grim? Was it necessary for the job perceived as the highest in the labor movement to be a humdrum slog of dealing with jurisdictional disputes between unions and backroom lobbying on trade policy? If the AFL-CIO was labor's equivalent of the White House, it was doing an awful job using the bully pulpit. Where was the *vision*? Though unions drew their power from solidarity between workers, the notion of solidarity between unions themselves—real solidarity, meaning coordinated strategy, funding, and action to organize the tens of millions of unorganized Americans—barely existed. And because of that, the labor movement's power remained splintered. The AFL-CIO seemed incapable of marshaling all its unions in a single, concerted direction. There could be great power in doing so, but it was hard to know if such a thing was even possible. The gap between the coalition's potential and its reality seemed to alternately energize and depress Nelson.

She considered her options. There was also the outside game. The upside of becoming AFL-CIO president would be the built-in attention and credibility that go with the job perceived as the highest one in labor, the ability to use it as a launching pad for a coherent strategy. On the other hand, the position also came with an explicit lack of actual power to make the member unions *do* anything, and with the responsibility to spend a potentially limitless amount of time serving as mediator-in-chief on internal spats. She was contemplating, again, the possibility of just launching a new, independent organization to do the things that needed to be done, without being held back by the AFL's thicket of competing interests. When John L. Lewis, the crusading leader of the United Mine Workers, faced similar frustrations almost a century ago, he had picked up and left the AFL and formed the CIO, which did the kind of industrial organizing that labor progressives still pine for. Instead of grasping for the top job at the labor coalition, or accepting some consolation prize as Weingarten suggested, would it be better to just use the visibility she had accrued to follow in the CIO's more radical footsteps—not a competing labor coalition, but at least a skeleton upon which new unions could be built?

"You have all this interest in organizing, but workers will reach out to unions and some unions will say, 'We don't have the bandwidth,' or 'It's not a fit with our union, and we won't be able to staff the representation, so it's not gonna work.' Or they just don't know who to call, period. So giving workers a path to actually reach out and have the backing of—whether it's the AFL-CIO, or something new that's created—that has a legal staff, a comms staff, and an organizing staff that helps see them through the election, and then their first contract. And even if they're forming their own independent unions, ultimately they'll come into the larger labor movement. That's what has to happen. That's what happened in the '30s." She pauses and gives a bitter chuckle. "All we have to do is extract the racism and sexism from that process!"

By March, Nelson had a small brain trust of union world veterans mulling this idea over. But she still had a lot to handle herself. She was up for reelection as president of her own union, the AFA, in May. The long-running quest to organize more than 25,000 flight attendants at Delta Air Lines, which had been one of the AFA's goals for decades, had reached the stage where it seemed like a true possibility. The Choose-Your-Own-Adventure book that was Sara Nelson's career was laid open before her, with only a few pages left. She had an eye on her own union, another eye on starting something new, and a head that was always quietly updating a mental list of where allies might be found among the other union leaders who would be voting for AFL-CIO president. She also nurtured, in the back of her mind, another, more dramatic option: to have someone nominate her for president from the floor of the AFL-CIO convention itself, creating a thrilling moment of old-fashioned unpredictability at the stodgy proceedings, a moment that she could use to air in a forceful way the platform that she could not stop thinking about.

March turned to April. The convention was seventy days away. She still needed to rest and let her body heal. But there was too much to do.

=

THERE IS NEVER A TIME WHEN SARA NELSON IS NOT TOO BUSY. TO RUN A union, in the most practical sense, is a full-time job. To then try to be the public voice of an entire industry is a job on top of that, and to try to be the public voice of the labor movement is a job on top of that. April 2022 was a fairly standard month. She spent many days dealing with the fallout of an April 18 ruling by a Trump-appointed federal judge that voided the federal mask mandate on airlines. That ruling had dropped with such little warning that passengers heard about it mid-flight, causing pilots and flight attendants and passengers alike to either shed their masks joyfully or glance around in panic as their potentially virus-spewing seatmates did. This was the sort of sudden, chaotic travel situation that caused Nelson to be booked for days' worth of nonstop interviews on every cable news station and *Good Morning America*, and to spend hours on the phone with newspaper reporters. These all-encompassing floods of media requests happen whenever some air travel issue floats up to the top of the national news: viral videos of unruly passengers, the airline rescue bill, bankruptcies, whatever. Nelson's dual role as someone that CNN will put on the air to talk about the dire need for Democrats to pass an essential worker economic rescue package, *or* as someone to discuss how early you should get to the airport during the spring break rush can feel a little jarring. But much of her ascent to the top of the minds of union members has been built on a foundation of media relationships that were forged over humdrum aviation issues. During the pandemic, even when she was being interviewed about nonlabor issues, Nelson would appear from her home office in front of a bookcase full of labor history, its shelves festooned with signs touting the latest strikes or organizing campaigns.

So April, as usual, was full of flight attendant–related work. But Nelson also took the time during the month to go to McCalla, Alabama, to speak at a rally for the one-year anniversary of the United Mine Workers strike at Warrior Met Coal, a strike she had repeatedly traveled to Alabama for in 2021; and to go to Richmond, Virginia, to drive around speaking to Starbucks workers who were unionizing at several different stores; and to go to Long Island, New York, to speak to the college class of Stephanie Kelton, the left-wing economist who has become one of Nelson's close allies; and to go to Staten Island for a big rally celebrating the victory of the independent Amazon Labor Union (ALU), which secured the first successful union election at any Amazon warehouse in America at the beginning of April.

That ALU victory, in which a completely independent, grassroots, scrappy group of workers and volunteers shocked the world by overcoming Amazon's incessant union busting to unionize more than eight thousand workers, was by far the most thrilling union news of 2022. But it was also a quietly uncomfortable moment for the union establishment, which had to face the fact that these scrappy independents had succeeded where none of the big and well-funded unions ever had. (To be fair, the Retail, Whole-sale and Department Store Union, which has spent millions trying to orga-nize the Amazon warehouse in Bessemer, Alabama, has always been vocally supportive of the ALU, rather than casting them as competitors. They and other unions have given ALU material support.) Every union leader issued hearty congratulations to the ALU when they won, but only a few both-ered to attend the celebration rally. Nelson not only went but leaned into the theater. She took the makeshift stage in a gray ALU sweatshirt and gripped the handheld microphone and started roaring. "They are fighting for the things we fought for a hundred years ago. Because somebody came up with a phrase called 'labor peace.' Let me tell you something: there is no fucking labor peace!" Then she peeled off the sweatshirt to reveal an AFA T-shirt underneath. A little sartorial solidarity. "I have to tell you that after twenty-five years of doing this work and praying like hell that people would wake up to their power, this union is the answer to my prayers!" she howled. Finally, she whipped off the AFA shirt, revealing a red ALU T-shirt under-neath, and led the crowd in a chant of "I've got your back."

I spent the pandemic years of 2020 and 2021 as a full-time labor reporter. As the Covid disaster oozed into every crevice of life, it was possible to look in any direction in America and find that there were two basic stories. One was, "I'm suddenly out of work, and I'm in a crisis." The other was, "I'm forced to continue working, and I'm in a crisis." The white-collar part of America, the part that worked on a computer and could easily work from home, was doing okay. Every other part of working America found itself in an economic crisis, a health crisis, or both, mixed in with unprecedented levels of stress. Working people learned in a very visceral way that their jobs did not care about them, or their lives. It was a time of death and struggle and awakening. Capitalism expected people to work and die, or to not work and die, but certainly not to be cared for, or shielded from harm, or rewarded for their sacrifice in continuing to work while others sheltered at home. The suffering of those two years was matched by a widespread and unavoidable realization that there was no safety net, that the system would not shelter you, that if workers wanted to be protected from the ravages of poverty and illness and uncertainty, they must seek out that protection on their own.

It was, in other words, a once-in-a-century advertisement for the value of organized labor. When I interviewed union leaders during the pandemic, I would always ask them whether they thought that this crisis would lead to a huge swell in labor organizing. And they always said, "Yes." And throughout 2021 there was a wave of very visible strikes that instilled in the news cycle a sense that labor militancy was rising, and going into 2022 there were some very visible union-organizing wins at name-brand companies like Starbucks, and then the win at Amazon. If you were a person who paid attention to labor news casually, you could see a sustained pattern of exciting things happening. But if you paid attention closely, you could see that reality was not shaping itself quite so neatly to expectation.

By April 2022, a Brookings Institute report found, the shareholders at twenty-two major American companies had gotten $1.5 trillion richer during the pandemic, while the workers at all those companies had only seen one-fiftieth of that amount in wage gains. The economic effect of the pandemic was not to mitigate the primacy of the investor class in our hierarchy, but to magnify it. In practice, this looked like all the warehouse workers and grocery store workers and meatpacking workers who received temporary "hero pay" raises for a few months during the scariest part of 2020, and then saw those raises phased out even though hundreds of thousands of people were yet to die from Covid. The inability of workers to reap the benefits of the enormous, stimulus-fueled boom of those years—to use their willingness to work during the pandemic as leverage for permanent gains, rather than settling for the lowliest pile of crumbs that could possibly be offered to induce them not to quit—is a direct result of the lack of organized labor power in America. Ninety percent of workers do not have a union that would have allowed them to collectively bargain at that key moment when everything was uncertain. And, it must be said, most of those that did have unions failed to seize the opportunity. The hundreds of thousands of unionized grocery workers, for example, could have asked for and received almost anything in March 2020 if they had threatened to strike for their own safety. But their unions were not organized enough, daring enough, or capable of enough long-term vision to do such a thing. And so both union and nonunion workers alike, for the most part, struggled through the pandemic as a pure matter of survival, while corporate investors experienced it as a time that supercharged their wealth. The gains that low-wage workers did achieve during those years were a result of simple supply and demand in a tight labor market to a far greater degree than they were the result of strategic action by organized labor.

At the beginning of 2020, when the coronavirus had not yet upended everything and inspired everyone and made all the union leaders so sure that their time was coming, 10.3 percent of American workers were union members. At the beginning of 2022, after twenty-four brutal months of proof of the absolute necessity of unions to millions of workers everywhere, 10.3 percent of American workers were union members. The needle did not move. In terms of raw numbers, in fact, there were 562,000 fewer union members in America on January 1, 2022, than there were on January 1, 2020.

So even with an extremely friendly president and a pro-worker National Labor Relations Board (NLRB) that was trying, for once, to enforce labor laws, and even though public opinion polls showed that public approval of unions was at a fifty-year high, and even though organized labor was receiving more positive media coverage than it had in decades, the inexorable downward slide of union density had continued right on schedule. This was not some great blow from the pandemic that was impossible to predict; it was perfectly in line with the trend of the past half century. Filings for union elections had shot up sharply through the first part of 2022, but the long-term impact remained to be seen. No matter how inspiring individual wins like the Amazon warehouse on Staten Island were, pulling back to look at the big picture was still grim. You could unionize fifty more gargantuan warehouses the size of the one on Staten Island and still not make up the loss in union members over those two years.

Everything that the labor movement was doing was not enough.

=

SARA NELSON IS A MOTHER JONES AFICIONADO. WHEN SHE SPEAKS TO labor groups, whether onstage or through a megaphone in the midst of a crowd, she is very likely to drop a quote from the woman who served as the moral voice of the early twentieth century's savage labor struggles. The quote that Nelson repeats most often is: "The capitalists say there is no need of labor organizing, but the fact that they themselves are continually organizing shows their real beliefs." The second most common, deployed when the news is not good, is: "You will fight and lose. You will fight and win. But you must fight." The exact wording fluctuates often in the telling, but the message is never hard to grasp.

On May 1, Nelson went to Illinois to give the keynote speech to the annual Mother Jones May Day event, put on by the nonprofit group that runs the Mother Jones Museum. (The group is also working to build a Mother Jones statue, and they have a giant inflatable Mother Jones balloon that they tote to picket lines and labor rallies around the country, where she often stands proudly next to her more menacing inflatable counterpart, Scabby the Rat.) It was a crowd of only the truest believers, and Nelson delivered a jeremiad, building in volume as it went on, about how unions, not the ballot box, would be the salvation of the working class, and about the need to shock the existing labor establishment out of its stupor. "It can't be about looking to politicians to save us today," she thundered. "Someone asked me last week, 'Do you think this is the one time that labor has in a hundred years to make the case to working people for unions?' And I said, 'No, the working people are making the case *to the labor movement* that they want unions!'"

The next night, as if to illustrate the folly of believing that the normal political process would move us toward justice, the draft of the Supreme Court's Dobbs opinion overturning *Roe v. Wade* leaked. Nelson's immediate reaction was emotional devastation. She was born in 1973, the year that the *Roe* ruling came down. Its looming reversal made a vivid case that America had regressed, not progressed, during her lifetime.

She is not the type of person to wallow for long. Her instinct, always, is to act. Yet this was a problem with no direct, immediate solution. It was, however, a direct and immediate reminder of the labor movement's traditional unwillingness to throw itself with full power at such all-encompassing (and controversial) political struggles. Organized labor in America has historically been a progressive force, in the sense of being a counterweight to unrestrained capitalism and a bulwark against economic inequality. But it has not covered itself in glory when it comes to larger social issues that cannot be solved within the narrow bounds of a union contract. The AFL-CIO, and its earlier predecessor, the AFL, have a long track record of racism, sexism, coziness with American imperialism, and other sins that result from the belief that unions exist to serve the specific interests of their specific members, and that if people outside of those bounds get screwed in the process, that is not the union's problem. The AFL-CIO today is far more progressive in its public presentation than it was in past generations. But without a shift in the fundamental belief that organized labor is only really responsible for itself, rather than for the working class at large—a belief that has always marked the boundary between conservatives and radicals—the labor movement is destined to follow, rather than to lead, on the hardest ideological fights.

On the last night of May 2020, in the early wave of Black Lives Matter protests that swept America after George Floyd's murder at the hands of the Minneapolis police, the AFL-CIO's headquarters building in Washington, DC, which sits right across from Lafayette Square, was set on fire by protesters. The building's lobby was boarded up for months after that as the protests continued, but the AFL did at least hang huge "Black Lives Matter" banners down the sides of its building while it was being repaired. The name of the street outside was officially changed to Black Lives Matter Plaza by the city of DC. (The AFL's leadership, however, forcefully rejected subsequent calls from individual unions and activists to kick police unions out of their organization.) Sara Nelson thought about the long, convoluted, and inexact effort to marshal the labor coalition's power on behalf of that, the biggest protest wave in American history. Two years later, in early May 2022, it felt like the imminent outlawing of abortion could foreshadow another period of hesitancy and heartbreak—the heartbreak of trying to wield the collective power of unions in the face of apathy or obliviousness.

"I've been very aware that we've been unwilling, as a labor movement, to fight for equal rights for women. More and more aware, the more that I do this work. Women's jobs are considered less valuable than jobs that are predominantly done by men. Period, across the board. Forget the wage gap. That's the real wage gap. It's not just people doing the same job, it's looking at the professions that are predominantly held by women and people of color, and those that are held by white men. That's where the major wage gap is. Of course that's right in my face on the airplane, because of pilots and flight attendants," Nelson said. She wanted the latest political atrocity to spur not just another single-issue battle—in this case for abortion rights—but a broader and more radical demand for society-wide equality. When she gave an off-the-cuff speech to this effect on an internal call with the AFL-CIO's executive council just after the Supreme Court's anti-abortion decision was leaked, she was not inspired by the response. "I said, 'This is the first step to authoritarianism.' That's where we're headed. If we don't understand that, and we don't understand that we have to step out right now, and not just say that we're for *Roe v. Wade*, but that we're for women—for women having equal rights in this country . . . It's not about health care. It's not about an abortion. It's about whether or not women have equal standing in this country, and whether or not we're going to claim that power as working people. That's the moment that we're in right now. And I don't think—I mean, maybe they'll surprise me. But I don't know that this labor movement, the leadership of this labor movement, is ready for this moment."

Though she still harbored a strong belief that she would be excellent at the job—and, perhaps, a few fantasies of a last-minute grassroots uprising to claim it—by May, it was becoming clear to Nelson and to the union world at large that there was probably not going to be a contested election for AFL-CIO president at the convention in June. The big union leaders who did not much care for Sara Nelson had mostly relaxed into certainty that Liz Shuler would be the only candidate, and that she would be a stable hand on the controls.

On May 14, at the AFA's own convention in Las Vegas, Nelson was reelected unanimously to a third term as president of her own union. She was in the midst of negotiating with Frontier and Spirit Airlines about what their proposed merger would mean for her members, and her attention was also on her union's enormous campaign to organize more than twenty-five thousand flight attendants at Delta, which would be one of the biggest triumphs of her career if they could pull it off. On May 23, a *New Yorker* profile of Nelson, written by Jennifer Gonnerman, was published; in it, she was quoted as saying that the presidency of the AFL-CIO was "not something I want."

Fate had made the presidency of the AFL-CIO retreat, month by month, from Nelson's grasp. She was an astute enough political observer to understand this. But the burning urge to change something an order of magnitude larger than her own union—the urge that comes about when you recognize the gap between what the labor movement could be and what it is—gnawed at her. By the end of May, the convention was only two weeks away. Sara Nelson knew that if she wasn't going to do that, she needed to do *something*.

CHAPTER FIVE

THE MACHINE
THE CULINARY UNION OF LAS VEGAS, NEVADA

We're in the Bellagio. We're *in* the Bellagio, right through one of the inconspicuous "AUTHORIZED PERSONNEL ONLY" doors, where the perfectly polished and unmarked floors of the marble-drenched casino end and the scuffed, dreary floors of a workplace begin. Down endlessly winding hallways with decommissioned slot machines and pallets of wine and head-high carts of clean linens and old tables and chairs and crates of bottled water stacked against the walls, each door leads to a different restaurant or snack bar or ballroom where the pretend world of Las Vegas unfolds. On one side of those doors is a fantasy. On the other side of each of those doors are the people who do the work that creates the fantasy.

Juston Larsen is a union baby. He has brown skin, a tiny nose stud, a low beard, and a forearm tattoo that reads "Never Grow Up" with a picture of Peter Pan. He is twenty-six years old. For twenty-five of those years, his mother has been a food server at the Las Vegas airport. For most of that time, she's also been a shop steward in the mighty Culinary Union—Local

226 of the international union Unite Here. Juston grew up playing at the union hall. In his early twenties, he took a job as a barista at Starbucks at the airport, which landed him in the union as well. He has spent the past year taking part in the union's Leave of Absence (LOA) program, in which they pull workers out of their day jobs, give them training, and teach them how to do union work. From 2021 to 2022, Juston has been working as an organizer representing the union's hundreds of members at the resplendent Bellagio, in the heart of the Vegas strip. Trailing him around there as he does his rounds is like watching Ray Liotta in *Goodfellas* breezing into the crowded nightclub through the kitchen, if that raucous scene had been accompanied by many, many more complaints.

In the center courtyard of the Bellagio, blissful guests lounge on padded pool chairs around a series of aquamarine pools, flanked by bars and cabanas. Little do they know the chaos that surrounds them, separated by a single wall. Everywhere Juston pokes his head, a crisis awaits. Minor outrages abound: management has removed the employee lockers; a bartender is forced to use a bucket for her tools because they moved her storage area too far away; a manager is out serving drinks, an ominous sign of understaffing. All the vacation fantasies playing out by the pool exist atop an unseen sea of pandemonium. In the kitchen behind one of the pool bars, a harried server with curly blonde hair and whose uniform is a bikini stacks a fantastic number of drinks on a serving tray and tries to check drink tickets while simultaneously narrating to Juston a litany of scheduling problems. "It's a shit show," she concludes apologetically, before whirling out toward the cabanas.

Though Juston is, technically speaking, just a twenty-something airport Starbucks employee, he strides through this palace of luxury with the confidence of a CEO, nodding to managers, stopping everywhere to talk to employees in hushed tones, and always making mental notes about the evolving landscape of possible contract violations. His power is the union button he wears. It is as good as any VIP pass that a casino company could bestow. The Culinary Union, you see, runs this fucking town. They earned their influence with close to ninety years of sweat. And they have as much to teach us about how regular people can build power as any union in the United States of America.

=

LAS VEGAS IS AN AWFUL PLACE. ITS EXISTENCE AS A PULSING, NEON-drenched magnet of excess set in a parched desert valley is an abomination against sustainability, good taste, and common sense. The Las Vegas Strip, rising out of the black desert like an evil electric eel, is the street that is most like America itself: grandiose, decadent, and infested by Midwestern tourists looking confused about how they ended up in a party bus. From the gold-windowed Mandalay Bay at its southern tip all the way up to the soaring tower of the Strat, which stands 1,149 pointless feet above the flat city and punctuates the Strip like a disappointing exclamation point, those four miles of manufactured glamour suck in billions of dollars a year and pump out an ultra-distilled version of the American dream. If the abiding belief that we will all earn a small-town home with a white picket fence is the opiate of the masses, Vegas is the cocaine. From a distance, the glare is blinding; look too close, and all you can see are the hard-faced men arranging their belongings on the hot sidewalk of Las Vegas Boulevard, and bedding down for the night under dirty blankets in the alley behind the Bonanza Gift Shop.

When you stand outside of the Strat, you can look one way down Las Vegas Boulevard and see all the world's neon and false promises. Then, you can look in the other direction, away from the Strip, and see a homeless man sleeping precisely within the small shadow cast by a thigh-high concrete wall in the early afternoon sun, a tiny oasis of shade that grows inch by inch as the long day wears on, allowing him to slowly roll from his side onto his back over the course of several hours. In every little crack of the city's facade lurks some sort of poison. When I got a haircut downtown, the barber stopped mid-snip when I told him I was staying at the Strat. "My mom worked there for twenty years. Whatever you do, don't use the ice buckets," he said. I laughed, but he didn't. His expression was urgent. "People put everything in those ice buckets, man. *Everything.*"

If there is a redeeming quality to Las Vegas, it is that it has allowed generations of regular working people—often immigrants with few opportunities elsewhere—to conjure a decent living out of the desert sands. The fact that such a thing is possible is due not to the casino moguls, who are experts at reserving every last ounce of profit for themselves, but rather to many decades of hard-fought labor organizing. The Culinary Union has led that work since 1935. Today, the union has sixty thousand members, including the housekeepers and porters and bellmen and food servers and cooks and other workers at virtually every casino on the Vegas Strip, as well as a large chunk of the off-Strip casino industry in Nevada. Those members are 55 percent women and 54 percent Latino, and 45 percent of them are immigrants. The union provides guaranteed contracts, free health care, and a pension to all these workers and their families. It is, in a very real sense, an independent social safety net, built from scratch, that has created a middle class where there otherwise would not have been one. To support and protect this mission, the Culinary Union has also built a relentless political operation that has made it one of the most powerful political forces in Nevada. There is now only one degree of separation between an immigrant single mother cocktail waitress at the Tropicana and the White House. Both are directly connected to the whitewashed two-story cement building on Commerce Street with "In Solidarity We Will Win!" painted across it, where the Culinary Union lives.

Inside of the cramped, mazelike offices, next to a floral couch and flanked by pictures of historic strikes, sits Ted Pappageorge, whose neat blue golf shirt and combed gray hair belie his history of agitation. Pappageorge took over as the Culinary Union's secretary-treasurer in 2022 after the retirement of Geoconda Arguello-Kline, a Nicaraguan immigrant who began as a room cleaner and rose to become a legendary activist who led the union for a decade.

Pappageorge was born in Vegas, the city his grandparents had moved to in the 1950s. His parents worked in hotels, and when he was old enough, he did too. In 1990, he was a bartender at Binion's Horseshoe, downtown on Fremont Street. The Binion family, who owned the place, were some of the last of the old-school, mob-affiliated Vegas casino bosses, the type who got the town going before the big corporations moved in. They wanted to break the union. There was a nine-month strike at the Horseshoe, which the union finally won—though the company refused to take back nine of the most incorrigible union activists after the strike, including Pappageorge. A single father with two kids who had just sacrificed his job in the interest of winning the strike, he joined the staff of the union shortly afterward and has been there ever since.

"This is a factory town. It's a company town," he says. "These giant casinos, they rule." The utter control of Las Vegas by a single industry has also been the fuel for its evolution into a strong union town. Just as the United Mine Workers, the United Steelworkers, and the United Auto Workers grew out of factory towns where workers chafed under the iron hand of all-powerful companies, so, too, has the Culinary Union's growth been driven by a clear-eyed understanding that they were the only thing standing between thousands of workers and a life of absolute domination by casino companies. The union's history is riddled with win-or-die organizing fights, contract battles, and strikes in which employers have tested the union's resolve, determined to break it. The most famous of these was the Frontier Strike, which began in 1991 and lasted more than six years, one of the longest strikes in American history. In February 1998, the union won the strike. Nobody crossed the picket line. All the strikers got their jobs back. And the entire industry was forced to recognize the fact that dealing with the Culinary Union, and treating workers fairly, would be the price of operating in Las Vegas.

The union, in turn, has learned through bitter experience what it actually takes to maintain its position in such a cutthroat environment. It is always, always working to organize the remaining nonunion parts of the casino industry, recognizing that every nonunion operation is a threat to the fundamental idea that the industry must operate up to union standards. And it has developed an almost military-grade level of *internal* organizing, keeping in constant contact with members to keep them mobilized for bigger political fights, and to identify, recruit, and train the most enthusiastic members as union activists. It is constantly pulling workers out on LOAs and sending them back to their workplace later with well-developed organizing skills. The Culinary Union's staff and leadership ranks (not to mention the ranks of friendly politicians sprinkled throughout the city and state) are overwhelmingly made up of people who started out working in hotels and casinos.

"We took the things we learned from the strike, and from the nonunion organizing fights, and we adapted them to our union organizing, our union contract fights. We call it our internal program," Pappageorge says. "House visits, recruiting committee [members], daily check-ins with the staff for accountability. 'What are you doing today? What is your goal for today?' And the next day, you come back: 'Did we hit the goal for today?'"

In practice, this process looks like forty Culinary Union organizers and members on LOAs gathered around plastic folding tables on a Monday morning, role-playing the conversations that they will be having with members later that day. Their mission is to rally attendance for the upcoming April "citywide," an all-union meeting held several times a year to keep membership informed and plugged into the latest campaigns. Over and over, the organizers take turns critiquing every bit of small talk—discussing how to best remind the members of everything the union did for them during the pandemic, finding precisely the best moment to tell the member to pull out their phone so they can enter the meeting date on their calendar. Then they all break up to scatter to the different properties on the Strip.

Juston Larsen, a seasoned pro at this work by now, drops his union button–festooned bag at a table in the Bellagio's subterranean employee cafeteria, "Mangia!" He takes a seat near the back wall. Sitting across from him is Cathy, a woman with short blonde hair, approaching retirement age, who works at the casino's Cafe Gelato. During Cathy's workday, her husband, who is having neurological problems, is being watched over by her eighty-one-year-old aunt. "I gotta stop stressing about it, 'cause it's not helping me," Cathy says, kneading a napkin in her hand. "What am I gonna do? I gotta work to get the medical insurance."

Cathy and her brothers run their own contracting business on the side, but she has maintained her job at the Bellagio specifically because of the union's pension and health care plan. She spends several minutes explaining to Juston a troublesome new policy at work: instead of rotating two tubs of gelato so she can scoop from one that is more thawed out, the cafe has started placing one tub of fake gelato in front, for display purposes, leaving her only one tub of real gelato to scoop from, which doesn't allow it time to thaw, which makes the scooping harder work. Juston makes a note of it. This is the sort of unglamorous but useful thing that separates a union job from a nonunion one. It's an avenue to convey to management the employee displeasure with the bad gelato policy.

Cathy agrees to come to the citywide meeting, dutifully entering the date and time in her calendar. Indeed, she makes it a point to attend every one of them. She's been married to her husband for forty-five years, and the scooping of gelato that she does every day is what allows him to access the health care he now desperately needs. Cathy used to be a chef, and was offered management jobs over the years, but she always chose to stick with a union position. "I said nope—I'm gonna stay with the Culinary till I get my pension," she says. "Nobody understands it till they worked their whole life, and they retire, and they've got no pension. They got nothing."

After the meeting, we once again walk up the endless internal hallway on our way to the employee parking lot. As Juston grumbles about having to trudge such a long way every day, a worker who Juston knows zips by on an (employees-only) electric cart. He gives a taunting smile and a wave as he zooms by. "Thanks to the 226, I get to ride!"

=

WE'RE IN NORTH LAS VEGAS, FIVE MILES NORTH OF THE STRIP. It's a neighborhood of humble, rectangular cement block homes, but in every direction there is a backdrop of spectacular mountains, the consolation prize for the sand-colored monotony of every Vegas suburb. The sun's heat is already wafting up off the blacktop at 10 a.m. We are here to do politics. Not the lofty philosophical part of politics, but the *work*.

Tewedage Yohanes, who often introduces herself as "TeeWee," is slim and effusive, with red nails and dark hair pulled up in a bun poking out above a black visor. She grew up in Ethiopia, won a visa, and moved to Las Vegas, where her brother was already living, in 2011. She got a job as a porter at the Excalibur for years and began saving money. She was able to buy a home just in time for her son's birth in 2021. The little slice of the American dream that her union job has provided to her has transformed her into an activist. "It just hit me when I had my son. I see other people, like my friends, cannot afford to buy a house. And I was like, no! Something has to change here!" she says. "There is people in the community who don't know where to go and what to do. At least if I learn something from the union, I can tell them, I can guide them."

She is wearing a light gray Culinary Union T-shirt, a red lanyard with a name tag, and spandex workout pants. Her partner for the day, in an identical uniform except for her big, floppy white sun hat, is Ermila Medina, a guest room attendant and union shop steward at the Tropicana. Medina, who is from Mexico, has serviceable English after a quarter century in Vegas, but her primary job is to handle the Spanish-speaking homes in this Black and Latino neighborhood. Her personality is that of the natural-born fighter; she only got involved in the union to get the benefits, but quickly became the go-to person at work who would help colleagues who were being mistreated by their bosses. "I need to know what I can do," she thought to herself, and soon she was enrolled in shop steward classes. She carries the simmering exasperation of someone who is constitutionally unable to tolerate injustice, wherever she sees it.

"In the casino, the majority don't know nothing. This I can't believe, because they speak perfect English—*why people don't do nothing for themselves?*" She throws up her hand at the very thought of not fighting for yourself at work. "I know my English is not so good, but they're coming to me: 'Ermila, what can I do?'"

Medina and Yohanes carry electronic tablets loaded with a list of names, addresses, and voter info from the union's database. They are both on LOAs, assigned to the union's political department. For the next two hours, they knock on almost every door in the neighborhood. Their mission today is threefold: to register voters; to drive voter turnout for Nevada's June primary elections, coming up in two months; and to begin laying the groundwork for an upcoming push that the union is planning to get rent-control laws passed. Those regulations would be a boon for the working-class residents of this particular neighborhood, suffering under the soaring post-pandemic rent inflation. (That rent-control initiative, dubbed "Neighborhood

Stability," would hit a wall in August, after the North Las Vegas City Council voted against adding it to the November ballot. That would not stop the union's door-knocking, which by then was transitioning into an even bigger statewide program to get Democrats elected in the midterms.)

Hello, we're from the Culinary Union. No, we're just here to speak to the community today. Is Danny here? He doesn't live here anymore? How about Doris? She isn't home? How about you, are you registered to vote? Yes? Anybody else in the home who wants to register? Did you know we have a primary coming up? Okay. So tell me, what do you think about the gas prices these days? Crazy, right? How about rent prices? So what do you think we can do as a community about that? Nothing? That's not true—we have our voice! We have to make our voices heard, right? So listen, we want to keep you informed about some work we're going to be doing, coming up . . .

To my surprise, almost everyone who answered the door engaged in this conversation in good faith; the pair even got a couple of new voter registration forms filled out and had close to twenty conversations with residents, who universally agreed that The Rent Is Too Damn High. The success of the door knocking was completely due to the absolute sincerity and seriousness with which Medina and Yohanes approached the process. They braved locked gates, barking dogs, and several residents who were clearly grumpy and had just woken up. The data for every single address was scrupulously updated on their tablets—who was home, who lived there now, what sort of contact they made, what conversation they had—information that would be used to guide future rounds of door knocking, for the primaries, for the general election, and beyond. The fact that the pair was representing the union, rather than a political party or campaign, seemed to soften the reception they received; everyone was familiar with the Culinary Union, and nobody yelled anything cynical at them.

This work, multiplied by dozens of door knockers in dozens of neighborhoods over dozens of days, is the most tangible expression of the political power of the Culinary Union, and the reason why any Democrat who wants to be elected mayor, governor, senator, congressperson, or president inevitably comes to bend the knee on the union's doorstep. They possess an army of door knockers with a direct and ongoing connection to voters. Everyone in that army is motivated by their own personal experiences in the workplace, experiences that have instilled in them a very practical understanding of money, influence, and power. The union's staff and leadership often say that they are not a political organization—they are a union that understands politics. That is true, though that distinction may be meaningless in practice. The Culinary Union chooses its battles, like its current push for rent-control-that-we're-not-calling-rent-control, by being aware of what its mostly female, minority, immigrant, working-class membership needs. In America, that means they will always land on the left by default. It is the only part of the political spectrum that cares about the basic justice they need.

If you see all this work as mere electoral politics, though, you miss the real effects of what the union has built in this city. Around noon, Yohanes strode up the driveway of a small, worn-out house with vinyl siding that had started peeling off in large sheets. Two older men, one of them very drunk, sat on faded armchairs in a patch of shade under a small plastic awning, smoking Newport Reds. She asked the sober man, who was wearing house slippers with one red and one green sock, if he was registered to vote. "I don't think I been out of prison long enough." He shrugged.

Yohanes, however, knew that in 2019, Nevada legislators had passed a bill giving convicted felons the right to vote as soon as they are released. "We just passed the law, you can vote!" she replied, pulling out a registration form. "Our voices matter!"

Both men dutifully began filling out the forms, their grumbles crumbling in the face of Yohanes's relentless exhortations. "It don't matter no way," one man said. "It is matter! It is matter!" she shot back. "We can stop them. We don't have money, but we have a voice." As the man finished up his form, he noticed the shirts that the pair were wearing. "Oh, you from the Culinary? 226? Let me ask you, how can I find out about my pension?" It turned out that he had worked for decades in union hotels before he went to prison. Now he was sixty-four years old, but he had never gotten around to inquiring about the pension money waiting for him. They assured him that it was there, if he had worked in the shops that long, and told him how to contact the union to find out. By the time they left, with friendly handshakes, they had helped a convicted felon register to vote, and helped a retiree access a pension that he had earned, which might have otherwise sat for years, as the vinyl siding continued flaking off his modest house in the hot sun. All of that in ten minutes. That is more than politics. That is the work of a social service agency, built from the ground up by thousands of working people, looking out for one another when nobody else will.

=

WE'RE IN THE DARK, TIDY LIVING ROOM OF A SMALL HOUSE IN NORTH LAS Vegas, not far from Nellis Air Force Base. The curtains are tightly drawn to keep out the punishing mid-morning sun. Children's toys are pushed up against the walls, but the underlying tile floor has been cleaned to a gleam. Little inspirational plaques are hung on the wall—*Las Buenas Amigas Son La Familia Que Podemos Elegir*: "Good friends are the family we can choose." On the couch, wearing basketball shorts and Raiders slippers, sits Sam Fletes, a thirty-year-old with a dark brown beard and a tattoo of the Raiders logo on his forearm. In the adjacent kitchen, his mother is chopping vegetables for soup.

When the pandemic struck in 2020, Sam was laid off from his job as a cook at a restaurant at the Palace Station Casino, a job he had held for years. (Two years later, he and seventy-five fellow laid-off coworkers filed a lawsuit alleging that the casino ignored state laws that entitled them to return to their former jobs.) He was a member of the internal committee of workers that the union builds during all of its organizing drives, and helped to convince his coworkers that they needed to join the Culinary Union—which they did, in a successful election in 2016. His motivation to get involved was rooted in a long pattern of the sort of petty dictatorial treatment from supervisors that prevails in many nonunion workplaces: capricious treatment, chefs playing favorites unfairly, lax workplace safety paired with a tendency to blame anything that went wrong on any workers that the boss of the day didn't care for. Sam saw employees who were the sole income source for their families cower in fear around supervisors. It bothered him. He became one of the most outspoken union supporters during the campaign. Once he started wearing his union committee button to work, he saw an immediate change in the behavior of the supervisors he had clashed with before.

"First thing I did, when they talked to me, I got my little coat and turned it and said, 'Is there an issue?' I made sure they saw the button. And they were like, 'It can wait for another time.' It got to the point where they were no longer trying to press their power on me." A smile plays across his lips, years later, at the memory of those first glimmers of union power in the months leading up to the ecstatic day of the successful vote. "At the end of the day, it's not just the union that got the victory there, it's the workers that got the victory. So whether they like it or not, they're going to have to come to terms with it."

Six years later, the company has very much not come to terms with it. Palace Station is one of six separate Las Vegas properties owned by Station Casinos, the biggest player in the off-strip, locals-focused casino market. Station is owned by Frank III and Lorenzo Fertitta, brothers who inherited the business from their father, Frank Fertitta Jr. Palace Station began its life in 1976 as Bingo Palace; from there, Frank Jr. built his mini empire.

The father was a self-made businessman, but the sons are caricatures of spoiled billionaire assholes. They bought the Ultimate Fighting Championship for $2 million in 2001, when it was a mere novelty, and sold it for $4 billion in 2016. They are major Republican donors, giving millions of dollars to Trump-related entities during the presidency of the world's most famous UFC fan. Their idea of a worthwhile charitable donation is the $10 million they gave to UNLV in 2016 to build a new football complex named for themselves. In 2018, Frank Fertitta III spent a reported $25 million on his daughter's wedding, held at one of his hotels, which featured performances by Bruno Mars and Seal and a million-dollar floral arrangement.

The Fertitta brothers are staunchly, deeply anti-union. They are the type of men who see themselves as Randian superheroes who must fight any labor organizing with the zeal of those who believe they are entitled to all the world's money as a birthright. The Culinary Union, aware that Station was the single biggest nonunion casino company in its territory (and the third-largest private employer in Nevada), began a long, hard, property-by-property organizing campaign at the company in the early 2010s. They won their first union elections at two Station properties, Boulder Station and Palace Station, in 2016. By 2019, workers at four more Station properties had voted to join the union, and by 2023 the union and regulators were seeking a "bargaining order" to force the company to recognize the union at three other properties. Station has, at every turn, fought as hard and as dirty as it can against its employees' efforts to organize. Threats, lies, dishonest cajoling, and cynically showering workers with incentives that are—surprise!—timed to coincide with union drives have been common tactics. The company has been cited for a slew of violations by the National Labor Relations Board as far back as 2012. An anti-union website that Station launched, the sort of goofy pastiche of worn lies that union-busting consultants can build in their sleep, once proclaimed that the workers who had unionized in 2016 had gone "Over 3½ Years and NO CONTRACT"—a delay that was wholly due to the relentless intransigence of the company itself.

The Culinary Union has built itself up to its current level of power only by waging, and winning, a regular series of existential battles dating back more than three-quarters of a century. The casino industry has never stopped trying to break the union, to cripple its hold on labor in Las Vegas, to find a weak spot through which they could pour enough money and political firepower to erode the whole enterprise. In 1952, Nevada went "right to work," making it much more exhausting to maintain union membership; the union has kept growing in spite of that ever since. The years between 1970 and 1990 saw several major citywide strikes that brought Vegas to a halt, culminating in a series of agreements with major casino companies to stay neutral in union organizing campaigns. In 1991 came the bitter Frontier Strike, not won until 1998. For the next two decades, the union waged many years-long organizing campaigns and strike authorization votes that allowed it to cement its hold on the properties of the Vegas Strip. When the pandemic struck in March 2020, virtually the entire membership of the Culinary Union became unemployed all at once. Though this posed the very real threat of financial ruin for the entire organization, the union redoubled its organizing and political muscle, winning members eighteen months of continued health insurance, guaranteed recall rights to allow them to return to their old jobs, and other benefits that allowed thousands of families to survive when no one was sure if enough help would be coming.

Each one of these fights, had they been lost, had the potential to destroy the entire Culinary Union. The union has grown used to the fact that it will always be in a "win or die" situation. There is just too much money and too many cutthroat capitalists in Las Vegas who would love to drive down labor costs for the union to ever rest. The quest to organize Station Casinos is only the most recent of these high-stakes fights. If the company is successful in keeping the union out, it will serve as a billboard to the entire industry that it is, in fact, possible to operate as a nonunion casino in this city. And so the fight must be won, no matter what. That's all there is to it.

That's the big picture. But the big picture is really a pointillist drawing made up of the individual efforts of thousands of Station Casinos workers. Julie Wolfe, a fifty-three-year-old woman with short, stylish blonde hair and a lot to say, has worked for twenty years as a cocktail server at Boulder Station, one of Station's mid-level Vegas properties. In 2016, Wolfe was making around twelve dollars an hour. She was raising five boys, three of her own and two stepchildren, with all the sports team fees and high school prom tuxedo rentals that entails. Family health insurance was costing her more than $360 a month. Raises at her job came irregularly, in increments of twenty-five cents. She couldn't afford to contribute to her own 401(k). When the Culinary Union opened a satellite office to organize her casino that year, Wolfe thought about the union health insurance and pension, and she went in and signed up for the committee.

Workers at Boulder Station voted by a 2–1 margin to join the Culinary Union in 2016. But that was only the beginning of a wearisome saga of corporate obstinance. The very day of the election, Wolfe remembers, Station management announced that they would be lowering health insurance premiums—but only for workers who weren't in the union. The company used this tactic to lean on employees at Palace Station, which the union was organizing at the time. In 2017, the NLRB ruled that this was an unfair labor practice and forced the company to reimburse the Boulder workers for the difference in their premiums, and to certify the union at Palace. Station lost further NLRB rulings concerning its behavior at other properties in 2018 and 2019. These losses, though, did not alter Station's basic strategy, which has always been to stall and litigate and refuse to bargain and threaten and lie and do every last little thing possible to avoid actually having to negotiate a union contract in good faith.

This strategy often works. It did at Julie Wolfe's workplace. After their union vote the years dragged on, as the union worked to organize the rest of the Station properties, and the company sought to exhaust every tactic in the anti-union playbook. By 2020, the company began to aggressively push for the workers at Boulder to decertify the union, offering new benefits and raises to make the status quo seem better. In August 2020, they succeeded in getting enough employee signatures to decertify the union. The union said that the company had used a variety of illegal tactics to get those signatures, resulting in more unfair labor practice charges. In February 2022, the union was picketing in front of Palace, demanding a contract; the next month, the union formally asked the state Gaming Control Board to consider pulling Station's gaming licenses due to repeated violations of labor law. All these things go on, and on, and on. Win, or die.

Meanwhile, every day that employees continued to come to work and do their jobs without a union contract constituted a small win for the Fertitta family. Julie Wolfe continued to act as a cheerleader for the union at work, but she suffered for her commitment. "2016 to present was a very tough time for me. It was not easy. Every manager that was in that property pretty much hated me. And you could feel it. It was torturous." She says this with a sigh, six long years later, sitting at the kitchen table in her apartment. She is a person who fully grasps the need for a union contract and has done everything humanly possible to get one for herself and her coworkers, but still does not have one. She does not have the tangible progress that she deserves. Sometimes union organizing is like this. It takes a commitment beyond what should reasonably be asked of anyone. When doubts creep in, Wolfe remembers what she did when Boulder brought in union busters to harangue the workers in mandatory meetings before the vote in 2016. "They were trying to tell me, like, 'What do you mean, you think that you guys deserve to have eighteen dollars an hour as a maid, and you guys deserve to have sixteen dollars as a cocktail waitress, just the same as a five-star resort, when they got high rollers going in there?'" The union busters, she admits, were intimidating. But she spoke up anyhow. "I stood up and I said, 'You know what? You know what? Yeah, I do feel that way. I work just as hard as them.'"

At each one of the Station Casinos properties, there are employees like Wolfe who have resolved to see this fight through to the end, no matter how unreasonably distant that end may be. Casiano Corpus, who grew up in the Philippines, has worked for thirty years as a porter at Palace Station, the casino where Station was grudgingly forced to recognize the union in 2017. Corpus is very short, with the shoulder-length hair, powerful forearms, and perpetual sunny smile of a surfer, though there are no surfers in Las Vegas. We sit on a big stuffed couch in his small living room as a YouTube video showing a tour of a Filipino food market plays soothingly on mute in the background. To speak to him is to receive a jolt of inspiration. He will describe an atmosphere of constant fear of layoffs or retaliation at work, then smile and recall in the next breath that when Culinary Union organizers first knocked on his apartment door in 2010 and asked him if he was interested in joining the campaign, his response was, "No doubt. Absolutely. There's no hesitation." Then he will smile again.

Corpus grasps the nature of his workplace power struggle with complete clarity, a clarity capable of cutting through any quantity of threats and obfuscation and leaving only the conclusion that a union is necessary. So whatever it takes to get one, that is what he must do. "This is not just for me. This is for all new generations to come. So that when they come here and work at Station Casinos, they won't struggle just like us," he says. He is a realist. "All of our kids are not gonna be successful, like become a doctor, a lawyer. No, they're gonna be cooks, porters, just like us!"

Twelve years after he joined the union committee, as the Fertitta brothers have grown hundreds of millions of dollars richer, Casiano Corpus and his coworkers at Palace Station still do not have a union contract. He is at the age when he thinks about retirement. If Station Casinos had followed the normal rules and negotiated a normal contract like a normal employer, he would already have a pension waiting for him. Instead, he only has a fight. He retains the ability to smile about all of this because, like a soldier seeking peace before a battle, he long ago decided that he would just continue this fight until he can't anymore, and that's that. When his coworkers get discouraged and cynical and ask what the union has done for them, he replies, "What have you done for yourself?" This answer sometimes makes his coworkers mad. But it makes him smile because he long ago accepted its truth.

Even sitting there in his living room, Casiano is wearing his union committee button. "I'm never going to take this off, until I'm finished," he says, tugging it on his shirt. "I hope I can taste that. If you want to fight, you gotta be serious. You gotta fight."

If Las Vegas is the sham version of the American dream, the version that grins and dazzles you and rips you off and leaves you broke, then the Culinary Union is the actual American dream in action. Out of nothing, this union has built a system that allows an immigrant to this country who works hard to provide health care to her children, support her family, buy a home, and retire with a pension. And while doing all of that, that person can talk and vote and participate in democratic decisions of an organization strong enough to make the mayor and the governor and the senators and the presidential candidates all come down to the union hall to hear what they have to say. One way to explain this accomplishment is to describe it as a finely honed and well-tested system in which power is built through workplace organizing based on collective self-interest; and then that power is nurtured and scaled up and protected by a parallel system of political organizing; and all of it is sustained by a nonstop program of internal education and training; and the entire system is a way to teach people *what democracy is* and show them its power and then make them the messengers of its continuation. But to honestly explain how this whole thing was conjured up, over nearly ninety years, in the midst of a city and an industry and an economy that absolutely did not want any of it to exist, it is important to say that the thing that did it more than any whiteboard full of strategy was: to fight. Fight, and fight, and fight. It is not a fight that ends. It's one that is handed off from one generation to the next. If you want to fight, you gotta be serious. You gotta fight.

A union is an organism. One day I went to lunch with a group of Culinary Union organizers at a burger place off the Strip—they couldn't stand to spend their lunch breaks in the same casinos where they spent their work days. One of the organizers, Miguel, had worked in a restaurant at the airport decades ago. While there, he had recruited a woman who also worked at the airport to become a shop steward. That woman was the mother of Juston Larsen, who now sat with us munching fries, training as a union organizer himself.

"You recruit one person. And they recruit somebody. It's like a branch of a tree," Miguel said. He had seen many fights, for many years. Some were lost. The branches, though, kept on branching. Everyone sitting around that table was a branch, flourishing somehow in a hostile climate. "It's not always really about winning," he said. "It's about people growing."

CHAPTER SIX

THE METHOD
UNITE HERE AND THE FORMULA FOR POWER

The Fontainebleau Hotel is a gleaming white wave, slotted in that narrow strip of Miami Beach that is really just a little spit of sand, where you could almost throw a rock from the inlet to the ocean if you could throw that rock through a luxury hotel. Across Collins Avenue from the hotel's front door, a long line of yachts are parked in Indian Creek, the same way that cars are parallel parked on the street. The whole strip seems perilous and ill-advised—a long, skinny ribbon of extravagance jutting out into hurricane territory. Just waiting for one good storm to blow it all out into the Atlantic, a mighty wind of Chris-Crafts and Maseratis and Patek Philippes and sea-green wall tiles, never to be seen again.

If you walk past the curvilinear front drive of the Fontainebleau where the valets park the Range Rovers, out the modest side entrance for employees with the "Welcome Team Bleau!" sign, and down the block, you come to a small sandy area next to a public parking lot by the beach. Eddis Feliz stands there chatting with a coworker after a long daytime shift. She is wearing long black pants and a gray button-up top, the uniform of housekeepers at the Fontainebleau. Feliz, who grew up in the Dominican

Republic, came to Miami almost twenty years ago. She has worked at the Fontainebleau for the past decade. She earns a little over fifteen dollars an hour for cleaning a dozen rooms a day. Since the pandemic, when hotels pulled back on daily room cleaning—meaning fewer housekeepers employed, but those who remain work harder because rooms are dirtier when guests check out—she has been working six or seven days a week. Her hands hurt.

When Feliz started the job, it was so onerous that she didn't think she would be able to do it for long. Yet she stayed, in large part, because she has a daughter to support—and because she has union health insurance. The workers at the Fontainebleau have been unionized since the 1960s. The union has not magically transformed room cleaning into a lucrative line of work. But it does provide benefits and some protections, and, for Feliz, something equally important: "What it comes down to for me is respect."

=

WHEN YOU STUDY WHAT THE CULINARY UNION HAS BUILT IN LAS VEGAS, it is natural to wonder whether it can be replicated in other cities. The Culinary's parent union, Unite Here, is the nation's foremost hospitality industry union, with about three hundred thousand members working at hotels, airports, casinos, and associated industries across the country. (The union was formed by the 2004 merger of UNITE, traditionally a textile workers' union, and HERE, a hotel and restaurant workers' union; five years later, a faction of the new union split off to form Workers United, which is affiliated with SEIU. Be warned that if you ever ask anyone who works for the union about this period of its history, you may hear recounted a thousand hours of grievances, feuds, and vicious internal rivalries that are still vividly remembered by everyone who lived through them. Readers of this book will be spared hearing all of that, on humanitarian grounds.)

On one hand, there is nowhere quite like Las Vegas: a geographically isolated city powered by tourist dollars but overwhelmingly driven by a single big money industry and full of tightly packed, large workplaces that offer the opportunity to organize workers industrially. It's the perfect place to build high union density in a small area with an outsized economic impact. On the other hand, the general strategy used to build and maintain union power in Las Vegas can be used to build and maintain power in any city that relies on a tourist economy. By organizing the workers in the places that make up the spine of any tourist city's business—the hotels, the airport, the convention centers, the stadiums, the casinos, the tourist attractions—a union can, in effect, wrap its hands around that city's throat and demand that the working class receive its fair share of the money flowing into town. Cities that rely on tourism are fragile. Any disruption to the flow of visitors and their open wallets will soon cause the entire local economy, and all its tax revenue, to collapse. If a union can organize in a disciplined enough way to be able to credibly threaten to go on strike at the places where the tourists fly in, sleep at night, and spend their money, that union is in a position to make political demands that must be respected, grumpy Republican local business owners be damned. Tourist-heavy cities therefore offer one of the best opportunities for building union power at municipal scales. Unite Here is the union best positioned to do that. And they know how.

Every union, of course, derives power from an ability to turn off the flow of business in its corner of the economy. Targeting the hospitality industry in tourist cities, though, offers some intriguing advantages: these cities are everywhere, meaning a union can truly build power coast to coast and not be geographically isolated; the workers are numerous, and they are typically the working poor, meaning that the gains of organized labor go to those who need it the most; and the issues at play are so intimately tied into the heart of local politics that a hospitality union's political organizing naturally tends to raise standards for vast swaths of workers across the city who don't have unions themselves. Instead of organizing relatively small numbers of skilled workers in specific places to create the sort of economic chokepoint that a union wants—think Hollywood screenwriters, or, for that matter, Charleston longshoremen—Unite Here has the ability to organize lots of workers in lots of places to achieve the same effect and watch its benefits ripple out more widely. As chokepoints go, the tourist economy is one of the most promising that organized labor can lay claim to.

No one is more aware of this opportunity than the leaders of Unite Here. But it ain't easy.

=

MIAMI INTERNATIONAL AIRPORT IS A HUGE HORSESHOE OF BUSTLE, THE southern door to America. It is the second busiest airport in the country for international passengers, and the busiest for international freight. It also has dozens of stores, fast food restaurants, and Cuban coffee joints. Unite Here intends to unionize every single one.

I met Wendi Walsh at a deadly drab and mostly deserted Burger King tucked into a nook of Terminal E. She was on a break from contract negotiations, which were happening at the Miami International Airport Hotel, also located in Terminal E. It evoked the dystopian undertones of the film *The Terminal*, in which Tom Hanks is unable to ever leave an airport. Walsh, a slim woman with medium-length brown hair and glasses, is the secretary-treasurer of Unite Here Local 355, which oversees all of South Florida. She grew up in a working-class family in Massachusetts, made it to Yale for grad school in 1992, and joined the grad student union, which was then locked in a mortal struggle with the Yale administration. The experience transformed her. She went to work for Unite Here straight out of school and never left.

When she came to Miami in 2008, Walsh's intent was to focus on driving up unionization of the city's hotel industry. "Miami is probably the most important unorganized hotel city in the country," she says. "The revenues per room here are much, much greater than they are in a lot of other cities. And the labor costs are very low. So it's a highly profitable city for the industry."

But the big hotel organizing plans had to wait. The union had just won labor peace agreements at five local pari-mutuel casinos, all of which then had to be organized. (Four of them eventually were.) Local 355 was also focused on organizing South Florida's airports, and successfully pushed local politicians in Miami-Dade and Broward counties to agree to labor peace rules at the airports, rules that require contractors to agree to neutrality in union campaigns. Since Walsh arrived, Unite Here has organized all the concessions workers at Fort Lauderdale Airport and about half of those at Miami International. Organizing the other half of those workers at Miami's airport is a top priority, and also an unimaginable slog: instead of a single subcontractor who can sign one contract that covers all the little stores in the airport, Miami has dozens of different subcontractors in the airport, many operating only a single store. Walsh estimates that fully organizing the airport concessions may require the union to organize and negotiate forty-five separate contracts.

Just outside of Miami's Terminal E, across the lanes of cars waiting to scoop up arriving passengers, is a small park with some landscaped plants, a circle of flapping flags, and one very visible dead rat whose corpse is bloating in the midday sun. On a petite bench, wearing a striped blue shirt and a Unite Here lanyard, sits Olga Bolanos. She works part-time for the union, organizing airport workers, and part-time at the Spring Chicken restaurant in the airport, where she has spent the past fourteen years serving fried chicken to travelers in Concourse D. Bolanos grew up in Cuba and still speaks mostly Spanish. She confirms something that several members of the union in Miami told me: Cuban workers in South Florida are often inherently skeptical of unions because they associate them with communism. Bolanos has some credibility on this front—she has actually been in unions in both countries. When nonunion airport workers complain to her about understaffing, overwork, and the unaffordable cost of their paltry health insurance, she tells them about how being in the union has allowed her to make almost seventeen dollars an hour, with free health insurance.

"People come with a mentality from Cuba to here, and we tell them it's different here," she says, speaking through a translator. "Here, you can stand up for your rights, and you'll get backup for it. Here, you'll have your voice heard. That's not the case there."

Local 355 grew to about seven thousand members before the pandemic. By the spring of 2022, membership had recovered to about two-thirds of that, in line with all of Unite Here nationally. For Walsh, her years in Miami

have hammered home how arduous the path can be between a good strategy, which the union has, and the actual transformation of a city, which is
very much a work in progress. Decades in the labor movement have taught
her patience. Her union already has some of South Florida's most prominent hotels—the Fontainebleau, the Hyatt Regency, the Diplomat, the St.
Regis—and she knows that it is possible to organize many, many more. But
hotel organizing is hard, and it would go a lot faster if she had one hundred organizers, rather than the half dozen or so she has now. Until more
resources pour into South Florida, she will do what she can.

"Sometimes I think, okay, we've organized maybe fifteen, twenty places
since I've been here. And one could say, in the sea of hospitality workers
in South Florida, or in the country, or for trying to move the Left where
we want it to go, that is such a little tiny impact, and that it's not good
enough. But I really feel like people should appreciate the victories we have
way more. There are workers who, when we won an 18 percent gratuity here,
they make $10,000 to $15,000 a year more than they made before that.
That's a big fucking difference for those workers," she says. "Sometimes you
do the work every day, you put on a stupid ass suit to do negotiations"—here
she gestures to the suit she is wearing, on her break from negotiations—
"and you can kind of forget what you're doing. We have always been at our
best here when we've had a campaign that is thinking about this really as a
movement—for racial justice, for immigrant justice, for bringing people into
the middle class. It has a broader vision; it reminds us why we do this in the
first place, why the fight is worth it."

Las Vegas and Miami are both magnets for first-generation immigrants
to America. In both places, many of those immigrants, particularly women,
end up working in hotels and food service. Miami draws heavily from all
the nations of the Caribbean, and the union's membership and leadership
reflect that. Rose Denis, a woman in her early fifties with tight, neat braids,
is the union's second-in-command. She was born in Haiti. Her involvement
in activism began when she was a teenager in the late 1980s, and she joined
the movement to try to force the Duvalier dictators out of power and install
Jean-Bertrand Aristide as president. In 2004, she moved to Miami, and
two years later she was hired by Unite Here as an organizer. She started by

organizing the casinos, then went on to the Fort Lauderdale Airport, where the workforce was heavily Haitian.

In the years that Denis has been with Local 355, its membership rose from two thousand up to a pre-pandemic high of seven thousand. Yet none of the union's fights are *won*, exactly—they are more like a house that is being built over years and years, brick by brick, in the hope that it will one day be big enough to shelter everyone. Years are spent organizing one airport, then years more organizing another airport; a living wage ordinance is passed in one county, then must be passed in the next county; elections make the government temporarily more friendly or less friendly, which makes the organizing either quicker or more onerous, and the material gains either easier or harder to come by. Recently, local politics have been promising, but Florida's state politics have gone the wrong way, and the state can preempt local ordinances, so any lasting legislative progress can be excruciatingly hard to pin down. While all this ebbs and flows, the organizing of workers in new places, and the training of already-organized workers to become organizers themselves, must always continue. All the union's political power is derived from that, and not the other way around.

"Anybody from Haiti, we know that the first thing you have to do is to fight to survive," says Denis. She dreams of seeing her local in South Florida become as powerful and ubiquitous as the one in Vegas is. She admits that she doesn't know if she'll see it in her lifetime, but has no doubt about the path to get there. "To me, organizing is organizing. You can organize everybody. Any race, any ethnic group, you can organize them. It's the belief in the fight that they have in front of them, and also being willing to tell people the truth. It's gonna take time."

Miami-Dade and Broward are the two biggest counties in Florida, approaching five million people between them. Numerically speaking, Unite Here of Florida is strongest in Orlando, where two separate locals of the union represent more than twenty-five thousand Disney workers. But politically and economically, the future of the state runs through South Florida. As the pandemic wore on, Miami saw such an influx of residents from across America that it became, by 2022, the nation's least affordable place to live, with rent costs exploding to 60 percent of the average family's income—double what is considered to be "affordable." The same thing fueling the revival of the area's hospitality industry was also making it ever harder for the people who work in the industry to live there.

The ability of a relatively small union to exert influence across this sprawling area will depend in large part on people like Duane Thwaites, a soft-spoken middle-aged man with dark skin and a neat goatee. We met at the Local 355 headquarters in an unglamorous office park in Miami Gardens, north of the city, next to a Skechers warehouse and a self-storage facility. Chairs were lined up all the way around the walls of the conference room after a committee meeting the previous night. Traffic roared by constantly on the Palmetto Expressway just outside the windows.

For ten years, Thwaites has worked at a concession stand at the ballpark where the Miami Marlins play. The employees at the park only work during baseball season, but they are unionized with Local 355. Thwaites joined the union after a few months on the job but paid little attention to it until a few years had gone by, when he grew frustrated that the union wasn't addressing his day-to-day problems at work. That prompted the realization that he'd better get involved, if he wanted anything to improve. He began going to meetings and cajoling his coworkers to join the union. Since Florida is a "right to work" state, employees must sign up voluntarily to pay the forty-dollar-per-month union dues, which Thwaites explains to them as "one soda a day. That's it, and you're covered." Now, he says, nearly three-quarters of his fellow concessions workers at the stadium have joined the union.

Duane Thwaites is homeless. For the past four years, he has lived quietly in a commercial warehouse. His situation is not only due to low pay, but also to the fact that he has spent time in prison and finds it hard to get landlords to rent to him. He suffered through the first half of 2020 when baseball season—and his job—were abruptly canceled. "Food became an issue," he says demurely. Yet he survived and continued working with the union throughout those especially lean times. He has been at the ballpark long enough to get health insurance, something only the most senior workers there have.

The small handful of full-time union employees is dwarfed by the number of people like Thwaites, who are the true source of Unite Here's power.

He rallies his coworkers to the union, and makes sure the union is aware of what's happening at the stadium, and goes to committee meetings, and participates in political rallies, and in turn—in theory—the union power he helps to build will accrue to his own benefit. It would certainly be easy for this promise to ring hollow to a man who is homeless. But Thwaites, who has many strongly held opinions about how the union can improve its communications and operations and strategies, has channeled all his energies into building the institution, rather than giving up. He hangs on to the realizations that he had eight years ago, when he first got frustrated enough to complain to a union staffer that the union wasn't doing enough.

"I realized two things: that there was no way they would know what my problems are if I didn't tell them; and, two, even if they did know, how would they know they're making effectual change, meaningful change?" he says. "So I made up my mind at that point, what I should do is take ownership. At least on my part."

When you get out past the jeweled pockets of affluence along the beaches, Miami dwindles into an endless expanse of flat houses with scraggly lawns clinging to sand separated by six-lane roads, further separated by parking lots. Its blatant tropicality is always seeking to transform the whole place into a sweltering jungle, a forest of snakes and banana leaves lurking forever in the wings. Money flows up from points south, and down from points north. The only reason that South Florida, a hurricane-strafed wildland hospitable only to sharks, mosquitoes, and roaches, has developed at all is due to the invigorating effect of that out-of-town money. And ever since the New York industrialist Henry Flagler used convict labor to run his railroad down to Biscayne Bay and founded Miami in 1896, there has been a struggle to see to it that all the money that washes into Florida is not sucked right back out again.

South Florida sprawls farther than rationality. It will not be easy to sew a net wide and sturdy enough to ensure that enough of the wealth that built Miami can be saved for the working people who make it all run. But Unite Here is trying.

=

IN 1892, WHEN THE CITY OF MIAMI WAS STILL JUST A FANCIFUL IDEA IN THE back of Henry Flagler's mind, the city of New Orleans had itself a general strike. For three days in November, commerce in the city shut down as more than twenty thousand workers in the city struck in support of a "Triple Alliance" of unions—two white, and one Black—that was demanding a ten-hour workday, overtime pay, and the right to have a union shop. The city's Board of Trade rebuffed the demands, then tried to split the white unions from the Black, and, having just pissed off the workers even more, earned a citywide, racially integrated strike. It was just months after Homer Plessy had purposely gotten himself arrested at a New Orleans railroad depot when he sat in a whites-only train car. His act led to the *Plessy v. Ferguson* decision, which cemented "separate but equal" segregation as the legal standard in the South for decades to come. New Orleans was then, as now, a deep South city that thought for itself. It is of the South, but so stubbornly attached to its own singular culture that it will put up a fight when the broader cultural mores are not to its liking.

No American city is more sui generis than New Orleans. It's a furious mix of Spanish, French, and a kaleidoscope of African cultures, its local cuisine and music both potent enough to be internationally famous, a place that always seems to grasp at life with an urgency driven by the fact that tomorrow you may die. In several important ways, though, New Orleans shares a set of characteristics with other cities that make them fertile grounds for Unite Here's brand of organizing: it is a blue city in a red state, where local politics can be friendly even if state politics aren't; its economy is driven by tourism and hospitality, an industry that, in normal times, employs more than sixty thousand locals directly (and almost the entire town indirectly) and brings in close to $10 billion a year; and it is a majority Black city, wracked by a history of poverty, inequality, and corruption, where the workforce that makes the city run for all those tourists has never gotten a big enough piece of the pie. Local 23 of Unite Here has a membership in New Orleans that is 90 percent Black and two-thirds women. For more than a decade, it has been patiently building power in a bid to transform this stubborn place from the inside.

On a sunny spring day in 2022, Marlene Patrick-Cooper sat wearily in an empty conference room on a high floor of the Loews Hotel on Poydras Street downtown. She has golden skin and short hair dyed blonde, and she wears chunky eyeglasses and a white button-up shirt with a big button that reads "LOCAL 23." Since 2014, she has been the union's president. She had spent all day in that conference room, putting the final touches on the new contract that the hotel's workers are voting to ratify. New Orleans is not, temperamentally or physically, a city of towers. But from that conference room high over the business district, Patrick-Cooper can gaze out toward what the foundation of a tourist city's union empire looks like.

Directly across Poydras Street sits Harrah's, New Orleans's only casino. Its staff belongs to Local 23. Two blocks down that street, where the Mississippi River begins its curve up against the Riverwalk, is the Hilton Riverside, the city's biggest hotel. It has more than 1,600 rooms and pulls a good portion of the guests who flock to New Orleans for conventions. Its staff belongs to Local 23. One block south, across a yawning parking lot, is the enormous convention center. Its staff belongs to Local 23. Head the other way up Poydras and you'll hit the Smoothie King Center, where the New Orleans Pelicans play their NBA games, and the Superdome, where the Saints play their NFL games. The workers at those arenas belong to Local 23. And the workers at the airport terminal—they're in Local 23 too. How can organized labor change a poverty-stricken southern city? Well, when the economy runs on tourist money, and you organize the hotel workers and the casino workers and the convention workers and the airport workers and the stadium workers . . . then, you just might have something.

Patrick-Cooper herself is something of a prophet for Unite Here's methods. After growing up in rural St. Mary Parish in southwest Louisiana, she moved to Las Vegas to attend UNLV in 1983. Her aunt was already there, part of a wave of Black Southerners who had moved to the desert mecca a generation before in search of opportunity. Soon, Patrick-Cooper landed a job as a cashier at a casino on Fremont Street, making her a Culinary Union member. She found herself drawn over and over into union actions, with peer pressure from friends transforming her from a mere dues-paying member to a picket line–walker to someone getting arrested for civil disobedience, all while she was still in school. She became a Culinary Union organizer, working on a team of twenty-five people who successfully organized the newly built MGM Grand. In 2001, Unite Here sent her to Chicago, where she stayed for eleven years. Toward the end of her time in Chicago, "there was talk of putting resources towards organizing the South. And I was like, 'Whew! That sounds good,'" she says. "I definitely have to be a part of that—going home and being a part of building something."

By 2014, she was back in New Orleans leading Local 23. Besides being a homecoming, it was a chance to put what she had learned in Las Vegas into practice. As a union organizer, she had seen Vegas nurse itself back from the effects of 9/11 and watched Chicago's employers trying to recover from the Great Recession. That was good training for New Orleans, where her union would be forced to weather not just the pandemic, which left almost all its members unemployed, but also devastating hurricanes that would force it to transform into its own quasi–social service agency. When she first got to town, her predecessor at Local 23 told her that Union organizing comes in waves. It ebbs and flows. At that time, it was a slow grind. Eight years later, leaning on a conference table high atop Loews, another contract behind her, Patrick-Cooper remembers the conversation she had with the same man in early 2022. "I told you it was coming back," he said to her. "Just get ready for the ride."

That comeback has been many years in the making. Scott Cooper, a tall, studious man with brown hair and black glasses, is Unite Here's chief of staff. He has been working for the union in New Orleans since 2009, when the wreckage of Hurricane Katrina was still an open wound on the city's workforce. At that time, Unite Here had three shops in New Orleans: the Loew's hotel, the convention center workers, and the concession workers at the airport. In 2014, they added the Harrah's Casino. The same year, they began organizing the Hilton Riverside, which would take until 2017 to actually win. Simultaneously, Local 23 was in a bitter and ultimately successful fight to unionize the Gulf Coast casinos in Biloxi,

Mississippi—including the biggest, the Beau Rivage, where 1,200 workers won their union in 2018. The tendrils of power stretching out from the Culinary Union in Las Vegas are evident here: pressure on casino companies—and personnel, and expertise—from the union in Vegas helped to secure the wins at Harrah's and at the casinos in Biloxi, incubating a new and growing center of union power 1,700 miles away from the Vegas Strip.

Cooper had heard stories of the Culinary Union while he was in college, and cut his teeth with Unite Here in the early 2000s on casino campaigns in Atlantic City and Mississippi. Though some workers he met in Mississippi had no idea what a union even was ("Do you mean a credit union?" some asked him), the ones who did often had friends who had passed through Vegas. In 2005, he was neck-deep in an effort to bring several thousand new Mississippi casino workers into Unite Here, a breathtaking projection of the union's formula. "The energy around that was incredible. People were like, 'We're gonna change the state of Mississippi, we're gonna change the country,'" he says. At the end of that summer, Katrina hit, wiping out the casinos and leveling the union's office into a flat concrete slab, with rain-soaked paper records strewn around for blocks. Cooper spent the next year as a sort of union-centric disaster relief worker, a skill that would prove to come in handy again in Louisiana.

On August 29, 2021—the sixteenth anniversary of Hurricane Katrina—Hurricane Ida made landfall near Port Fourchon, Louisiana, a tiny town jutting perilously out into the Gulf of Mexico. It carried 150-mile-per-hour winds, making it the fifth-strongest storm to hit the United States in recorded history. Its eye passed less than fifty miles from New Orleans, stripping roofs from houses, tearing down billboards and power lines, and knocking out power to the entire city for more than a week. Because the storm had spun up with unusual quickness, few people had evacuated from the city before it hit. Hundreds of thousands were left with no electricity or air-conditioning in the sweltering late summer heat. The city's commerce ground to a halt. People were suddenly out of work, in need of food and shelter, and hot as hell. Many of those people were the city's hospitality workers.

So Local 23 swung into action. In the weeks immediately after Ida—with its own money, as well as money raised from its national parent union and a galaxy of allies—the union put together, on the fly, a grassroots disaster relief campaign that helped a lot of people survive until the federal government's creaky wheels could turn fast enough to reach them. Many of the people who were helping the union help displaced workers were, themselves, displaced members of the union. One of those people was twenty-four-year-old Katelynn Gordon, who had joined the union when she got a job as a barista at the Hilton as a nineteen-year-old. Covid got her furloughed. When Ida barreled toward the state, Gordon evacuated to Arkansas, where she was sharing a hotel room with a friend, the friend's mother, a dog, and five cats. She was there when the union asked her if she could help out. She went to Walmart with her credit card and bought the cheapest laptop they had. Then—armed with a rudimentary cheat sheet with information about how to contact FEMA and apply for various forms of government assistance—she began making calls to members, asking them what they needed.

"It was hard because we were also all going through it. Trying to help people, while needing our own help," says Gordon, who had been evicted shortly before the storm and was forced to couch surf for a while when she returned to New Orleans. "That was so difficult. Plans just kept changing every single day."

Still, the relief program kept expanding until the union had more than a dozen people making calls full-time. They were nimble—for those who were stuck with nothing more than a cell phone and in dire need of help, the union sent cash directly via Venmo or CashApp. They also held an event in town, handing out cash and $150 gift cards in person. The program not only helped its recipients, it also put a group of union members to work in the immediate aftermath of the storm, when hospitality work itself was scarce.

After a few weeks of that, it was election season. The union, already running hard, directed its efforts toward knocking on tens of thousands of doors on behalf of JP Morrell, a former state legislator running for an open city council seat. Morrell—whose father was a longtime Louisiana state legislator and whose mother was on the city council—had been an ally to Unite Here in the statehouse. He had a solidly progressive reputation and helped to spearhead a successful 2018 amendment to the state constitution that brought Louisiana into the modern age by requiring unanimous votes of juries to convict people of felonies, ending the practice of nonunanimous jury convictions that had persisted since the Jim Crow era. Morrell won his three-way election in November 2021 with 51 percent of the vote, squeaking through with just enough of a margin to avoid a runoff. There was little doubt that Unite Here's months-long work to focus distracted, storm-battered residents on the election through the oppressive days of late summer heat had been decisive.

"When you get a lot of political endorsements from other politicians, it sounds great, but most people are like, 'Look at those politicians endorsing each other.' When you've got somebody there who's like, 'We've worked with JP and he's made our quality of life better by being pro-union,' you can't really pay for that," Morrell says, lounging on a couch in his city hall office, wearing the aggressively colorful high-top kicks of a longtime sneakerhead. He has a dark beard and dark-rimmed eyeglasses, and his office walls are festooned with Marvel action figures and memorabilia: a plastic Captain America shield, a plastic Thor's hammer by the desk. It's a fully developed cool nerd vibe. He believes that closely embracing a hospitality union in a tourism-fueled city should be common sense for the Democratic Party, particularly in red states like Louisiana. "I think the pandemic actually presented a pretty significant opportunity in that everyone saw collectively—when I talk to Republicans *and* Democrats, they're all pissed about how little they're being paid. They're all pissed about their hours. They're all pissed about being classified as an independent contractor so they have no insurance. These are all commonalities that the Democratic Party has really done a very poor job of bringing people together over."

While it was knocking on doors for Morrell's campaign, Local 23 was also organizing the workers at the Superdome and the Smoothie King Center. That campaign is a good example of the union's methods: long-term civic involvement coalescing into a broad, iron-fist-in-a-velvet-glove political campaign, with labor power as the end goal. Organizers had forged relationships with a number of those workers during its Ida relief efforts, when they turned up in need of help. In early October, the union decided to forgo its usual measured approach and strike while the sentiment was hot. Members began leafleting in front of the stadiums on weekends. For several weeks, they were met with stiff resistance, including private security and local police officers demanding that they move away from where they wanted to stand. The workers at the stadiums were employed by Centerplate, a division of the institutional food giant Sodexo—a company that Unite Here already had many contracts with at cafeterias, dining halls, and event venues across the country. In New Orleans, Centerplate also ran the convention center, where Local 23 had had contracts in place for many years. But the company did not seem inclined to make things easy at its stadiums.

The union, however, could apply pressure of its own. Using a combination of the community goodwill built up by its hurricane relief, the political influence of allies like Morrell, and the labor influence it already had with Sodexo, it forced (or, you know, *persuaded*) the company to sign a card check neutrality agreement. That meant that once the union got a majority of the workers to sign union cards, the company would agree to recognize the union and begin negotiations without a long, drawn-out, anti-union fight. The success of the union campaign at the stadiums would not only bring better wages and health insurance to more than five hundred of the city's workers—it would also, finally, bring Local 23's membership numbers back above where they were in March 2020, when the pandemic sucked away so many union hospitality jobs. By the beginning of 2023, the stadium workers had won their union recognition and began bargaining their contract.

For all its devastating effects, the Covid crisis was a stark demonstration of how unions can act as stabilizers when everything begins to crumble. "After Covid, Centerplate Convention Center—unionized—was fully staffed, and rocking and rolling. Centerplate at the Superdome was not unionized, and it was devastated," says JP Morrell. "They couldn't get anybody to work there at all. It became a running joke that what they were paying people was less than what it would cost to buy nachos. The benefit that businesses downplay is that unions and the people they represent have a sense of agency, and wanting to get back to work to maintain the standards they've earned. When I look across the city and across the state, the only areas of industry that haven't had dips in employment are the areas that are unionized."

=

WILLIE WOODS IS A STOUT MAN WITH SHORT, GRAYING HAIR AND THE HINT of a gold tooth peeking out from his parted lips. He grew up in the Treme section of New Orleans, and at a young age joined a community group called Tambourine & Fan, which was started by Jerome "Big Duck" Smith, a Freedom Rider and a famed leader in the city's civil rights movement. At the time, Black children were not allowed to play in some of the city's parks, so Smith would have all the boys in his group go out to the football fields on Saturday mornings, sit down on the fifty-yard line, and refuse to move. "If we couldn't play, nobody played," says Woods. "So I've been organizing since I was a little kid."

Woods spent his life working in hospitality in New Orleans, including a long stretch at the Fairmont Hotel, which was unionized. He liked it there. Later, he got a job at the Hotel Monteleone, a nonunion hotel, which he remembers as "awful." He went on to work at the convention center, which he helped to organize with Unite Here, and then, in 2006, to the big Hilton Riverside. There, he was a banquet server. Despite his experience, he found himself stuck with the less lucrative breakfast and lunch shifts, due to what he says was rampant favoritism and racism from a bad manager. Favored waiters would get better shifts and access to work private parties, while others languished.

In 2014, a union organizer knocked on Woods's door. He was more than ready. He had the place all scoped out. He spent the next several years diligently helping the union organize the hotel and sharing information about who made how much, and why. "We had a certain set of waiters making like $80,000 a year. And we were making thirty," he remembers. "When we organized, we went up thirty more thousand dollars. We went from $30,000 to $62,000 a year after we got our contract."

Woods is a living, breathing example of someone who experienced the benefits of being in a union, understood that workplaces need to be organized for workers to have a decent life, and went on to do just that at multiple places. That organizing work was in addition to the actual work of his jobs. To dig into the membership of Local 23 is to find person after person who has been transformed into a union stalwart by life experience, and who now works to keep the union strong because they want to. Because they believe in it. It is downright inspiring.

On a muggy spring morning, Trinice Dyer sits on an overstuffed couch in the living room of her tidy New Orleans East house. Soon she'll be going to work, but for now she's relaxing in fuzzy pink slippers and a purple T-shirt that reads "Live Your Life," perpetually glam even when she's at home. Dyer, born and raised here with the accent to prove it, has a vivacious disposition that served her well as a bartender in the French Quarter for a decade. The money was good, but she was a single mother, and she got tired of having to come home at 2 a.m. So fifteen years ago, she got a job as a server at Drago's, the seafood restaurant at the Hilton Riverside that advertises itself as the creator of charbroiled oysters. There, she chafed under the same rampant favoritism by managers that bothered Willie Woods. When she heard that the hotel would finally be getting a union, she—despite having only a vague idea of the details—was thrilled. "I'm like, 'help me!'" she says. "That's what came into my mind: a union's coming, we get help."

Having a union is not a panacea, but it has smoothed out some of the most egregious aspects of the job. Dyer is a shop steward, serving as a combination of an agent, career counselor, and therapist for her coworkers. Gone is the climate of favoritism; now, managers are so used to the need to negotiate workplace disputes with the union that when things happen, they will often seek Dyer out to preemptively explain to *her* their side of the story, knowing the offended employee will soon be coming to her as well.

One of her most vivid memories of her career as a server is the day that a group of tourists from Europe ran up a $500 bill at lunch. When they were leaving, a young man from the group handed her the payment book with a smile on his face. She opened it to find that the tip was a fresh, uncreased one dollar bill. She was so crushed that she started crying and went home, even though it was only a couple of hours into her shift. Now, thanks to the union, the restaurant automatically adds a tip to the bill of large parties. Such small improvements can make a big difference in workers' lives.

Dyer was out of work for a year and a half thanks to the pandemic. During that time, the union kept her afloat, hiring her to phone bank for its relief efforts. She is a recipient of the union's help, and a giver of it. To her, its power is biblical. She invokes the story of Abraham, whose faith was rewarded: "When I was out of work, they found work for me. God always keeps a ram in the bush."

A union with 1,500 members or so would be a blip in a major metropolis. But in a city of modest size and international renown and many overlapping social networks, Local 23 manages to reach into every facet of civic life. New Orleans is one of the few noncoastal cities with enough film and television activity for a community of actors to sustain itself. One of those actors is Kamille McCuin, who moved to New Orleans in 2014 and has booked a series of commercials and small roles in movies and TV shows, along with modeling work. (No matter how many jobs she gets, she finds she's recognized most often locally for the ad she did for Morris Bart, a personal injury lawyer whose face blankets this part of Louisiana like the morning dew.) Like many actors, she has a day job—in her case, a night job. Since 2016, she has been a cocktail waitress at Harrah's Casino. For much of that time she has worked the "sunrise" shift. The shift's name is misleadingly happy, since it starts at midnight and ends at 8 a.m. That leaves her the daytime to go on auditions. The hustle is real.

McCuin, who does have the statuesque posture, gleaming white smile, and carefully applied makeup of an actress/model/cocktail waitress, is more than just those things. She is also a shop steward in Local 23. When she was unemployed for a full year and a half during the pandemic, she spent her free time phone banking and door knocking with the union leading up to elections. One of those was Jason Williams's successful 2020 race to become New Orleans's progressive, reform-minded district attorney, a race that felt personal for McCuin. Her brother is incarcerated, and the right of felons to vote is important to her. The union gave her a vehicle to put that belief into action.

Even with the late hours and the grind and the demanding customers, McCuin vows that she won't leave her job until she books a steady acting role on a big show, big enough to bid adieu to the normal working world for good. A large part of what makes her entire career setup palatable is the union. It has helped her get better shifts, and better pay, but she has also seen it functioning as a true civic institution: giving her a chance to participate in the campaign, hand out gift cards for hurricane relief, and in general to *be a part* of something that has power, to participate in making her city better in a way that would simply not be possible if the union didn't exist.

"New Orleans was one of the major slave trading ports in the United States. I don't think people understand that that history still resonates in every fiber of the city today. When you don't teach a people that you are powerful, and that you have the right to certain benefits, and that if something isn't working for you, you do have the right to stand up and say something without facing retaliation—then you create a certain worker that doesn't really push back too much, that just accepts things as status quo," she says. "A union helps you not do that. It helps you realize that you are powerful, that you are deserving."

More than most unions, Unite Here's strength is rooted in its ability to build a staff made up of people who started as the most passionate members. The organizers look like the members because they *were* the members. They understand the members' struggles, and they can speak to them not from a script, but from shared lived experience. One of those people is Thanh Dao, a short woman with long black hair, kind eyes, and the nervous energy that comes with genuine enthusiasm. Her family migrated to America from Vietnam after the war in 1975, when Dao was a young girl, and then moved in the '80s to New Orleans, where they had family members who were part of the city's large Vietnamese community. She went to work at a series of Louisiana casinos in the '90s, ending up at Harrah's in New Orleans, where she first encountered Local 23.

At Harrah's, she had an abusive manager. He would yell at her, harangue her while she was on break, and threaten to fire her, just to exercise his own power. As traumatic as it was, it was a dynamic that she would have taken for granted until then. But the union set up a sit-down meeting with Dao, the manager, his supervisors, and HR, at which Dao got to denounce his behavior. That taste of worker power was eye-opening for her. "I walked out of that meeting, I was like, 'Wow! This is what it means to have a union.'"

Soon, her enthusiasm was so evident that Unite Here pulled her out of her job on a leave of absence to help the union full-time. She was sent to Denver, where a branch of Local 23 was organizing United Airlines catering workers. Dao could speak to Vietnamese workers in Denver in a common language. Many of the catering workers were from the Pacific islands of Micronesia, and Dao could discuss their shared stories of immigration's harsh challenges. A staple of corporate anti-union rhetoric is the assertion that the union is a "third party," trying to stick its bureaucratic beak between the employees and managers in order to siphon off dues money. That lie tends to wither when the union is represented by someone like Dao, who overflows with earnestness, who has lived the struggle herself, and whose motivation is to bring to others the mechanism she found for salvation.

What corporate America fails to understand is that unions, real unions, spread like religions, not like businesses. The evangelicals of unions like Unite Here are those who have had the union extend its hand to pull them out of dangerous waters, and they feel obligated to do the same for others. It is one of the most unadulterated things you will ever find in this nation of scammers and grifters and omnipresent commerce. Companies cannot grasp it because there is no parallel to it in the business world. It is pure.

When Dao was out talking to those immigrant workers in Denver, she could hear her own family's story. People came to America with no money, with children in tow, with no savings. Many of the women were marginalized, shunted aside in patriarchal homes. Groups of twenty people lived in a single house, all the adults working for United, none of them with any health insurance. They had come to the land of the free, and it was brutal.

Dao saw how being a union could change their lives. She saw women who learned how to speak up for themselves at work, and brought the same attitude back home, breaking free from dysfunction. She saw empowerment, not as a buzzword but as a living process that took hold of entire families. She had been through it all herself. One day, a man broke down in tears describing to her how he had had to stand in the snow in the dark, waiting for the bus to go to work. "He asked me, do I know what that feels like?" Dao remembers. "And I told him, I do. Because my dad was the same way. Didn't speak English. Didn't understand. You come to a country where you just want to provide for your family. To share that with these people . . ." Her voice catches in her throat. The union is bigger than a contract. It's love.

—

To immerse yourself in Unite Here is to see the outlines of what the entire labor movement could be. If you take the Culinary Union of Las Vegas as your model—one built with almost ninety years of deep organizing, bitter strikes, militaristic discipline, and collective sacrifice by tens of thousands of working people—you can look across the nation at every other city in turn and imagine the possibilities. Miami and New Orleans are each at an early-to-medium stage of development in which the union has established itself and has a number of key properties in hand, but has not yet achieved the density necessary to fully bend the political gravity of the region in the way that the Culinary Union can.

Here is the formula: You go to a city. You organize the hotels. You organize the airport. You organize the people who make the sports and entertainment and convention infrastructure run. You now control a good part of the economic activity that keeps cities running. Politicians and business leaders must take you seriously because if you decide to strike you do not merely inconvenience a single business—you threaten the entire intricate system that makes these cities rich. With this strategic power, you can ensure that those who do the necessary work share fairly in the proceeds. You can build a middle class where none would exist otherwise. By demonstrating your value to workers, you can also build a coherent political bloc. Your members will vote, and they will also go knock on doors, and serve as an army for politicians who are willing to help them. Thus, the candidates will come seeking the union's endorsement. Thus, the working class has achieved political power it would not otherwise have. In this way, an effective union can be the difference between a two-tier city full of the working poor and a more equal city with livable wages and affordable housing and elected officials who are obligated to care about the majority. And when you can take political power in the cities, you have political power in the state-houses. And when you put this model into effect in swing states, your power automatically becomes national.

Unite Here's model works in any fair-sized city, and indeed the union has strong locals across the country. But it works most powerfully in cities that depend on tourism to underpin their economies. When you understand the model, it is easy to look at a map and see how many places could be changed if the effort to do the necessary organizing were applied. The most promising opportunities are in places that fit all the above criteria, but where unions in general are weak, and where politics are hostile: Savannah and Charleston and Nashville and Branson and Moab and Boise. The model can work as well in red states as in blue because it derives its power from labor organizing, which can be done anywhere that people have shitty jobs, which is everywhere. The labor power then applies itself to politics and creates a virtuous cycle. In every Republican-controlled state where poor people are oppressed and forgotten, this opportunity sits, waiting to be exploited.

How to accomplish this is not a secret. The people of Unite Here under-stand it perfectly well. The limiting factor is resources. To organize, say, the next twenty largest unorganized hotels in Miami or New Orleans, enough to truly be able to exercise sectoral control, will take dozens of professional organizers quite a few years. In addition to the new organizing that's neces-sary, the union relies on constant *internal* organizing of existing members to maintain a unit that is actually capable of pulling off the strikes and the marches and the door knocking and the enforcement of contracts necessary to keep the union formidable. With about three hundred thousand mem-bers nationally, Unite Here is a moderately sized union. Even with a philo-sophical commitment to new organizing, it can only grow so fast. The gulf between what cities could be and what they are is one that can be filled by union organizers.

In the months leading up to the 2022 midterm elections, Unite Here rolled out its most ambitious election door-knocking campaign in history. About 1,200 members spread out in the swing states of Nevada, Arizona, and Pennsylvania, knocking on what the union estimates were 2.7 million doors on behalf of Democratic candidates. And it worked: the Democrats succeeded in holding onto control of the Senate, thanks to close wins in each of those three states. When the Senate election in Georgia went to a runoff, the union redirected all its efforts into that state in advance of the December 6 voting, which the Democrat Raphael Warnock won. It was, all in all, a massive demonstration of how valuable organized labor can be to a friendly party—not just for donations, but for its ability to provide an army to fuel a refined ground game that many candidates could not pull off themselves.

One of the architects of Unite Here's political program is Gwen Mills, the union's former political director and now second-in-command. Mills, whose blonde hair is just long enough to brush the shoulders of her glaring red union hoodie, grew up in New Haven, Connecticut, where the three Unite Here locals represent thousands of workers and grad students at Yale. In New Haven, a decade of labor and community organizing led to a city election in 2011 in which a slate of Unite Here–affiliated union members took control of the city's Board of Alders, effectively making New Haven a union-controlled city. That process of organizing-to-politics power building was a laboratory for Mills, and she brought its lessons with her when she became a national leader in the union.

"The goal is to transform the economy to be one that works for working-class people. Politics is a tool in that struggle, just as unionization is a tool in that struggle," Mills says. Unite Here has not discovered any secrets, but they are unique in how explicitly conscious they are of the fact that all the internal organizing they do with members is meant to prepare them not only to be leaders at their jobs, but also to participate in electoral politics and become elected officials themselves. "I feel like the decline of small-d democratic politics in the country—not about Democrats, but engagement in politics—maps to the decline of union density. It's a cycle that builds on itself. You'd start losing elections for pro-worker candidates in Ohio and Michigan and Wisconsin and Pennsylvania. It's not a mistake that the attack on unions has led to a weakening of the democratic operation."

Since 2012, the international president of Unite Here has been D. Taylor, a salty union veteran whose squinty look and baseball-cap-and-T-shirt wardrobe give him the air of a hardboiled high school baseball coach who has arrived to yell at you for loafing on the basepaths. He is a man given to plain talk. I once saw him climb on the back of a flatbed truck on a Las Vegas picket line just before the 2020 Nevada Caucus, and—in front of an array of visiting Democratic presidential candidates—raise a bullhorn, point toward the Palms Casino, and holler about its owners, "These guys are scumbag liars! The only way we're going to win is to kick the ever-loving crap out of them and beat the shit out of them!"

Taylor spent decades in Las Vegas with the Culinary Union before ascending to higher office with Unite Here. He would not have taken the big job, he says, if he didn't believe that what the union has done in Vegas could be replicated in other cities. He knows the formula and understands the opportunities for change that exist not only in New Orleans and Miami, but in Seattle and Minneapolis. Scaling up the union's model can make red states less red, and blue states more blue, and can offer working people the chance at a middle-class lifestyle that they never, ever would have had otherwise. All these things have been demonstrated. Unite Here is one of the clearest examples of the promise of the labor movement itself. We know it works. So why isn't it everywhere?

Money, to be blunt. "It's a resource question," Taylor says. As devastated as its membership was by the pandemic's near-total unemployment, it is a small miracle that Unite Here got back on its feet as fast as it did. By 2022, Taylor could look out at America and see a high demand for workers and the most enthusiasm for unions that he had seen in his forty-year career, but he simply did not have the money or personnel to flood the zone with organizers in every city that could put the trends to use. And there is no real mechanism for getting him those resources because there is no coherent national labor organization capable of thinking that strategically, or of doing anything material about it if they did. So Unite Here will just continue to do its best.

"I don't think there's any sector that's not able to organize. You have a labor shortage. You have a workforce that's pretty discontent. You have an economic structure in our industry that relies on low wages, and people aren't gonna take it anymore. And you have the most pro-union administration ever in my life," Taylor ruminated. The question of whether all of that promise would just slip away hung over the conversation. He had been around long enough to know that good times don't last forever. He spoke of the need to be bolder, to take more risks, to do everything, everywhere, without fear of losing. To fail, and to come back and try again. "We will become completely irrelevant if we don't grow," he says. "A union is like a shark. A shark dies if it sits still. We've got to keep on moving."

CHAPTER SEVEN

THE CONVENTIONAL WISDOM

The twenty-ninth quadrennial AFL-CIO Convention began by talking about death. Not the long, slow death of American unions, which might have been appropriate, but rather with a Saturday night memorial service for Richard Trumka, the former AFL-CIO president who had died suddenly of a heart attack in August 2021, before the conclusion of his term. This convention was supposed to be his opportunity to pass the torch to a handpicked successor. (Some also speculated that he would change his mind and run for another term. We'll never know.) Instead, it was a more permanent goodbye.

In a large ballroom on the third floor of the Philadelphia Convention Center, Trumka was remembered as a Pennsylvania coal miner, a fiery union reformer who won control of the United Mine Workers of America at the tender age of thirty-three and rose through the ranks of the AFL-CIO for more than a decade before being elected president in 2009. Trumka spoke slowly, had a dark, bushy mustache, and narrowed his eyes in an endearing way when he smiled. His son, Richard Trumka Jr., has the same mustache as his dad and is the head of the Biden administration's Consumer Product Safety Commission. He gave the most touching speech at the ceremony, remembering Trumka as a dad who always made time for football games and soapbox racer rallies. There were video tributes from Nancy Pelosi, Joe Biden, and Labor Secretary Marty Walsh, who woodenly read a speech while staring straight into a webcam.

Though there may have been some things to quibble with, the memorial was nice. It showed Trumka as a man who, at least, tried. He came to the labor movement through the UMWA with genuine fervor. In the end, he was not capable of replicating that fervor on a national scale. During his tenure as the highest labor leader in the land, union density in America fell from 12.3 percent to 10.3 percent. His death was announced the day after a big Alabama rally to support the United Mine Workers on strike at Warrior Met Coal; by the time of his memorial service, ten months later, those workers were still on strike. At the memorial service's opening invocation, the chaplain, Clete Kiley, said of Trumka, "He knew righteousness was right around the corner." After his best efforts, it remained around the corner.

The AFL-CIO convention was ostensibly the biggest organized labor convention in America during a year in which public enthusiasm for organized labor was at a generational high—when high-profile organizing victories at companies like Starbucks and Amazon were lending a new level of visibility to the idea that anyone could unionize their own workplace. It was noticeable, though, that the crowd at the AFL-CIO convention was, generally speaking, indistinguishable from the crowd at the Mid-Atlantic Insurance Industry Convention. A lot of middle-aged white guys in blazers and golf shirts with "Southeast Regional District Council President" stitched on a corner of the chest. I do not begrudge the existence of middle-aged white guys, nor of unions having regional district councils. But it was clear that this was not an organization that saw itself as the vanguard of a radical, powerful new labor movement. This was unions' version of middle and upper management. The revolution would not be televised here.

The featured, headlining speakers of the convention were Stacey Abrams, Marty Walsh, and Joe Biden. Not appearing on stage at the convention: any recently unionized Starbucks or Amazon workers. The seeming explanation for this was that neither the Starbucks workers (who were members of Workers United) nor the Amazon workers (who were their own independent union) were members of unions that were affiliates of the AFL-CIO. Another more honest explanation is that the AFL-CIO did not—no matter how much it should—see itself as anything more than a friendly spool of red tape. There is one sort of vision in which the AFL-CIO is a mighty coalition of labor that flings open its doors to all the workers of the world and says, "Join us! We are all one! Together, we will fight the vital battles against the capitalist class that is murdering the dreams of all working people!" And there is another sort of vision in which the AFL-CIO is, you know, a tepid coalition of several dozen disparate unions that needs someone to lobby for them and rule on the occasional boundary dispute. A Kiwanis club for unions. The idea that the most vibrant, exciting, recognizable people in the labor movement at a given moment should not be invited to the biggest stage of the biggest labor convention because they do not meet the conditions set forth in Article III, Section 1 of the bylaws makes perfect sense to the sort of people who tend to find themselves running the AFL-CIO. And that is the problem. The AFL-CIO is not bad, it is just *blah*. Watching the procession of truly inspirational members who did appear on the convention stage— the nurses, the flight attendants, the auto workers, the public defenders, the Amazon workers (those who were organizing with an AFL-CIO member union), all fighting the sorts of fights that never end—made it even more painful to grapple with the seeming futility of the federation as a whole. It takes many admirable constituent pieces and adds them up to less than the sum of their parts. It offers pleasant bureaucracy when we need heroics.

On the evening of Sunday, June 12, after a string of laudatory nominating speeches, Liz Shuler was elected as president of the AFL-CIO. There was no opposing candidate.

In her acceptance speech, Shuler announced what she presented as a bold commitment to new organizing. "We have a visionary way forward," she said from the stage. "Just as the AFL invested to create the CIO for industrial organizing in the 1930s, today we are launching the Center for Transformational Organizing—the CTO."

This was an odd setup. The CIO did in fact begin its life as a committee inside the AFL in 1935, to try to encourage the federation to do bold, industrial-scale organizing. But what happened next? The AFL suspended all the industrial unions because it despised their approach, and those unions eventually broke away from the AFL to form their own independent organization because the AFL was conservative, insular, and unwilling to organize as necessary. John L. Lewis, the head of the United Mine Workers and the founder of the CIO, famously punched the leader of the United Carpenters union in the face at an AFL convention when the man made disparaging remarks during an organizing report. The founding of the CIO was hardly a story of the AFL offering kind support for industrial organizing.

After this rather ahistorical intro, Shuler announced the goal: "In the next ten years, we will organize and grow our movement by more than one *million* people!" It was reminiscent of Dr. Evil in *Austin Powers* demanding, as his ransom request for the entire world, "One *million* dollars!" Because if you did one minute's worth of math, it became clear that adding one million union members over the next ten years would cause our country's already paltry union density—the percentage of American workers who are union members, which is the single most important measurement of union strength—that existed at that moment to *decline*.

In fact, the addition of a million union members between 2022 and 2032 (a time period during which it was estimated that something like thirteen million additional total jobs would be added to US employment rolls) would mean that, at the end of that decade, union density in America would have fallen under 10 percent, into the single digits, the last stop before true irrelevance. The official organizing goal of the AFL-CIO, therefore, represented the acceptance of the fact that unions would continue their multi-decade fade into feebleness. Shuler and other officials argued that the important thing was the mere *act* of setting a goal that all the federation's unions would agree to, and that the figure of a million people in ten years was a floor, not a ceiling. The problem with that excuse was that the floor was in the basement. America's most powerful organized labor group was acting like an unhealthy person who celebrates the act of joining a gym, with the goal of lifting one pound. Yes, the goal is achievable. But it's not gonna help you very much.

Joe Biden showed up to give a speech on the last full day of the convention. There was a running bet among some of the reporters about whether he would say anything newsworthy. He didn't. He talked about how much he loved unions. And that is true: he does, at least in an aesthetic sense, love unions, more than any president since FDR has. Like a broke husband, though, love sometimes felt like all he had to give. The big labor law reform bill, the PRO Act, couldn't get through the divided Senate. Biden had appointed a number of very good regulatory officials at the Labor Department and the NLRB, and he had issued a number of meaningful but not sweeping union-friendly regulatory changes, and he had used much more pro-union rhetoric than the average Democratic president. The huge domestic spending bills he got passed were good for workers in general but did little to permanently alter the balance of power between labor and capital. Apart from the bully pulpit, he had pretty much exhausted his ammunition. Barring a shocking midterm election season that would grab Democrats a bigger majority in the Senate while retaining control of the House—and we all knew that wasn't going to happen—the legislative playing field was set. The slogan of the AFL-CIO convention, plastered on signs and podiums and souvenir water bottles, was "Building the Movement to Meet the Moment." But beneath the fanfare, it was difficult to discern any actual plans that would indicate that the AFL-CIO's leadership was ready to do such a thing. The movement to meet the moment would have to be built offsite.

On the second floor of the Philadelphia Convention Center, just outside of the main meeting room, dozens of unions and various union-adjacent groups had set up display booths. The Airline Pilots Association had a flight simulator. The Machinists had a shiny motorcycle. The Screen Actors Guild had a red carpet and a step-and-repeat. Roaming the cavernous space for several days was one of those Boston Dynamics robot dogs, for no apparent reason I could imagine, except to remind us that all our jobs would be automated out of existence soon enough. Right off to the side of the entrance, setting the tone, was a booth with a large, open metal grid for a roof. Hanging down from each of the squares in the grid was a chain of multicolored plastic rings. "OUR MOVEMENT is built on connections," a sign read next to the booth. "Add your ring to show you are ready to link up and take on the future. Let's see what happens when we join together." With each passing day of the convention, the hanging chains of red and blue and yellow rings drooped longer and longer, eventually reaching the neutral gray carpeting below. It felt like a display at a convention of kindergarteners, a hanging forest of sterile plastic symbolism from the AFL-CIO. When the attendees finally went home, I assume, all those chains went in the trash.

=

Two days after the AFL-CIO convention ended, in a hot parking lot in Chicago, the labor movement's redemption tour began. The concrete lot sat in the middle of "Teamster City," surrounded on three sides by low office buildings belonging to Teamsters Locals. The buildings only partially blocked the day's brutal, ninety-six-degree sun. By 6 p.m., as "Summer in the City" blared on the loudspeakers, the arriving crowd was huddled on the half of the lot that was in the shade; by seven o'clock, the shadow had crept over most of the rest of the lot, and attendees could spread out in its wake.

Bernie Sanders, who understands the importance of unions to America's political landscape as well as any elected official in America, had come to do his part to try to push organized labor into the mainstream conversation. He was launching what amounted to a barnstorming tour with union leaders, lending his own star power on the left to the cause. This, the first of the events, was headlined by Bernie, Sara Nelson, and Sean O'Brien, the barrel-chested, bald-headed Bostonian who was the newly elected head of the Teamsters Union. In front of a building-sized blue and yellow mural of the Teamsters horse-and-wheel logo, Nelson—her voice amplified to eardrum-shattering levels—thundered to the group of more than a thousand people about solidarity, the power of strikes, and corporate greed.

Milling about in the crowd were quite a few people who had flown in directly from the AFL-CIO convention. They were the itchy ones, the true believers who had rolled their eyes and muttered under their breath about the AFL's many tepid disappointments. They had all come to Chicago for the Labor Notes convention, the grassroots union gathering populated by organizers and activists, whose spirit of urgency and democratic action was only enhanced by its temporal proximity to the AFL-CIO's top-down declaration of mediocrity. This was very much Sara Nelson's target demographic. The more that righteous anger crept into her speech, the happier they were.

"If you just want to tell the boss to kiss your ass, build your union!" Nelson hollered. A young guy in front of me in a Bernie T-shirt leaned into his girlfriend's ear and hissed, "I *love* this!"

After Nelson, the partially deafened crowd heard from O'Brien, an equally vehement speaker, who railed Bostonianly against the "WHITE CAWLA CRIME SYNDICATE known as corporate America." There was one particularly funny, telling moment that night, especially for everyone who had just come from the AFL-CIO convention. O'Brien (who had not been at that convention because the Teamsters are not AFL-CIO members and was therefore missing some context) had clearly misunderstood something that Nelson had said to him sarcastically while they were waiting in the wings. Near the end of his speech, he tried to reference that conversation, saying, "We have a little wager going on, where my sister, Sara Nelson, said to me, looking in my eyes sincerely, 'Do we have the ability to organize one million new members over the next ten years?'"

Then Bernie Sanders took the stage, with O'Brien and Nelson standing behind him. In the midst of his remarks, he glanced over his shoulder at them. "I kind of think a million new union members over a ten-year period is pretty conservative," Bernie said, sounding a little confused. Nelson, who was wearing a red T-shirt that read "ORGANIZE," leaped forward to clear things up: "TENS OF MILLIONS!" she yelled.

"Yeah, that's right," Bernie replied, satisfied. Most of the people there were oblivious to the subtext of that exchange, but its meaning jumped out at me. The AFL-CIO's stated goal for new organizing had, in two days, already become a punchline.

=

A DREAM WAS DEAD. IT WAS NOT THE ONLY DREAM, NOR WAS IT, PERHAPS, even the best or most important or wisest dream, but it was a dream that had existed in the minds of many people for several years, and so is worth acknowledging. It was the dream that the long-awaited revival of the labor movement in America would take a very specific path: that it would be ushered in by one dynamic leader, and that that leader would be Sara Nelson, and that the job she would have would be president of the AFL-CIO. It was a flame of hope that was nurtured in many of the progressive corners of the labor and politics worlds, where people had grown righteously impatient with the inability of labor's existing institutions to grapple with the reality of being on the losing side of a fifty-year war against workers.

Now that path was closed. And who knows? Maybe it would be for the best. It is unhealthy for movements to become too invested in the idea of having a savior in human form, when what is really necessary, always, is the action of thousands and thousands of people in a common direction. By the middle of June, when all the union presidents had left Philly, and all the union activists had converged on Chicago for Labor Notes, it was clear that they would have to find a different path to the same goal.

For Nelson herself, there was a period of coming to grips with missed opportunity. She had also thought about getting that job for years, and now the last flickers of hope had been snuffed out. It was not that she craved the political side of the job so much—the endless need to soothe five dozen different unions, the constant litigation of personality disputes. It was the *resources* that the AFL-CIO had, resources that she had planned to marshal and direct in service of a plan to revive union organizing and power. The federation, for all its flaws, had an existing infrastructure, and central labor councils in every state, and a big bank account, and a direct line to the White House. The potential to put all of that to use would remain out of her hands. That was tough to swallow. When the AFL-CIO convention finally came, she showed up and participated and cheered on Liz Shuler's election as president, as she was obligated to. But before she put it all behind her, she gave herself a few days to chew over the what-ifs, to dwell in the excruciating land of What Might Have Been. What gnawed at her most was that she hadn't been able to give it a proper try.

"[One] thing Covid did was, it made sure that I wasn't meeting with people on a regular basis. I mean, when I meet with people, most of the time they like me! I always knew that I would have to run a big, grassroots campaign that had never been done before at the AFL. That would probably, in a best-case scenario, be about a year-long campaign," she sighed. The pandemic, and her two hip surgeries, saw to it that that campaign never happened.

Even as the likelihood of Nelson grabbing the job had dwindled throughout 2022, the possibility that she could mount a run for it gave her some political capital inside of the AFL-CIO. If she had wanted to, she could have made it a messy election, even if she had not won. Her decision not to run had smoothed the way for the AFL-CIO to get fully behind the AFA's campaign to unionize the Delta flight attendants. That was something of substance—the biggest private sector union organizing in the country, at the time—but not the sort of substance that would produce millions of new union members. Before the convention, Nelson had had dinner with Shuler, who asked what the AFL could do to bring her into the fold. At that moment, Nelson thought to herself, "My place is not in the fold."

There was no denying that Nelson had wanted it. She had wanted to run the AFL-CIO because that had seemed, for a while, to be the most direct way to change the world. The night before Shuler was officially elected, Nelson, racked with adrenaline and second-guessing, could not sleep. When that day passed, though, a sense of peace began to return, along with a growing certainty about where the movement would go next.

"I started to feel like, okay, I'm going in a different direction. And that's okay. I started to feel like a leader again. It was pretty torturous just sitting there and feeling like I wasn't *doing* what I was supposed to be doing. But the next day, when people started to talk to me again, I felt real clarity," she said. "There was a decision to be somewhat irrelevant. What I mean by that is to keep the AFL as a service model to the affiliates, rather than a place that can serve as a strategic hub—a real voice, strong voice, leading voice for the American worker. That's just not gonna happen there. But there's all this other organizing, and all this other action, and it just feels like it's gonna happen in a different way."

For months, Nelson had been informally plotting out the formation of a new group that would do the things she wanted to do with the AFL-CIO in the event that she didn't get ahold of the AFL-CIO job. She envisioned an organization that would do four things. First, it would be an open door that any worker who wanted to unionize could come to—a first stop for inquiries, a sort of "1-800-UNION" that anyone could reach out to and begin the process of organizing. (This seems like something that would have been built decades ago, but alas, the process of matching casually interested workers with appropriate union organizers remains mostly ad hoc and inadequate.) The workers that came in could be funneled to existing unions, or affiliated with the new organization itself, which would offer them legal, communications, and organizing resources to help them form their own unions.

Second, it would have a "solidarity fund" to support workers who wanted to organize their own unions, as the Amazon workers in Staten Island had done when they formed the Amazon Labor Union. Though they made a national splash by winning their first union vote, they lost their second union drive at an adjacent Amazon facility, largely because the new organization was just stretched too thin. "The only way they're going to have the time to spend to do the organizing that's necessary that you heard about at ALU, where people were driving back to the warehouse on their days off, or spending time after work organizing, is if you can actually supplement their income," Nelson said.

Third, the new group would give assistance to workers on strikes, with the aim of ensuring that strikes were victorious and not just noble struggles. Finally, there would be some component of pushing labor history education in schools and universities, and a media relations program to make unions more visible in the news—something Nelson was already gifted at.

By the time the AFL-CIO convention was wrapping up, Nelson was already thinking of fundraising avenues for this new organization. It would take a lot of money. She went to dinner with Bernie Sanders after their rally in the Chicago parking lot and discussed it with him. He was willing to help raise money for it, the same way he often used his vast email list to raise money for labor groups and strike funds. She had close relationships with other pro-union senators as well, like Elizabeth Warren and Sherrod Brown, and she was fairly sure they would help out too. (In an idle moment, Nelson once remarked how realistic those ubiquitous political spam fundraising text messages that we all get on our phones were becoming, how hard they were to distinguish from real text messages from friends. I realized that they seemed realistic to her because actual senators *do* text her on a regular basis.) And she was convinced that there was a vast pool of politically engaged potential private donors lurking out there.

One can bicker, in a chicken-and-egg sense, over whether the Democratic Party should support organized labor because it is good for working people and it reduces inequality, or whether their motives are always self-serving because unions tend to align politically with Democrats. The answer is that it doesn't matter. The only thing that matters is turning around the crushing descent of union density. Sara Nelson believed that the AFL-CIO was not going to do it, so something else would have to. And she believed that the leaders of the progressive political universe would help because they would understand what was at stake. Her mind was already moving.

"Some of the people are steeped in labor and have always understood in their career that labor is important, and they don't see the kind of leadership that's necessary right now to make sure that the labor movement doesn't just die out," she said. "It's that existential."

CHAPTER EIGHT

THE HARD FIRST STEP
TUDOR'S BISCUIT WORLD, ELKVIEW, WEST VIRGINIA

From Charleston, West Virginia, take Route 119 north, winding alongside the Elk River, whose greenish-brown waters amble along at a walking pace. In fourteen miles, past the airport, past Mink Shoals, past Big Chimney, just after the road leading to Pinch, you will pull into Elkview, which is, technically speaking, not a town but a census-designated place (pop: 1,095). Right at the corner of Frame Road, which marks the turn toward Main Street, there is a small white wooden gazebo with the words "WELCOME TO ELKVIEW" in raised blue letters, framing a hanging outline of the state of West Virginia. And directly to the left of that, screwed to two metal poles stuck into the dirt, is a large yellow road sign reading "DEAD END."

Elkview proper is, like many of West Virginia's tiny towns, just a few blocks running parallel to the river. Besides a smattering of houses, downtown consists of a church, a sheriff's department office, a musty community center in the old elementary school, a bank, a barber shop, and an abandoned, weed-choked building with an "Expert Repair- Jewelry- Custom Designs" sign. That ramshackle building has an unusually large cluster of gravestones in its front yard, which could mean it's either a gravestone dealer or a family cemetery. To the west there is a small shopping center with a grocery, pharmacy, and a Family Dollar. Most of the activity on Main Street centers on the two restaurants there: a Dairy Queen Grill & Chill, and—most popular of all—a Tudor's Biscuit World, a faux barn–shaped building with a green roof and a sign outside advertising two biscuits and gravy for $4.99.

Besides that great price, something else remarkable happened at this Tudor's. Its flour-choked kitchen, in forgotten little Elkview, is the site of the kind of spontaneous worker uprising that should, in the best of worlds, be a prototype of how labor organizing can spread into even the tiniest and most neglected corners of America. What happened here could happen anywhere. What *didn't* happen here can teach us a lot about why so many Americans are toiling at bad jobs every day with very little money, power, or hope.

=

TUDOR'S IS NOT JUST SOME FAST FOOD RESTAURANT—IT IS *THE* UNOFFICIAL restaurant of West Virginia, the homegrown chain ubiquitous enough to become a state mascot. Its stores stretch out into Ohio and Kentucky, but most are clustered in West Virginia, from the university town of Morgantown down to the desolate coal country of Mingo County, and everywhere in between. And it's not quite fair to call it fast food—they bring your food to your table after you order it and bus the tables when you leave. Sometimes people leave a dollar or two on the table for this, but just as often they don't.

You can get three meals a day at Tudor's, but breakfast, available all day, is the star of the show. There are more than a dozen different biscuit sandwiches with names like "Dottie" and "Duke," comprising every mathematical combination of eggs, cheese, bacon, ham, sausage, and hash browns stuck inside a biscuit. You can get biscuits on a plate with gravy (or, if you're in the mood for something sweet, with fried apples or blueberries) poured on top. Or you can get the fried apples inside the biscuit, as a sandwich. There are breakfast platters like the "Big Tator," which is a lot of diced potatoes covered with eggs and bacon and cheese, or the "Little Tator," which has slightly fewer potatoes. There is a "Low Carb" platter with eggs, bacon, sausage, and no biscuit, for health nuts. For lunch you can get a BBQ or ham or chicken or fried bologna sandwich, or burgers or hot dogs or a bowl of pinto beans with a hunk of cornbread for five bucks. The dinner platters, of country fried steak or meatloaf or roast beef, also come with a biscuit. A single biscuit, which has five hundred calories before you put any butter on it, will fill you up for half a day, which is nice if you're broke. I ate Tudor's biscuits for three days in a row, until some of the employees told me about how dirty and bug-infested the kitchen was. Nevertheless, they said, for some of their coworkers, the food at Tudor's is the only thing they get to eat all day because they start out there earning nine dollars an hour. Employees receive a 50 percent discount.

The Tudor's in Elkview, which opened to much local excitement in 2019, is done up in country kitchen–style decor inside—short plaid curtains, bright yellow walls, six booths surrounding a bunch of tables with wooden, slatted chairs. The walls are decorated with cutesy little signs like "Keep the Kitchen Clean. Eat Out" and framed historic photos of Elkview's past. Next to my table was a picture captioned "Boys Playing Cards, 1925," showing four young boys perched on a log next to an empty railroad track. It was one of the bleakest photographs I've ever seen. Elkview has not added a significant amount of development since then.

In June 2016, powerful rain produced a terrifying flood in Elkview as the Elk River surged over its banks and swallowed much of the town. Homes were underwater to their rooftops. The local high school, Herbert Hoover High, was completely destroyed; six years later, students were still attending classes in portables, so kids at rival schools derisively called it "Trailer Park High." The bridge that leads to a shopping center just outside of town washed away, leaving hundreds of people who were working and shopping at the Kroger and the Goodwill utterly stranded. Locals still talk about which managers of which stores did or did not hand out free food to all the people trapped that day, and how the La Quinta Inn didn't give people free rooms. Elkview is a hard place to live. There is often more bad news than good. People remember who helped out and who was only looking out for themselves.

CYNTHIA NICHOLSON ALWAYS WEARS A RED BANDANNA. SOMETIMES SHE wraps it around her neck like a choker, and sometimes she ropes it around her long brown hair, in the back. She has almost reached the age of Social Security, but her straight bangs and dark eyeliner and silver bracelets give her the vibe of a (very polite) rock and roller. The bandanna looks stylish on her, a punchy accent to her white blouse, but she does not wear it just for style. She wears it as an homage to the most famous piece of West Virginia's rich labor history. In the early twentieth century, when the state's Mine Wars between coal miners and company bosses were raging, the red bandannas that miners wore became a virtual uniform for union supporters. Those bandannas were worn prominently by more than ten thousand angry miners who marched south toward Mingo County in August 1921, determined to fight against the coal company's private armies of thugs and help spread the United Mine Workers union into that ruthless and oppressive part of the state. The marchers ran into notorious anti-union Sheriff Don Chafin's hired gunmen at Blair Mountain in Logan County, and there, had the largest armed clash in the United States of America since the Civil War. After three days of fighting, dozens dead on both sides, and some bombs dropped onto the revolting miners from airplanes, the fighting ended when federal troops arrived on September 2. The Battle of Blair Mountain, though experienced as a defeat for the UMWA at the time, went down in history as the closest thing that unions in America have ever had to an actual war. It is one of the bedrock stories of West Virginia's long annals of class conflict. In the state museum in Charleston today, right next to the gold-domed capitol building, you can see a neatly folded red bandanna that one of the miners wore at Blair Mountain on display in a glass case. Some say that the term "redneck" originated with those miners; that may be apocryphal, but the meaning of the red bandanna in West Virginia is recognizable to everyone there to this day.

The struggle that it symbolizes is not one that has ever been won by the state's working people. (When I went to write a story about the legacy of Blair Mountain a few years ago, I found that I could not get onto the mountain itself because it is still private coal company land.) Cynthia Nicholson was born in 1958 in Madison, West Virginia, a town that the mine workers army had marched through on its way to the battle. She moved to Elkview when she was ten years old, and has lived there, off and on, ever since. Her father was an installer of communication equipment, and a member of the Communications Workers of America. Her late husband was a union coal miner and UMWA member who later became a pipe fitter and joined the Pipefitters Union Local 625. Nicholson had an entire career as a dental assistant, retiring after thirty years.

After a while as a retiree, her dad told her she was becoming a hermit. She needed to get out of the house. So she wandered downtown to the newly opened Tudor's and got a job there in 2019. It did not turn out to be an easygoing, part-time retirement gig. "Never have I been through as stressful a job in my life," she says, shaking her head. "I thought dealing with patients and knowing I gave them the right stuff was stressful, but no. Nothing like the restaurant business."

Nicholson, who was going into Tudor's at 4 a.m. to open the store, was certainly not afraid of hard work. But she found the way that the store was run to be dictatorial and disrespectful. After she began working there, her son, Daniel, got a job in the kitchen as well; one day, as he was singing a song in Spanish (Nicholson's family is Spanish-speaking on one side), a manager told him to knock it off because it was "un-American." Daniel was coming in at four thirty in the morning to get all the biscuits ready, along with the bacon and the homemade cinnamon rolls, before the breakfast rush started at 5:30 a.m. It was 2020, and everyone was required to wear masks, and the flour floating in the air constantly made it hard for him to breathe. Still, he took pride in making the prettiest biscuits of anyone.

Schedules were made weekly, and they were inconsistent. The number of hours anyone could get would fluctuate wildly from week to week. Daniel would get close to forty hours because he was one of the only biscuit makers, and Cynthia once worked sixteen days straight without a day off—but that could drop off without warning in any given week. The employees took whatever they were given when the weekly schedule was posted on Sunday. Normal life planning was impossible. Cynthia remembers a coworker trying desperately to balance her unpredictable Tudor's schedule with the government meetings she needed to attend in order to get her children back from Family Services.

As a retiree, Cynthia was not quite as economically dependent on the job as most of the people she worked with, but the numbers are a stark illustration of what people have to do when their need for money is desperate. Cynthia made nine dollars an hour. While she was working at Tudor's, she had a tractor accident that seriously injured her leg, keeping her at home for months. At one point, the boss told her she should come to work and just wheel herself around as she recovered, but she declined. Daniel was making $9.30 an hour and could barely afford to buy the gas he needed to get to work. Another friend who started at the same time as Daniel, Danna Withrow, says it took her so long to get the company to give her a printed check stub that she lost her food stamps because she couldn't prove her income. When Cynthia began looking at various coworkers' checks, she started to suspect the company was not paying everyone the overtime they were due, or taking out taxes properly. Some employees were going hungry, too poor to buy food, yet still weren't allowed to eat at Tudor's for free. Nevertheless, one hated manager—who everyone called "Miss Trunchbull" after the sadistic elementary school principal in *Matilda*—would sanctimoniously inform the staff that they should be able to live and raise a family just fine on twenty-five hours a week at Tudor's, if only they managed their money properly. (That would be $225 a week before taxes—well under the federal poverty line for a single person, not to mention anyone supporting children.)

"We always used to say working there was like how they used to do revolutionary warfare, like they just shoot each other and step over the top of each other," Daniel Nicholson says. "Just put some dirt on top of it! That's literally what it felt like."

It was all too much for Cynthia. Her father had been a union member. Her husband had been a union member. She had seen the union protect and support them. What Tudor's needed, she decided, was a union of its own. She picked up the phone and called Local 625, her husband's old union for pipefitters. The rep there was, reasonably enough, mystified about how to go about organizing a fast food restaurant, so he put her in touch with someone who might know what to do: Alan Hanson, the burly, goateed organizing director for Local 400 of the United Food and Commercial Workers Union (UFCW). It was a sprawling local with more than twenty-five thousand members, most of them grocery store workers, across seven states. Including West Virginia.

We should pause here and make it clear just how unusual this all was. In November 2021, when Nicholson got in touch with the UFCW, fast food unions were still incredibly rare. The Starbucks union campaign that was soon to spread across the country was only just getting started; Burgerville workers in Portland, Oregon, had just signed their first union contract, which drew national attention because it was such a rarity; the Fight For $15 movement had spent a whole decade agitating and winning wage increases for fast food workers, but did not unionize any stores. There were more than three million fast food workers in America. It was one of the most common low-wage jobs in the country. And it was almost completely untouched by organized labor. Though Nicholson was doing nothing more than following her instincts about basic fairness, she had launched one of the very few active fast food union drives in the United States at the time.

It is not a coincidence that such a campaign popped off in Elkview, of all places. "It's a very West Virginia story," says Hanson, the organizer who agreed to take on the Tudor's campaign. "West Virginia is a really unique place to work, in how connected so many people are to the labor movement. It seemed like everybody you talked to there has a friend or a relative or a neighbor that is getting a mine worker pension, or something like that." Indeed, coal's historic stranglehold on the state's economy had the salutary effect of making the United Mine Workers union one of the state's most important and respected institutions for many, many decades. Though the union's membership in West Virginia has declined alongside the coal industry itself, family connections to organized labor are still common. No other rural state in America has such a rich pro-union history.

High union density is also the reason why West Virginia remained a blue state much longer than its poor, lightly populated counterparts. In 1981, according to the West Virginia Center on Budget and Policy, 38.3 percent of West Virginia workers were union members, well above the 21 percent national average. Right at that time, as Reaganism took hold, the state's average wage fell below the national average and has never recovered. By 2021, union density in the state had fallen to 9.6 percent, slightly below the national average. As unions disappeared, so too did the population's affinity for the Democratic Party. West Virginia had the second-highest voting percentage for Donald Trump in the 2016 presidential elections (though it is worth noting that the state's stubborn anti-establishmentism also enabled Bernie Sanders to win every county in the Democratic Primary). Republicans took full control of the state legislature in 2014 and soon passed bills rolling back the state's "prevailing wage" laws—which served to drastically decrease wages on public contracts—and, egregiously, torpedoed mine safety laws. They also passed a statewide "Right to Work" law, aimed directly at weakening union membership, which took effect in 2020 after surviving a court challenge. Between 2010 and 2020, the population of West Virginia declined by 3.2 percent, more than any other state. It is hard to find a clearer demonstration of what happens to working people when union density collapses: wages go down, pro-worker regulations get scrapped, and the political situation darkens into a futile downward spiral.

"Instead of doing things like making sure more people get a higher education, I think it's a very low road version of economic development. Like, 'If we pass Right to Work, if we eliminate the income tax, these are things that will make companies come here.' Rather than thinking, 'Our people are healthier and more educated. We have, you know, nice infrastructure, and good schools, and parks and things,'" says Kelly Allen, the executive director of the West Virginia Center on Budget and Policy. Her organization spends its time analyzing the state's often appalling political and economic choices and lobbying for improvements, which can be dispiriting. "It's this disconnect that businesses want something different than families want—which some maybe do, but are those the kind of businesses we want?"

The current policies of the West Virginia power structure have produced, for the poorer residents of Elkview, a job market in which fast food is the most prominent opportunity. Many of the employees at Tudor's have also worked at every other fast food place in town, along with a whole constellation of other gigs that fall under the rubric of "hustling." Everyone is hustling. For some that means a second job at a gas station, or cleaning houses, or taking care of other people's kids, or doing handyman work wherever it can be found. For others it might mean occasional prostitution, or selling some pills. The distinction of what is and is not a respectable form of hustling recedes into absurdity when you consider the hard absence of options in all these little towns along all these little rivers in all these little valleys. Scraping together enough money to pay the bills for another month is a win. The only people getting rich around here are people who aren't around here.

Cynthia Nicholson wanted a union. She wanted everyone she worked with to be paid properly, and she didn't want them to be disrespected by managers, and all of that sounded pretty damn good to most of the other people at Tudor's when she first spoke to them about it. There were about twenty-five employees at the store who would be eligible for the union, a manageable number for a respected worker like Cynthia to pull together quickly. After only a couple of weeks of her talking to coworkers, Alan Hanson left his home in Maryland and drove down to Elkview with a batch of union cards.

He parked his car and set up shop in an empty lot by the community center, adjacent to Tudor's on Main Street—a lot that was, several people hastened to tell me, locally famous for once being featured in an episode of *16 and Pregnant*. It only took a single day for Hanson to collect signed cards from 80 percent of the store's workers. With those in hand, Hanson and the organizing committee planned a dramatic little demonstration of unity. A group of six Tudor's employees piled into cars and drove twenty miles to the Tudor's in neighboring Sissonville to demand union recognition directly from the district manager. Phone cameras in hand, the group entered the store bristling with fervor. When the manager came out, Cynthia began reading aloud a speech she had printed out on a single sheet of white paper, in all capital letters: "WE ARE HERE TODAY TO ASK YOU TO RECOGNIZE OUR UNION AND IMMEDIATELY SIT DOWN WITH US TO BARGAIN A CONTRACT. HERE ARE OUR SIGNED UNION CARDS. AS YOU CAN SEE, WE HAVE A MAJORITY." There is an excellent photo that captures this moment: Cynthia in a red-and-black-checkered lumberjack shirt, red bandanna looped around the back of her head, standing amid the Tudor's dining room tables, mouth open as she looks down at her speech, with her left hand raised and pointer finger extended to punctuate her words; and, two feet in front of her, the district manager, a stout, gray-haired woman in a black polo shirt, turned theatrically in the opposite direction, caught in the act of fleeing from what she was hearing, her hands extended, palms up, toward Cynthia, as if to block any more of the words from reaching her ears.

"That's when she threw her hands up like, really, 'EEEEEEEEE!'" Cynthia remembers, trying to recreate the sound of someone freaking the fuck out. "Oh my god, it was awful. And then Alan says, 'When she goes to walk off, you walk behind her, and you keep continuing your speech.' So when I did, when I got to the swinging doors, she turned around real fast and went, WHAM!" She mimes a slamming door and squeezes her own fingers in memory of the pain. "And caught my hand in the door. I still have trouble with that bugger." The manager then called police to the store, but everyone was allowed to leave without any arrests.

That, it turns out, was the easy part. As most anti-union companies do, Tudor's refused to recognize the union voluntarily and instead demanded an official NLRB election. Ballots for that were scheduled to be mailed out at the end of December. That gave the company a solid month to threaten and cajole against the union, which they did with zeal. Several Tudor's employees told me that some of their coworkers were offered cell phones or promotions in exchange for voting against the union. A mysterious new management guy, with suspiciously clean hands, showed up in the store, pulling workers into individual meetings and handing out discipline. Everyone assumed he was a hired outside union buster. One of Cynthia's coworkers was, she says, given tacit permission to harass supporters of the union. "One time he called me a 'union bitch,'" she says. "I told him, oh yes, I wear that one proudly."

The organizing committee made up a flier headlined "It's Union Time!" with a picture of them standing outside of the store in Sissonville with raised fists. It ended with the exhortation, "Remember, it's illegal for management to cut your hours, write you up, or intimidate you in any way just for being a union supporter. We have rights, and it's time that Tudor's respects them!"

In such a small restaurant, though, it was impossible for anyone to keep their union sympathies anonymous. Word got around. Alan Hanson says that one organizing committee member was told by a supervisor that her son's status as a student at Marshall University could be threatened by her participation in the union drive. He also says that the company "prominently reposted" its drug-testing policy in the store during the campaign and started a whisper campaign implying that union supporters could find themselves drug tested at any time. "What they were experiencing was truly egregious," he says, "and Tudor's counted on the fact that it was a small town, that they could bully those employees, because there were relatively few job prospects in the city."

April Redman, a sunny woman with a bright smile and a short red ponytail, began working at Tudor's in April 2021. She had worked at gas stations, Subway, McDonald's, and other fast food outlets in the past, and was not fazed by coming into Tudor's in the dark hours of the morning to make eggs, sausage, and gravy. Her father was a union bulldozer operator—"best one you'll ever meet," she says with pride—and when he died, the union paid for his headstone. When Cynthia Nicholson approached her with the idea of unionizing, Redman was all for it. She went out to deliver the union cards to the manager in Sissonville, standing right behind Cynthia as she read her speech. When she was speaking to her more uncertain coworkers about why they should vote yes, Redman would ask them if they were happy. Because she knew that they weren't.

She herself was driven by a conviction that she should not be treated as a replaceable cog by her employer. There were days when Tudor's was shorthanded, when she had gotten out of bed and come in at four in the morning in her pajamas to help open the store, just because they needed her help. In the summer of 2021, Redman got sick after working the Fourth of July rush and ended up falling into a diabetic coma. Three weeks later, she was back in the Tudor's kitchen, and happy to be there with her friends. In December, she got disciplined for something she thought was unfair and got so mad that she quit. The ballot she cast for the union, therefore, didn't count. Did she feel like the company was targeting the union supporters for harassment at work? "Completely," she says.

On January 25, a small knot of Tudor's workers gathered in the UFCW's office in Charleston to watch the NLRB count their union votes. It was a short party. About half of the store's workers had voted, and the union lost,

7–5. The vote was cold proof of how important a company's efforts to scare individual employees about unionizing can be. If only two people had voted differently, the union would have been certified.

The UFCW filed a formal complaint with the NLRB, charging Tudor's with a slew of unfair labor practices and saying that the results of the vote were therefore tainted. The complaint said that Tudor's managers in Elkview told workers they were not allowed to talk to one another outside of work; told them that the workers and managers alike would lose their jobs if the store unionized; threatened to fire workers who were organizing the union; told workers they would have their wages reduced to six dollars an hour if they unionized; suspended Cynthia Nicholson and another pro-union employee in retaliation; and "told employees that anti-union employees were permitted to give the pro-union employees 'as much hell' as they wanted to give them." In May 2022, the NLRB's office in Charleston found that there was probable cause to believe the charges were true and filed a complaint against Tudor's in district court. The workers who had been disciplined unfairly during the union drive were vindicated, but the burst of enthusiasm that had created it had flagged. Nicholson and Hanson couldn't even track down all the Tudor's workers who were supposed to go and testify against the company in court. They were off in the wind. So the union and the company agreed to settle. Disciplinary records were wiped. A Tudor's executive came into the store and read aloud a statement acknowledging the company's labor law violations during the campaign. That was, at least, a moral victory.

By the summer of 2022, only about a quarter of the workers who had been at Tudor's when the organizing campaign began were still there. April Redman was working as a cleaner overnight at a day care center, making more than she had at the restaurant. Cynthia Nicholson, however, was still at Tudor's, after everything. The same stubbornness that propelled her through the union drive has kept her there in the kitchen, thinking about what comes next. By the end of the year, she was the only Tudor's employee who had participated in the union election who was still working at the store. The managers had given everyone a dollar-an-hour raise. Cynthia knew that was only a small balm compared to a union. Even as her coworkers celebrated, she tried to refocus them on the bigger picture. "Who knows if this dollar is gonna be the only dollar raise you get for ten years?" she asked them.

Her mind keeps working. She has not given up, even though she would have to start the whole thing over again from scratch. She thinks about more than biscuits. One hot afternoon, she and her son gave me a tour of Elkview, which did not take long. As we wheeled past Tudor's, Cynthia declared, "It's not over with. Not at all."

=

THE SUDDEN, SPONTANEOUS FLARE-UP OF UNION SENTIMENT AT A FAST food store in a tiny town was unusual. That is part of a large problem. The insight that drove Nicholson to try to organize in the first place was a simple one, which applies to thousands of workplaces across the country: "We are being mistreated, and we need help." Yet the chain of events that led that commonplace thought to turn into something tangible required a lot of uncommon things to happen.

First, and most crucially, it actually *occurred* to Nicholson to want a union. She knew what a union was, and how it could help her. In a nation where 90 percent of working people aren't union members, that first and most basic condition is often unmet. Try to imagine how many moments of outrage over various injustices on the job happen everywhere, every day, and then fade away into nothingness. Until it becomes natural for regular people in regular jobs facing regular difficulties to automatically think of a union as the solution to their problems, most of America's latent opportunities for organizing will not be taken advantage of.

Second, Nicholson knew how to contact a union, even though it didn't happen to be one that might organize her specific job. Third, the person she spoke to at that union gave enough of a damn to take the time to track down another organizer, at another union, for her to talk to. Fourth, when she finally got in touch with Alan Hanson at UFCW Local 400—a man who oversees organizing at a union that spans seven states and has tens of thousands of members, almost none of whom are in the fast food industry—he took the time to engage with her, and, furthermore, made the decision to invest the time and effort to go to West Virginia and carry out a union drive for a group of two dozen workers. Which is, in the context of a big union, not very many people.

There are countless potential union campaigns that never come into being because of the failure of one of the links in this chain of events. The most common, by far, is the simple fact that most people in bad jobs do not decide to take it upon themselves to try to organize a union. Of those who do, many of them don't know how to do it, or who to even ask. Of those who do manage to get in touch with someone about it, many find that existing unions have little interest in trying to organize a new industry not directly tied to their core membership, so many or most requests like Cynthia's would probably just fall through the cracks. And even those motivated workers who do connect with a receptive union organizer may well find that the higher-up decision-makers of the union make the judgment that a small workplace in a small place is just not a "strategic" investment of resources for the union. Every time one of these small failures occurs, an opportunity is lost, and the labor movement itself grows a little bit weaker than it should be. These failures happen all the time.

And even if all these things fall into place, as they did at Tudor's Biscuit World in Elkview, West Virginia, the lucky workers still do not have a union. They haven't even started to fight the boss! That's when the real battle starts. At that point, we ask a group of people who may have very little money in the bank and who are making very little money and who are thinking mostly about how to pay their own bills and take care of their kids and manage the daily struggles and indignities of being poor to take a big, material risk to their own livelihood based on what can seem like an arcane, ideological desire for a more perfect world. If, based on long life experience, you have concluded that work sucks and the boss will always try to screw you, and that you just need to make the best of it as much as possible if you don't want to end up broke and starving and homeless, it can seem dubious, bordering on absurd, to imagine that you should put your whole job at risk to undertake an extremely uncertain process that might, months or years from now, produce some undefined gain for you, if you manage not to get fired by then. Maybe if you knew some people who had unions already, who had better wages and better health care and protections from mistreatment at work, who you could use as a mental reference point, you might feel more comfortable making such a bold leap of faith. But do you? Probably not. Especially if you didn't grow up in West Virginia.

"It's really tough, right? These are small establishments. There were twenty-four workers at this store. At the entire company, there's maybe a [few] hundred employees. In a right to work state, with turnover probably exceeding 100 percent in each location. Just the economics of representing workers in those industries is challenging for a union," says Alan Hanson. He is an organizer who did the right thing, who took on the challenge, who helped the fast food workers when they asked—he is a true union man. But not a naive man. "Would I launch an organizing campaign with them again? Absolutely, every day of the week. But, the way that labor law is structured in this country . . . it's gonna be a long time before the fast food industry is unionized." He ticks off the challenges of hostile state laws, of the grueling process of organizing individual stores one by one, of the unfriendly math of devoting the time of paid organizers to tiny shops. "I would still do it," he concludes, "but it was tilting at windmills, to some degree."

Hanson, though, as a true believer, understands that unions must have some Don Quixote in them if they want to escape their downward spiral. Viewed in isolation, any organizing campaign with the characteristics of Tudor's in Elkview can seem doubtful, even foolish; but that is the same sort of calculation that has sapped the power of organized labor in America. It is far worse for unions to give up on the long shots than to give them all a try. It is a long shot, after all, for a single fast food worker to believe that they can change a whole store, or company, or industry. But that is what unions promise. If they give up on that, they have little left to offer.

=

JOSH SWORD, THE HEAD OF THE WEST VIRGINIA AFL-CIO, HAS ONE OF those perpetually youngish-looking faces. But after six years at the job, gray streaks are creeping into his brown chin hairs. Like many of his counterparts who lead chapters of the union federation in mostly Republican states,

Sword's job can be thankless: trying to prevent the state legislature from passing *too* many horrific laws, smiling at Joe Manchin through gritted teeth as he explains why he won't back anything decent, things like that. Sword has suffered through the solidification of the Republican Party's control of his state's politics and its attendant damages to organized labor. His ambitions have been somewhat sanded down by Charleston's grim electoral politics.

"We would like to reinstate the prevailing wage. We would like to reverse 'right to work.' We would like to prohibit charter schools. We'd like to unravel the new school voucher bill they passed. We would like to reverse the prohibition on payroll deduction for public employee union members. The reality is, we're in no position to do that. We're mostly playing defense," he says. When he speaks about the ideas that emerge from the legislature for revitalizing the state's economy—like, for example, cutting unemployment benefits in half during a pandemic—his voice takes on an exasperated tone. "Nothing that they've done has helped the economic situation in West Virginia whatsoever. One of the things they said when they were trying to pass 'right to work' laws was, 'This is gonna be a huge jumpstart to our economy.' And the data, the real data, suggests it made absolutely no difference. Except that it's much more difficult for workers to find jobs with fair wages, good benefits, and a safe workplace, because they lose that leverage at the negotiating table."

Indeed, the West Virginia Policy Center found that, by the end of 2019, West Virginia had the slowest economic growth rate in America, along with the sixth-highest poverty rate, second lowest median household income, and fourth lowest median hourly wage. It is painfully clear to anyone in their right mind that the state is in dire need of both public investment and an increase in the power of workers to improve their own wages. The Republican determination to do the exact opposite of those things is less a reasoned policy choice than a bootlicking, quasi-religious belief in fundamentalist coal boss worship. For the past century, the major share of the state's natural wealth has been sucked out by corporations and investors who do not live there, leaving the citizens who do live there with crumbs. Crumbs can get you a biscuit. But people want more.

Bookstores in West Virginia have sections of books about West Virginia itself, and the majority of those books always tend to fall into three categories: organized labor, coal mining, and the drug epidemic. Those three forces all still jockey for control of the state's soul, and the deep vein of labor solidarity is the only one of the three that offers any hope for the future. When you stand on the street in Elkview—or in any of the small towns like it—you can look up in any direction and see the dark green hills looming right over you, like seething waves frozen just before they crash. Cynthia and Daniel Nicholson will tell you about hundreds of people in those hills, all the way up the Elk River, living in tents, or in their cars, just hanging on. A single union at a single biscuit restaurant in a single dot on the map can seem like a small thing. Really, though, it's a big thing: proof that, no matter who or where you are, you can make a union, and it can change your life. The workers at Tudor's may never see their Quixotic union dream come true. But they have already set a bar that the labor movement must live up to, or die.

CHAPTER NINE

THE STRIKE
THE NABISCO WORKERS OF PORTLAND, OREGON

Donna Jo Marks has a round, soft face that slips easily into a beaming smile and long, gray braids that cascade down over the shoulder of her blue work shirt, their untamed tips reaching the sewn-on name patch that reads "Donna" in cursive script. Most of her mother's family came from Louisiana, but Donna Jo, whose father was in the army, was born in Portland, Oregon, in 1965. She grew up there as one of the few Black faces in an overwhelmingly white city. As a young adult, she spent time in Arkansas and Ohio, seeing for the first time places where Black doctors and dentists and firemen were common. When she moved back to Portland, she returned with a new understanding of the loneliness that the city's racism of her youth created.

Marks has always worked. She cleaned up her uncle's nightclub on weekends as a kid. After dropping out of college, she worked as a manager at McDonald's, and at Wendy's, and at Payless shoes. She was, for a time, a licensed dog groomer. In her mid-twenties, in search of better pay, she got a job at a Wonder Bread factory in Portland, which had a union. It was a white and male-dominated place, and she was the only Black woman at the plant at the time. One of her supervisors was discriminating against her, giving more hours to people with less seniority. Marks studied her union handbook and then met with her shop steward. He was one of the plant's few Black men and had worked there for decades. Instead of helping her file a grievance, he cautioned her against making waves: "You're making good money. Keep your head down. Just do your job." This was a formative experience for Marks.

"He got treated any kind of way," she says of that shop steward, who struck her as a pitiful figure. "He came from a different era. I didn't come from that era."

Though many people might have concluded at that moment that the union was a waste of time, Marks did just the opposite. She had the union hold a new shop steward election, campaigned for the position, and won. The Wonder Bread factory later closed, but the knowledge stayed with her. In 2004, working at a Pacific Foods manufacturing plant that made soups, Marks was shocked when she saw the raise she had gotten: thirteen cents an hour. Outraged, she began talking to a coworker, who dismissed her complaints. Thirteen cents sounded pretty good to him, he said. His raise had been a penny.

That conversation was enough to finally kill the attitude that had been drilled deeply into Marks from her days grinding hard to be promoted to manager of a fast food outlet. "I still had what I call the slave mentality: if I work hard, they'll see me working, and I'll get the raise!" That myth was replaced by the realization that she and her coworkers were not going to get a damn thing if they didn't take it. It prompted her to call her old union rep and launch an organizing campaign at the plant—a campaign that only ran out of steam when she left to take a new, much better-paid job at the biggest unionized bakery in town: Nabisco.

The Nabisco plant is a long building of beige bricks that sits on Portland's northern outskirts, next to the railroad tracks. It makes Chips Ahoy cookies, Ritz and Saltine and Chicken in a Biskit crackers, and vast quantities of crumbled Oreos destined for America's cookies-and-cream ice cream supply. About two hundred of the workers at the plant—those who run the production lines, pack up the products, and keep everything clean—are members of Local 364 of the Bakery, Confectionery, Tobacco Workers and Grain Millers (BCTGM) union, which represents workers at all of Nabisco's American bakeries and shipping depots. The union and the company both share parallel histories as survivors of more than a century's worth of changes in the American economy. The BCTGM began in 1886 as a union of journeymen bakers and over subsequent decades picked up confectioners, tobacco workers, and grain mill workers through a series of mergers. Nabisco's roots stretch back to the 1890s, when businessmen in search of market dominance consolidated forty cracker bakeries across the country under one brand. The company has in modern times been the target of a staggering amount of corporate maneuvering, moving from Standard Brands to RJ Reynolds to Kraft to Mondelez in a series of multibillion-dollar sales, mergers, and spinoffs since 1981. Today, thanks only to the dogged efforts of the BCTGM, Nabisco factory work remains as one of the few surviving examples of that once-common thing: the blue-collar, middle-class job. But the intense, cutthroat financial engineering directed at the makers of such pedestrian products has rendered those jobs an endangered and hunted species.

When Donna Jo Marks was hired at the Nabisco plant in 2005, it was (despite the storm of dealmaking raging on Wall Street, where Phillip Morris was preparing to spin the company off under Kraft) seen locally as a desirable job. Turnover was low, and many workers stayed at the plant for several decades. The union contract guaranteed a "Golden 80" pension, meaning workers could retire with their full benefits when their age plus years of service added up to eighty. It was a powerful incentive for workers to stay and build a career at the plant. It also meant that seniority was important, and new employees like Marks had to toil for some time to get the more coveted jobs. She started out on the graveyard shift, from 11:15 p.m. until 7:15 a.m. the following morning. Workers could be "forced over" for five hours of mandatory overtime, so she was often ordered to stay until 12:15 in the afternoon. Workers were contractually guaranteed eight hours between shifts, so on those overtime days, she would drive home, sleep for five hours or so, and be back at work by 8:30 p.m. Not long after she started, the factory moved almost all the line workers to a schedule that persists to this day:

twelve days on, two days off. Everyone works a full week, through the weekend, and all the next week, and then everyone gets the second weekend off.

This was an exhausting combination. Up to twenty hours of extra forced overtime per week, before workers even had the option of saying no, and twelve straight days without a break. It meant that working at Nabisco was a job that required people to commit their entire lives to it. That suited the company, which saves money by piling more hours onto a smaller workforce rather than by hiring more workers who must all be paid benefits as well as wages. Hearing for the first time a description of the hours the job demands can be a shock, but the workers accepted it because the money was good. There was plenty of overtime, plus time-and-a-half on Saturday, and double time pay on Sunday. The union had negotiated wonderful health insurance, with no out-of-pocket contribution from workers and only three-dollar copays. Veteran employees now make thirty dollars an hour as their base rate and more for overtime. It amounts to a high five-figure salary for most, and those who aggressively pick up overtime can make well over $100,000 a year.

This is the working-class version of golden handcuffs. "I always say my job is the easiest job I hate the most," says Marks, who raised a daughter while working at the plant. "It's easy money. We make a decent wage. So I can afford my family . . . but you always tell people, 'If you're striving to do more, if you plan on going back to school, don't get caught in the trap.' Because the trap is, you get paid every week. You get caught. But we make cookies and crackers. We run machinery." The job's material adequacy was paid for by forsaking most of life's other pleasures.

The gravity of this trade—your whole life, in exchange for a secure career—created in employees a fierce attachment to the benefits they had written into their union contract. They were benefits that they had sacrificed significant things to earn. The Portland plant was not as big as the Nabisco bakeries in Chicago or Richmond, Virginia, but it was considered the most ferocious when it came to labor battles with the company. This was due in part to the political radicalism that infuses all of Portland, but also to the personalities at play in the union hall. Local 364's business representative, who works closely with the Nabisco employees, is Cameron Taylor, a gruff, plainspoken man with a long, luxurious goatee that is light gray on his chin but darkens to a deep brown as it curls down past the bottom of his chest. Taylor himself began working at the Nabisco factory as a nineteen-year-old in 1983 and became the union local's lone full-time employee in 1998. He is a living encyclopedia of the plant's history. He has witnessed the relationship between its workers and its management slowly curdle over the years, worsening under the steady pressure of each new owner to extract more profits for distant shareholders. Though there have always been workplace grievances and contract battles, no owner in Taylor's four decades has been as hostile as Mondelez International, the gargantuan self-described "global snacking powerhouse" that took over Nabisco when Kraft spun off its snack food division in 2012.

BCTGM signed a new four-year contract for its Nabisco workers just as Mondelez assumed control of the company. The new owners chose not to wage a hard fight at that time, but it quickly became clear to Taylor that they were laying the groundwork for war when the next contract negotiations rolled around. In 2013, Mondelez announced it would be building the "world's largest cookie plant" in Monterrey, Mexico, a city brimming with foreign factories. Six months later, the company said it would be closing the Nabisco bakery in Philadelphia. It was not hard to see what the goals of the new owners would be. Mondelez began requesting information about how much it might cost for the company to get out of the BCTGM's pension plan. The plant manager in Portland tried to get workers to participate in a "Lean Six Sigma" program, a popular management strategy for eliminating "waste" in the manufacturing industry, which the union wisely declined to do. Soon, union reps were barred from visiting the factory floor, a new low in the labor-management relationship. In July 2014, Local 364 sent a letter to all its members warning them that things could get grim: "We have a contract through February 2016 but, if the Company's inquiry [about the pension] is any indication, the members need to plan for a battle at contract time and need to start preparing now."

By then, Cameron Taylor was already telling his members to start saving up money in preparation for a possible strike. Barack Obama was president, and 22 Jump Street was atop the box office rankings. Few could have imagined how long the looming saga at Nabisco would actually take to unfold.

In the summer of 2015, Mondelez announced hundreds of layoffs at its Chicago bakery, along with the installation of four new production "Lines of the Future" in Salinas, Mexico. The following year, the union's contract expired—and, as predicted, the company set out to claw back as many benefits as possible. Typically, the BCTGM's negotiations at Nabisco ended with contracts that continued the benefits of the previous contracts: pension, good health care, maybe a small raise. Mondelez was determined to get rid of the pension. From 2016 to 2018, negotiations went nowhere. In May 2018, Mondelez declared an impasse and announced that it would freeze contributions to the multi-employer pension that Nabisco workers belonged to, and begin offering 401(k)s instead. The company dangled a $15,000 cash bonus in front of workers if they would agree to a contract giving up their pensions and accepting worse health insurance. The union angrily refused. They knew the same thing that Mondelez's own advisors did: a pension meant that the investment risk was on the company, and the benefits for the workers were guaranteed, while a 401(k) meant the opposite.

Still, with negotiations stuck and with no substantive help from the National Labor Relations Board, the union was unable to force Mondelez to keep up its pension contributions. For veteran employees at Nabisco in Portland—those who had reached retirement age but who would have preferred to keep working—that meant that they needed to retire soon if they wanted to lock in their pension benefits. Three dozen workers did just that, a significant loss in a workforce of two hundred.

For four long years, the stalemate dragged on. By 2020, the union had been without a contract for the entire length of time that a contract would have lasted if it had been signed on schedule in 2016. Finally, the pandemic forced the company's hand. Desperate to keep the plant operating when Covid struck in March 2020, Mondelez began hiring temp workers in Portland, something that would have been a clear violation of the contract during normal times. Since the company was disregarding that precedent, the union responded by staging a sickout. Workers on the late shift began calling out sick, and so did workers in the next shift, and the factory was forced to shut down for a day. This alarmed the company, which started calling around to other locations, frantically asking if this was the start of a strike. In fact, it was just a one-day action, and a release valve for Portland workers who had lost patience with the company's intransigence. Those in Portland were wondering why all the other Nabisco workers around the country weren't as fed up as they were.

"People were ready. They were so angry. The company was doing everything they wanted to do. I kept telling everybody, pardon my language: 'Let's fucking strike 'em! What the fuck are we waiting for?' And my members were saying the same thing," Taylor says. Hundreds of grievances had piled up on his desk over the past four years, and all of them were being ignored by management.

The sickout, along with the company's pressing desire to staff up temporarily to keep the lines going when people began getting Covid, prompted Mondelez to offer an emergency one-year contract. To the Portland workers, it sounded like a terrible deal: the contract meant agreeing to give up the pension, and the unit would be watered down with temps. Only two union members in Portland out of two hundred voted for the contract. But they were outvoted by workers at other Nabisco locations, who found the temporary stability of simply having a contract, and the modest signing bonus it came with, too attractive to pass up after years of uncertainty.

In February 2021, Mondelez announced that it would be closing its Nabisco factories in Atlanta and in Fair Lawn, New Jersey, both of which had been staples in their communities for more than a half century. That move only heightened the tension between labor and management. Shortly afterward, the one-year contract expired, the pandemic was grinding on, and the underlying anger between BCTGM and Mondelez was still boiling. The company continued to ask for takeaways in order to sign a new long-term contract. It wanted to weaken the health insurance coverage, it sure didn't sound like the pension was coming back, and the two-dollar-per-hour "appreciation pay" increase for working during the pandemic had only lasted three months. The temp workers were still there, and Mondelez wanted to introduce new, alternate workweek schedules that many feared would create separate and unequal tiers of employees inside the bakeries.

The relationship between the workers in Portland and their new plant manager was bad. "It became such a dysfunctional place," Marks remembers. "I was stressed. A lot of us were stressed, and walking on eggshells."

The national Nabisco contract negotiations were not encouraging. Portland, the radical ones in the company, had long been pissed enough to walk out, and now it was becoming clear to all the other workers across the country that the situation was not tenable. How much more shit should they be expected to eat?

=

On a sweltering summer day in 2022, Mike Burlingham sits at his desk in the crowded, yellow-walled Local 364 offices, not far from the Nabisco plant. The most visible decoration, a souvenir from a nearby Frito-Lay facility that the union represents, is a hand-drawn poster propped on a shelf showing an orange, muscular Chester Cheetah with "BCTGM 364" carved into his chest and blood dripping from his claws. The picture seems a tad too gory for Burlingham, a smiling dad with a short brown beard and two kids at home who has the soft-spoken patience of someone used to dealing with conflict.

When he relives those weeks one year earlier that led up to the Nabisco strike, though, intensity begins to creep into his voice. "So this is what we know. The company shoved a one-year contract down our throat that, at least here in Portland, we didn't want. There was some things in there we didn't like, such as the temp workers. Those temp workers were supposed to be gone. The company kept them anyway. So they clearly don't care about what contracts say. They're closing down two facilities, so we got roughly nine hundred workers that are now out of work. Who's next? They have a pattern of just shutting down bakeries. They moved production down to Mexico. They have two facilities down there," he says. Burlingham has supported his family for the past fifteen years by working at Nabisco. He is now Local 364's elected secretary-treasurer, a job he does each weekday after he finishes his work at the plant at 2 p.m. The year before, he was the local's vice president. He speaks in careful, measured tones, but he leans forward recounting the vivid memory of that fateful summer of 2021. "We have a company who is unwilling to negotiate with us. They've got, already, a long history of not being willing to negotiate, takeaways, shutdowns, violations. So, what's going to get their attention?"

In June 2021, there was a meeting for Local 364's members at Nabisco. Cameron Taylor told them that negotiations weren't going well, and the members cast an affirmative strike authorization vote, which would allow the union to call a strike at any time. On July 5, they got a boost of inspiration when more than five hundred of their fellow BCTGM members who staffed the Frito-Lay plant in Topeka, Kansas, went on strike for the first time in decades. The similarities to the situation at Nabisco did not escape anyone's attention: a snack food factory, owned by an international food conglomerate (PepsiCo, in Frito-Lay's case), which had once been considered a good job with a family atmosphere, had deteriorated into a nightmare situation of staffing shortages, insane hours, forced overtime, stagnant wages, and a palpable disinterest by management in addressing those quality-of-life problems. The strike in Topeka lasted twenty days. It ended when workers voted for a contract whose centerpiece win was heartbreakingly modest: one day off per week.

The workers at Nabisco felt the tingling sensation of looming action. It was not one or two things that had pissed them off recently; it was a grinding, years-long accumulation of inhumanity. Those who gave up their family time and free time and hobbies and everything else to spend day and night inside a factory to make a middle-class income were also capable of reading the news. In 2017, as Mondelez was busy killing the Nabisco employees' pension, the company gave its new CEO Dirk Van De Put a $42 million compensation package, so cartoonishly oversized that shareholders took the unusual step of rejecting it in a (nonbinding) vote. The toll of those years of toiling sixty or seventy or eighty hours per week, with no contract, as the company exhibited pure contempt for the concept of having a respectful working relationship with the union, ran directly into a pandemic during which workers risked their own health to keep cranking out cookies and crackers. Patience had run out.

"You have people being worked to the bone. Being put in situations where they're being exposed [to sickness]. When you're underpaid, overworked, fatigued, getting sick, enough becomes enough. You hit a breaking point," Mike Burlingham says. Mondelez's sales were profitable and growing during the pandemic's first year, as millions of people trapped at home feasted on the snacks that the workers in the bakeries produced. Burlingham can quote the company's multibillion-dollar annual profits figures, and the tens of millions of dollars that the CEO was bringing home at the same time the company was demanding takeaways in the Nabisco contract. In recent years, BCTGM had not been known as a particularly bold union. But the gross imbalances of Covid-era reality had animated them. "It's a David and Goliath story, really. You've got this monster of a company, who's got the deepest pockets, and they have no problem fighting you tooth and nail on everything, because they got the money to do it. Their mindset is, 'Well, we'll bankrupt you fighting you, so we can have it our way.' This is a good job. This is a fight for the middle class. If you don't fight and stand up for that, it's gonna go away. It's gonna be rich versus poor. These jobs are not even gonna be jobs worth fighting for. That's the motivation right there. Do you keep giving your lunch money to the bully? Or are you going to punch them in the face?"

All hope that the company might become reasonable had faded. In early August, Cameron Taylor was given the green light by the BCTGM's national leadership to call the strike whenever he was ready. He had been ready for years. And he decided to add an extra little turn of the knife with the strike's timing. Because almost everyone at Nabisco was on the same twelve days on, two days off schedule, the Portland plant always shut down its production lines every other Friday night—leaving them off for maintenance during the weekends when all the production workers were out, and then firing them back up again on Monday. So Taylor waited until Tuesday, August 10, to send a text blast to all his members telling them that the strike was on, just to be sure that the company had just restarted all its lines, right before being forced to abruptly close them down all over again.

At that, the thing that Taylor had been warning his members about since 2014 had finally happened. Workers streamed out of the plant, boisterous. Both Taylor and Burlingham described that moment to me with exactly the same words: "I've never seen so many smiling faces." The last nationwide

Nabisco strike happened in 1969. There was, as far as Donna Marks knew, only one person still working in the Portland plant who had lived through that strike. For the other two hundred people walking out that day, they were facing a complete unknown.

It was easy to be excited, at first. Many Local 364 members had been building up their emergency funds and getting increasingly pissed off at the company for years. The breaking point, for them, seemed long overdue. The need for secrecy meant that none of the workers knew exactly when the strike would be called, and none of them knew how long it would continue, or what the precise contract demands would be. People took up positions on picket lines outside of the plant, and made signs, and waved them. But it was not clear, at first, whether the rest of the city would pay much attention. The factory, sandwiched between railroad tracks and several busy roads in an industrial area, is not well-situated for foot traffic. Taylor, supervising the picketers, was stressed that someone would get run over. "It was treacherous as hell. These semis are driving by at fifty-five miles an hour, and my members are out there waving signs," he says. "It's like, holy crap, someone is going to get killed!"

Donna Jo Marks felt giddy, but also acutely aware that she didn't really know what she was in for. Her enthusiasm was unbreakable, but she could see some coworkers start flagging after only a few days as the reality of the drudgery of standing on a picket line through endless hot summer afternoons began to sink in. On one of those sweltering early days, though, a woman that Marks had never met walked up and asked if she could help her picket. The woman had seen a story about the strike in the news and driven all the way from Idaho just to show solidarity. After a few hours of sign-waving and woo-wooing at passing trucks, the woman packed up and drove home again. It was the first hint to Marks that the Nabisco workers were not out there all alone.

Well-intentioned Portland locals would drive by and drop off donuts for the strikers. Donuts, donuts, donuts. One can only eat donuts for so long before they start to sicken you. That's why Marks remembers so clearly when a man showed up one day with fruit, which thrilled her. He told her he was a member of the Democratic Socialists of America—a group she had never heard of. The leftists of the DSA were to become one of the biggest mobilizers of support for the strike, though she did not know it at the time. "I still didn't understand the gravity because I lived in Nabisco world," says Marks. "All I could see was Nabisco problems."

Supporters from other local unions began to show up. The second Saturday of the strike, the DSA member organized a rally to build community support and asked Marks to come speak. She blew him off—she had a picket line position to hold down. She had to man that post. Everything else seemed like an indulgence, a distraction.

A week went by, and then another. There seemed to be little progress toward a resolution at the bargaining table. Marks was coming to the picket line every day, picking up extra shifts, but she could see the attendance dwindling. Her daughter, who has an autoimmune disease, was in the hospital, and she couldn't be there with her because of Covid rules. She was also taking care of her mother on the side. It looked like she was about to lose her health insurance. The overwhelming stress of the situation, mixed with her growing anger at her coworkers who didn't seem to be giving as much to the strike as she was, was curdling into a toxic brew. September came. It was a Saturday, and yet another rally was scheduled. This time, she asked the organizer if she could speak. Her plan was to give her fellow BCTGM members a piece of her mind—she was out here sacrificing, and they didn't seem to give a fuck. But shortly before the rally, she felt a sense of calm descend over her.

There is a shaky, grainy cell phone video of her speech at the rally on that summer day. Hundreds of people had shown up to support the strikers. Marks, in pink tennis shoes and a long gray dress, leaned into the portable microphone and began telling the crowd about her stresses: her elderly mother, her ill daughter, her fears over health insurance, the part-time work she was putting in as a driver to try to supplement her lost income. "When I woke up this morning, I hopped in the shower to come do my duty here, and you guys, it hit me. I got overwhelmed. I broke down and I cried, and I crawled back into bed. And I just couldn't get up, and I wasn't gonna come today. And I always come! I always fill a gap in because I know people need a day off. But I got up, because I'm fighting for *this*, right here. I'm fighting for this insurance that we have. I don't want to lose it. I can't afford my daughter being sick. This is *important* to me, to be here every day."

Her voice began to crack, as a sob crept up her throat. One of her coworkers walked up from the crowd and placed his arm around her. She began to speak about the strength that she drew from coming and seeing such a large and diverse group of workers from different companies and different unions at the rally, after a week on a picket line where attendance felt increasingly slim. "They're trying to show us our place. It's not about money. It's about where we belong in society. We 'have a place.' But we don't," she said, her right hand gesturing back toward the factory for emphasis. "I got up today to be here because I needed my brothers and sisters to see that they will not break me. They will not break me. I'm here. And I'll be here tomorrow. And I'll be here every day, until we win."

Mondelez had hired a despicable firm called Huffmaster, which specializes in supplying scab workers to keep businesses operating during strikes. Huffmaster was busing in nonunion workers to the Portland Nabisco factory every day and providing a force of blue-coated security workers whose tactics grew increasingly nasty as the strike dragged on. A local reporter, Sophie Peel, published a series of photos and videos of the guards acting aggressively: two of them sandwiching in a lone picketer standing by the railroad tracks; another one, unarmed but pretending to pull a gun; a group of guards violently pressing a megaphone-wielding Teamster up against an incoming van full of scabs and yanking protesters away from a bus trying to bring scabs into the plant. Another video shows a Huffmaster guard slinging a strike supporter to the ground and punching him repeatedly after a minor scuffle in front of a scab-filled bus. After the fight, a union supporter jeers, "Lick those boots!" to the guard, who glances back over his shoulder and mutters, "Gotta make money."

No strike—at least none with a high chance of success—is a solo operation. The web of support for Local 364's strike in Portland stretched wide. The Portland DSA staged rallies. Sympathetic residents came to bolster the picket lines and did some of the things that the union members themselves couldn't, for legal reasons. Some blocked the buses full of scabs. Others used creative tactics to stop the delivery trucks bringing ingredients into the plant, like the guy who pulled his own truck into the road, blocking it, and then proceeded to change his "flat" tire with great sluggishness. Other unions joined the picket line, and donated money, and showed solidarity in more direct ways. Truck drivers who were members of the Teamsters would sometimes pull up to the plant, see the picket line, make a phone call to their own union, and then turn around and leave without making their delivery. BCTGM set up a small picket location by the railroad tracks specifically to target the delivery trains, and Railroad Workers United touted an incident when a train conductor spotted the picket line, stopped, and put the train in reverse. (There are also members of several other unions who work in specialized jobs inside the Nabisco plant. Most, but not all, of them supported the BCTGM strike.) Portland's politicians, who range from centrist Democrats to fiery socialists, were vocally and predictably supportive. The local women's professional soccer team, the Portland Thorns, who had recently unionized themselves, came out en masse to the picket line. Danny DeVito, one of the union world's favorite celebrities, tweeted, "NO CONTRACTS NO SNACKS," a phrase that quickly became a motto of the strike. By the fourth week, the strikers had arranged for a projector to beam images onto the side of the factory at night, including an enormous circular picture of DeVito's smiling face with "NO CONTRACTS NO SNACKS" surrounding it in a motivational garland.

Most important of all was the fact that the strike was nationwide. The workers in Portland were not alone. They set the hard edge by walking out first, but within a week, they were joined by fellow BCTGM Nabisco workers at plants in Aurora, Colorado, and Richmond, Virginia. On August 19, workers at the big bakery in Chicago went out, and they were joined a few days later by workers at a Nabisco distribution center in Norcross, Georgia, effectively covering all the company's production in America. A national strike, and national attention, was good and necessary for a national contract, but it also meant that the workers in Portland would end up as a minority vote in the final decision to accept a contract offer from the company. And, as had happened before, Portland would prove to be an outlier.

The strike was having its intended effect. After a month, Bloomberg reported that Nabisco was having more trouble filling its orders as more product shipments had to be canceled. The damage to global supply chains that the pandemic had caused only made it easier for the work stoppage to inflict pain on the company. The Mondelez CEO admitted at a conference that Nabisco was not producing as much product with its scab workforce as it had before. In the middle of September, the company offered the union a deal that included modest raises and a $5,000 signing bonus—but which did not resurrect the pension, and which gave Nabisco the ability to hire weekend-shift crews who would work a three-day schedule, for twelve hours per day. The inclusion of this "alternative workweek" language, in particular, upset many in Portland, who feared that it would destroy delicate and hard-won precedents that the union had cemented based on the "twelve days on, two days off" schedule that they had all worked for years.

"We work Monday through Friday, and then we're working Saturday and Sunday and we're earning premium pay on those two days. We're only working eight hours. And this guy who's gonna be right next to us on the line, he's working twelve hours at straight time," Mike Burlingham says. It was not just money at stake, but the underlying principle of respecting workers' humanity, which served as the justification for many of the existing benefits. "The reason why we get premium pay on weekends is because weekends are premium time for your family. If the company is taking that time away from you and your family—weddings, funerals, barbecues, birthdays, most people celebrate on weekends. So if you're going to be forcing us to work, we're earning premium pay for that."

Union contracts are an act of collective memory that is always in danger of fading away. Even in placid times, contract negotiations are an exhausting matter of transmitting and upholding the knowledge of provisions that were created in response to crises that can be easily forgotten as they recede into the past. There are always new problems, and the current problems will always feel the most urgent. Those who have worked somewhere for a long time may be seared with the knowledge of past battles, but newer workers are not. Contracts must be renegotiated every few years, and each time, there will be a temptation to bargain away what once seemed like uncrossable red lines. It is arduous to create, even within a single workplace, a culture in which the history and values of the union are impressed upon everyone and upheld throughout years of turnover. It is harder still to do this with a workforce spread across many locations from coast to coast. And it is harder still to do it while under the pressures of a strike, when every single worker is being squeezed by loss of wages and expiring health insurance and sheer, grinding tedium with each passing day. The temptation to say, "the hell with it" and give things up in order to end the strike and get back to stability can be intense. The determination of Local 364 to defend its existing contract after more than five weeks on the picket line is, in that light, an impressive feat.

When Cameron Taylor brought the company's contract offer to his members, they weren't happy. "The meeting was, uh . . . pretty colorful. The general tenor was not positive," he says, grasping for a diplomatic description. "I mean, I'm swinging a gavel and they're yelling and screaming." Many members—who had, for years, sacrificed their own personal life in exchange for long but well-compensated hours at the plant—viewed the "alternative workweek" proposal as unconscionable, an unacceptable reversal of something they considered sacred. (A minority, though, who were less in need of the extra income, took the opposite view: working thirty-six hours a week, getting paid for forty, and not being forced to do overtime sounded pretty good to them.) But even though most of the Portland workers voted against it, three-quarters of the Nabisco workers nationally voted in favor of the contract offer, which largely preserved the benefits of the previous contract. On September 18, after five weeks and four days on the picket line, the strike was over. Across Portland, Local 364 members quit their temporary survival gigs driving for Uber and delivering for DoorDash and prepared to go back to the plant.

The sting of seeing themselves once again overruled by their less radical BCTGM coworkers would dissipate with time. It began to sink in just how much had been accomplished. The most practical gain was the mere fact of *having* a contract in place—something the Nabisco workers had only had for one solitary year of the previous six years. The absence of a pension and the addition of weekend crews were significant chinks in the union's armor, but not unexpected ones. The contract preserved the excellent health care coverage and decent wages that the union had maintained for decades, and it restarted the rusty machinery of formal relations between management and the union. It provided the hope, at least, that basic things like grievances would start being processed again as usual.

The fact of the matter—which can be seen as either grim or inspiring, depending on your attitude—is that the monumental task of a nationwide strike was necessary just for the BCTGM to maintain most of what it already had. These Nabisco factory workers, who do classic blue-collar jobs day and night but earn, in return, a minimally decent middle-class life, are an endangered species in the United States of America. They are a throwback to the golden postwar decades when such things were normal. That is no longer the case. Today, Local 364 and their Nabisco counterparts across the country are the inhabitants of a rare and shrinking walled garden of those who can still, with much sweat and sacrifice, enjoy what was once carelessly called the American dream. They walked the picket line week after week not to gain great riches, but rather to preserve something that was taken for granted by their parents' and grandparents' generations: the ability to go to work full-time at an industrial job and not live in poverty. They are some of the few remaining holdouts against the ceaseless action of global capitalism to suck up the dollars that used to go toward pay and benefits for these working people, redistribute those dollars to far-flung investors, push those wages and benefits down into the gutter, and then, when that gutter bottoms out, to ship the jobs off to poorer countries where more desperate people will do them for even less. That is the story of the past half century in America. That is what happened to most of the blue-collar jobs that once animated the towns in the middle of this country that are now husks of their former selves. That process of the upward redistribution of money and hope has done incalculable damage, and it has not stopped. But it would be held at bay at least a little while longer, for the Nabisco workers. They had a contract.

Cameron Taylor, whose career in the Nabisco plant coincides almost perfectly with the beginning of the Reagan era, recalls that there were eleven Nabisco bakeries across America when he started. Now, there are three. The fact that the bakeries in Atlanta and New Jersey were shut down for good shortly before the strike of 2021 only adds piquancy to the defiance of those who remained. Many people assume that the constant threat of outsourcing means factory workers like those at Nabisco have no leverage. In 2021— with successful strikes at Frito-Lay, and then at Nabisco, and then at Kellogg's—the BCTGM showed that that is not quite true. Even as the cold, relentless machine of global capitalism grinds on, there are opportunities for human beings to build fortresses of solidarity strong enough to withstand its grasping claws. At least for a little while longer.

With the benefit of time, the workers in Portland are able to see their strike as part of something much larger than themselves. Throughout the latter half of 2021, much news coverage flared around America's "strike wave" as a symbol of renewed labor militancy in the post-pandemic age. The strike wave of 2021 was not numerically large by historic standards, but the perception that it created—that working people had at last decided to draw a line in the sand—was priceless. The strike at Nabisco, and at the other BCTGM strikes that year, played a significant part in the nationwide realization that workplace organizing offered a path for regular people to *do something* about the crippling sense of instability that had gripped us all. Portland, with its soaring rents, bitter street protests, and homeless people strewn in tents throughout downtown, embodied the fears that Americans everywhere suffered during the pandemic—that the entire social order could start crumbling all around us. In that environment, every single strike becomes an urgent symbolic battleground, a set piece that people watch to renew their belief that all is not lost; that people power is still real. When the history is written, the gripes between specific Nabisco plants over specific contract provisions will be less important than the strike's role in proving to America that blue-collar industrial union strength not only still exists, but is still able to be a bulwark against the vampires of capital.

Donna Jo Marks had spent many years in the union, but 2021 was her first strike. Just getting through it is one of the most remarkable things she has ever done. The experience has given her a survivor's sanguine view of struggle. "I'm one of the people who think that we won. A lot of my brothers and sisters don't. The reason why I think that we won is because the company came like such gangsters: 'We're gonna take this, we're gonna take this, we're gonna take this.' In the end, all we asked for was for everything to stay the same," she says. "How can we lose, when we didn't know we have power? We got what we asked for." She admits that there was fear after the pension disappeared, the fear that the Nabisco workers would lose everything they had worked for. She admits that she had gotten complacent before the strike and stopped saving her money in preparation for that day of reckoning. She wishes that they had asked for more.

More vivid than any lingering regret, though, is the sense of possibility that the strike has given her. She feels infused with an entirely new understanding of how the world works, and how it *can* work. When she was waking up and going to the picket line every day, with all the stresses of family responsibilities hanging over her, she was scared. But she could also see, unscrolling in her memory, the years and years of sacrifices made by other workers before her. Those sacrifices built and fostered and defended and preserved the union that she had now. The feeling of responsibility to past and future generations of working people was, to her, very tangible. Her career dreams now extend beyond the factory, and toward a job in the labor movement itself. Sometimes all the labor movement hands you is a heavy burden—an order to fight long and hard, and take drastic risks to just hang on to what you already have. That may have struck her as an unfair bargain before the strike, but now, she is at peace with it.

When Marks was a child, she used to get in trouble in class. If she felt that the teacher was wrong, she had to speak up. Even if she tried to stifle it, she couldn't; her stomach would begin to ache, and eventually the words would just come bursting out. She used to see that as something of a curse. Now she sees it differently.

"I'm a troublemaker. It doesn't sound like a good term, but it is a good term. I am a troublemaker to a lot of companies that I've worked for. Because I want to right a wrong," she says. The strike, for all that it demanded, did not just earn a contract for the workers. It earned the labor movement a new soldier.

"Most people get involved in the union because they've gone *through* something," she says. "They already have the fight in them. They just don't know it."

CHAPTER TEN

THE HOUSE OF LABOR
POLITICS, UNIONS, FRIENDS, AND ENEMIES

In Washington, physical proximity to the White House is a public statement of power. By that standard, the AFL-CIO stands atop this thirsty city of strivers. Its headquarters is a seven-story building of glass and stone, the same white stone that government buildings use. It sits on Sixteenth Street just above Lafayette Park, almost as close to the White House as it is possible to get. It is closer to the White House than the embassies, and the white-shoe law firm offices, and the headquarters of Bain & Company, which fill the streets behind it. It shares a prized block with the Motion Picture Association of America and the Ronald Reagan Foundation. The only building on its side of the street that is closer to the White House is St. John's Episcopal, the little yellow church that Donald Trump stood in front of holding an upside-down Bible after he had ordered his troops to violently clear away and tear gas the surrounding throngs of Black Lives Matter protesters, in his most Mussolini-esque moment.

That was on June 1, 2020. The night before, protesters had set fire to the lobby of the AFL-CIO's headquarters on one of the hot, early evenings of the anti-police rebellion following the murder of George Floyd. That episode had prompted a prickly sense of outrage from the union federation, which felt that it should have been immune from such chaos, since it was on the right side of things. Richard Trumka, who was the AFL-CIO president at the time, called the attack "senseless" and "disgraceful." But in this country where nine out of ten working people are not union members, it is not a surprise that all the protesters that night would have gazed down that block between H and I streets, seen the opulent Hay-Adams Hotel and the glassy MPAA and the motherfucking *Reagan* Foundation, and lumped the AFL-CIO building in with all the rest of them. They looked at it and saw just another fancy office building that they had never been invited to, and never believed they would be.

I went to DC on a reporting trip shortly after that. The protests were continuing day and night. The AFL-CIO's entire first floor had been boarded up, and the federation had hung a gargantuan Black Lives Matter banner from the top floor. The city of DC had officially renamed that block and the one next to it "Black Lives Matter Plaza," and the words "BLACK LIVES MATTER" were painted in thirty-five-foot-high letters all the way down the middle of Sixteenth Street. The street was an ongoing protest and concert and dance party. Over it all, though, hung the unmistakable whiff of the establishment desperately trying to insulate itself from the fallout of an antiestablishment uprising. I snuck through a door manned by a muscular security guard to peek inside the AFL-CIO's first floor, which still bore scorch marks from the flames, and snapped a couple of pictures. On a white wall underneath a "Union Plus" sign at one end of the lobby, "Fuck 12" was spraypainted in red letters—and, next to that, in a curving arc with an underline, "JUSTICE."

When I returned in the waning days of August two years later, all was sedate again. Black Lives Matter Plaza was empty. The AFL-CIO headquarters' lobby was clean, quiet, and bathed in soothing air-conditioning. Two months had passed since the group's convention in Philadelphia, and Liz Shuler was settling into her role as its new president. As I sat in a low chair just past the security gate, waiting to be escorted upstairs, a familiar sight caught my eye: it was the sign from that goddamn booth that had stood in the display hall at the convention. The one with all the plastic fucking rings. The one that had given me a queasy sense of angst every time I walked past it. It had been packed up, shipped back from Philly, and reerected right there in the lobby, directly in front of my sight line. It was following me. "OUR MOVEMENT is built on connections," it still said. "Add your ring to show you are ready to link up and take on the future. Let's see what happens when we join together." The rings themselves were nowhere to be seen.

On the top floor of the building, the president's office was getting a makeover. Gone were the cluttered shelves of photos and football memorabilia that had accumulated around Richard Trumka's desk during his twelve years there. Shuler had replaced it with custom wallpaper that was an exact replica of the enormous tile mosaic in the building's entrance hall by the artist Lumen Winter—a tableau of gods and workers bearing the Virgil quote *Labor Omnia Vincit* (work conquers all). It now serves as her Zoom background when she takes video calls from her standing desk.

Shuler, an unflashy woman who radiates a sense of practicality, is quite frank in saying that she never really envisioned herself ending up in that office. It seemed, even to her, that life had deposited her there through happenstance. Her father was an electric lineman, and a member of the International Brotherhood of Electrical Workers; her mother was a clerical worker at the same company. Shuler worked at that company too when she was in college, and helped her mother with an ultimately unsuccessful campaign to unionize those clerical workers. Then, Shuler went to work for the IBEW union local. She rose up to become chief of staff for the IBEW's international president, Ed Hill, and got to know Trumka by attending executive council meetings as Hill's staffer. When Trumka ran for the AFL-CIO president's seat in 2009, he handpicked Shuler for his ticket—because, she admits, she ticked several boxes: she was a woman, she had organizing experience, she worked for the building trades, and she was considered young by the standards of union leadership. Just like that, she was the second-highest official of America's biggest labor federation.

"I was thirty-nine years old. Did not aspire to that job. And he sat me down in his office basically in the beginning days of our administration and said, 'I'd like to see you succeed me.' At the time I was like, 'Haha, yeah right' . . . I thought it would be a pretty big stretch just to do that job competently," she says. By 2020, she had decided to run to succeed Trumka. His unexpected death the next year forced her into the seat sooner than she thought, but when no challenger arose, she won her formal election without a struggle.

For years leading up to 2022, everyone in the labor world would talk (off the record) about the potential of a leadership race between Sara Nelson and Liz Shuler. When it didn't materialize, that conversation died out, like the infinite quantum possibilities of a particle's position collapsing into a single point. Shuler is quick to dismiss any discussion of rivalry, but her description of her own leadership style—"I am not someone who's generally out front, I'm not the person who seeks the spotlight"—points to the fact that the unions that make up the AFL-CIO do not particularly *want* a popular, fiery president who will try to drag them up to the mountaintop. The most frustrating flaw in the AFL-CIO's structure, one that is almost impossible to remedy in a purely voluntary federation, is that each individual union is pretty much free to do whatever it likes. The president of the AFL-CIO can cajole and wheedle, but outside of very limited circumstances cannot force unions to follow commandments they dislike. One can imagine an LBJ-style master of power politics bringing recalcitrant unions to heel with a velvet glove over an iron fist, but Liz Shuler, who speaks of her goal as "keeping the machine moving, keeping everybody unified, moving in the same direction," is not that sort of leader.

Instead, Shuler is the sort of leader that you can find throughout the top level of the union world: one whose heart is in the right place, but who seems to have resigned herself to what she sees as the inescapable constraints of reality. This is perfectly normal. But it means that the question, "What would a true visionary do in this daunting situation?" is never answered. To her credit, Shuler seems to understand that the incessant decline of union density in America is a crisis, and that the AFL-CIO—which has long excused itself from responsibility by shrugging and saying that new organizing is the job of the individual affiliate unions—must be directly involved in the fight. She is eager to discuss her plan to increase the dues that each union pays to the AFL-CIO and use that money to fund the splashy new

"Center for Transformational Organizing." This CTO, she says, will have the staff and resources to build multi-union coalitions to carry out the sort of sprawling, national campaigns necessary to unionize hard but strategically important targets: Amazon, the gig economy, the budding green energy industry. This is all great, in theory. But there are reasons to doubt whether the perpetually paralyzed AFL-CIO is willing to change itself enough to pull unions out of the grave they have been sinking into for half a century.

The fact that the incoming AFL-CIO president grasped the need and the opportunity for new organizing is a good thing. But the fact that the Center for Transformational Organizing launched with a formal target of organizing one million workers in ten years, a paltry figure that would ensure that union density continues its decline, is not. (The Center's starting annual budget was $11 million—better than nothing, but hardly adequate to be "transformational," an adjective that would require unionizing millions of new workers.) Shuler says that this is the highest figure that it was possible to get all the federation's member unions to agree on. That's depressing because it is flat-out proof that existing unions do not appreciate the scale of the problem they face, in the same way that property developers who continue happily building condos on Miami Beach as the sea levels rise will one day be in for a rude surprise.

Gaping in horror at the nonstop decline of union density is not a new pastime. When John Sweeney became president of the AFL-CIO in 1995, he understood the urgent need for new organizing. He pushed all the federation's unions to dedicate 20–30 percent of their budgets to organizing new workers. (That level of organizing spending was normal earlier in the twentieth century, but by the 1990s it had become rare.) That didn't happen because the unions didn't want to do it. They wanted to spend the money on other stuff, and the AFL-CIO did not control their internal budgets. Union density has fallen by a third since then. When Sweeney died in 2022, Liz Shuler spoke at his memorial service. "He was an innovator, always pushing our movement forward," she said of her predecessor. "That's a spirit I hope to channel day in and day out by being bold, taking risks, and pushing for the future we all want to live and work in."

Sweeney indeed pushed the movement forward, but the inertia of the organized labor establishment pushed back. Like others who have grasped the problem, he ultimately failed to rectify it. Shuler may understand the need to organize, but when you sweep away the words and look at the actual substance of the plans, you find the same old AFL-CIO. When I asked Shuler if it was possible today to organize the five or ten million new workers necessary to push union density back to where it was even in Sweeney's time, she replied, "With the laws the way they are? Absolutely not."

It is very true that America's labor laws are tilted against organized labor. They ensure that companies can threaten, lie to, harass, and fire workers who want to organize with very little fear of meaningful consequences. And they impose a thicket of restrictions on who can legally unionize and how workers can exercise their collective power on the job. This has been true since the Taft-Hartley Act, designed to rein in a short-lived period of nascent union strength, was passed in 1947. It's obvious that we need to reform these laws. It is equally obvious that unions can't rest their strategy for revival on their ability to fix something that they have continuously failed to fix for seventy-five years. The AFL-CIO has long poured resources into lobbying for better labor laws—often to the exclusion of pouring resources into organizing workers—and yet here we are. Joe Biden has been far more enthusiastic than the last few Democratic presidents about actually spending political capital to help unions. After Biden took office, the AFL-CIO made it its top priority to pass the PRO Act, which would be a transformative package of labor law reforms. That proved to be impossible, even with a Democratic Congress, so long as the filibuster remains in place. An effort to get some parts of the PRO Act inserted into a reconciliation bill during the first half of Biden's term also came to nothing.

Historically speaking, getting no significant labor law reform passed even in the most favorable possible legislative circumstances is right in line with expectations. Yet there is little evidence that any of this has prompted the AFL-CIO to metamorphosize from an organization rooted in electoral politics to one rooted in organizing working people into unions. A couple of days after I interviewed Shuler, the AFL-CIO blasted out a press release with a headline trumpeting the "Largest Organizing Drive in History." Was this the launch of the big national Amazon union drive? I clicked to open the email. It was announcing a drive to mobilize voters for the midterm elections. Some things never change.

Shuler spoke of the need to meet the moment, to spread the good word about unions, to be the organizer-in-chief who quietly unifies the movement around a broad goal. There is a circular element to all of this. After many decades of decline, what is needed is a sharp and powerful break with the strategies of the past; it is hard to know how such a thing can arise from within the very structure that has been built to perpetuate what already exists. "It's a collective responsibility. We are nothing at the AFL-CIO without our affiliates," Shuler says. "We can make all the plans in the world. We can make all the declarative statements we want. But they're empty, if you turn around and there isn't anybody there."

In January 2023, the Bureau of Labor Statistics released statistics showing that in 2022, union density in America had declined to just 10.1 percent, from 10.3 percent the year before. The raw number of union members rose by more than two hundred thousand, but failed to keep pace with the growth in jobs. In a year in which unions were historically popular with the public, and high-profile union organizing drives were heavily covered in the mainstream press, and Democrats controlled Washington, union density had not risen, nor even stayed the same, but declined. It was plain evidence of the fact that organized labor itself had neither a plan nor the capacity to organize workers at a large scale, even when conditions were in its favor. In response to this dispiriting news, Liz Shuler said on Twitter, "2022 saw working people rising up despite often illegal opposition from companies that would rather pay union-busting firms millions than give workers a seat at the table. The momentum of the moment we are in is clear." Her words brought to mind the meme of the cartoon dog sitting in a chair with a plastered-on smile on his face as his house burns down around him, declaring, "This is fine."

Speaking on a webcast about the new statistics the same morning, Sara Nelson had a different reaction. "These numbers are incredibly disappointing, considering the moment that we're in, and the real desire for workers to join unions," she said. "We have to recognize that we're not meeting the demand of the American worker right now. We're going to have to do something pretty extraordinary . . . the labor movement is not meeting the moment."

The window of the AFL-CIO president's office looks directly out at the White House, with the Washington Monument rising to one side. It is certainly one of the most flattering views of any office in Washington. The contrast between the grandeur of that view and the desperate inadequacy of the existing labor movement is jarring. We have to consider the possibility that the theory that success for organized labor means insinuating itself as closely as possible into the existing American power structure is wrong. All those protesters for racial justice who flooded Sixteenth Street in 2020 were not impressed by the AFL-CIO's proximity to the White House. They burned the place. The building meant nothing to them because they were not union members, because unions long ago dismissed as impractical the idea that every single worker needs a union, or that it is the responsibility of those of us in unions to give a union to everyone who doesn't have one. Such utopianism is not taken seriously. After those protests, many activists inside the labor movement—including my own union, the Writers Guild of America, East—pointed out that the AFL-CIO has a police union as an affiliate, and police as members of more than a dozen of its unions. It is impossible to represent the interests of both workers at protests and the police who body-slam those workers. In recognition of that, my union and others urged the labor federation to expel those police unions and recommit to the priority of organizing the people in the streets—the ones who were angry at the injustices that many of those police unions had helped to enable. (Nobody said that police can't have unions; we just argued that those unions shouldn't be included in a labor federation that they relentlessly poison with the opposite of solidarity.) Instead, the AFL-CIO convened a "Racial Justice Task Force" that met for a year and then produced a report calling for increased funding for police, more police training programs, and the continuation of police unions as members in good standing. That task force was led by Liz Shuler and Fred Redmond, who would soon be elected as the AFL-CIO's top two officials. The Black Lives Matter movement would get itself a big banner on the side of the building, but it lost on the substance.

The AFL-CIO's headquarters are the "House of Labor." Sometimes this feels a little bit like calling the White House "the people's house." Most of the people never seem to make it into their house. It's possible that we would all be better off if the AFL-CIO sold that proud, shiny building, moved its offices to the poorest, cheapest neighborhood in the city, and spent all of its money hiring union organizers. The headquarters feels very grandiose, for a labor movement that can barely provide one in ten working people with a union. It is indeed a beautiful building, as beautiful as the people deserve. But—as Liz Shuler said—it can feel very empty, if you turn around and there isn't anybody there.

=

THE WAY THAT POLITICS IN AMERICA IS TYPICALLY DISCUSSED IS WEIRD. IT is a result of the long-standing norms among the national media that they should appear to be unbiased, which has led, for many decades, to the practice of covering "politics" A) purely through the lens of elections, B) as a sport, and C) without commenting directly on the rightness or wrongness of policy choices. Reporting critically about policy itself is denigrated as "taking sides." Thus, the messy, cutthroat battles for material resources and the distribution of wealth that characterize our capitalist society get transformed into narratives in which everything is spoken about primarily in terms of how it will affect politicians and elections, rather than how elections and politicians will affect the world. Will the outlawing of abortion drive Democrats to the polls? Will the climate change–fueled storms devastating our coastal red states be a risk factor to the Republican Senate caucus? Is the meteor that just struck your home bad news for the president?

This media tic—so ingrained that most people who have digested the news their whole lives barely even think about it—makes it difficult to properly frame the impact of movements. Movements do not succeed or fail based on their ability to get friendly politicians elected. Rather, movements are their own sort of institution, persisting through generations as permanent standing armies engaged in battle with monumental problems. The purpose of strong movements is not to change politics in order to change the world; it is to change the world in order to change politics.

There is always a danger that long-standing movements become so institutionalized that they start thinking of themselves as just another entrenched political player. That sort of self-limiting view can guarantee a long life that is also a slow death. The labor movement, one of America's oldest, has fallen prey to this. But labor is not a special interest. It is a common interest. It represents almost all of us. And the movement that exists to empower labor errs by failing to use most of its latent power when it allows itself to become a mere lobbying-and-door-knocking mobilizer. In fact, organized labor holds the tantalizing but still unrealized possibility of being a transformative force in American politics not through electioneering, but through changing the electorate itself. A true revival of unions—say, a doubling of current union density, taking us back to where unions stood when the Reagan era and its attendant supercharging of inequality began—would exert a tremendous natural force to move the political center left. This is not because union members tend to be more Democratic, but because the process of unionizing, coming together with coworkers as one, fighting the boss, and winning a contract *changes* people. It demonstrates what are inexactly called "progressive values" not through haranguing or sophisticated media campaigns, but through lived experience. There is no better way to make people understand class war than to have them participate in it. (A 2022 working paper by the labor economists Johannes Matzat and Aiko Schmeisser found that unionization of a workplace shifted employees' campaign contributions to the left and increased support for Democrats over Republicans among both workers and managers.)

One curious implication of this is that the future of the Democratic Party is tied to the future of the labor movement, but not for the reason that the Democratic Party or most union leaders think. The Democratic establishment and the union establishment both more or less buy into the view that unions are politically valuable because they give money and volunteer personnel to Democratic candidates. This is a blinkered view, that of a child who grudgingly agrees to go to the dentist because they know they will get a piece of candy afterward. The real potential, which the labor movement should be focused on and the political party should be aiding, is to purge the poison of inequality out of our society by organizing millions of working people into new unions and watching America's flirtation with fascism become less appetizing. Change rising from the bottom up is inherently more stable than trying to push change from the top down. That's why you do squats if you want to be strong, and that's why the key to organized labor's politics must be to *give* power to many more regular people, not to try to use laws to save us from the already immense power of capital.

The only high-profile national politician who really appears to understand this potential is Bernie Sanders. By this I mean he seems determined to throw his own political capital into helping the labor movement, rather than demanding the opposite. Many Democrats will show up for photo ops on picket lines, or issue supportive statements for unions in contract fights, but ever since 2020, Sanders has been pursuing the cause of unionism itself with a fervor unmatched among his peers. He held Zoom panel discussions with labor leaders and striking workers. He used his own email list to fundraise for labor groups. And he continued scheduling his rallies co-featuring Sara Nelson and Sean O'Brien. These rallies, fueled by one of the only Democratic politicians in America who can reliably turn out a crowd, did not dwell on the looming midterms. They sought to inject into the public consciousness, at high volume, the idea that a fighting union movement had to exist in order to achieve all the things that Bernie's supporters wanted.

Even more than Bernie, Sara Nelson seemed maniacally driven to drag this vision into existence. She said yes to every invitation, and never stopped moving. On August 19, she was onstage in Pittsburgh at the Netroots Nation convention, next to Disney heiress-turned-enlightened-liberal Abigail Disney, saying, "What we have to understand is that democracy is on the brink of collapse because we exist in a system of capitalism." The next day she flew to Philadelphia for a rally with Sanders and O'Brien outside Independence Hall. That night, the whole group of them flew to Boston, in preparation for a Sunday rally in O'Brien's hometown. On the flight out of Philly, Bernie and Nelson lounged in the waiting area as little knots of onlookers screwed up their courage to run over and ask Bernie for a selfie. He obliged. He boarded early and sat close to the front of the plane, and people high-fived him as they filed down the aisle to their seats.

At ten thirty the next morning, Nelson, wearing her oversized red "ORGANIZE" T-shirt, stood in front of a Starbucks store on Commonwealth Avenue amid a crowd of a couple dozen young people wearing Starbucks Workers United and DSA T-shirts. The store was closed, thanks to the 24/7 picket line that its workers had been maintaining for more than five weeks, to protest what they said was illegal retaliation from a manager after the store had unionized earlier that summer. (The strike would eventually continue for sixty-four days before Starbucks acquiesced to the workers' demand for a new manager.) Nelson spent an hour listening to the employees. She spoke about her own ongoing campaign to organize Delta and how all these fights were intertwined, and led chants on an impromptu, boisterous sign-waving march. Finally, Bernie himself pulled up, shaking hands with the enraptured strikers, hugging Nelson, and grabbing a megaphone for a quick pep talk. "What Sara and I and others are trying to do, we're trying to create an economy that works for everybody, and not just the people on top. And the only way we're going to be successful is if we build a mass grassroots movement, and at the center of that movement is a strong trade union movement. And that's what you guys are doing," he said.

True, and rare to hear from a politician of national significance. Bernie hopped back into his ride, and everyone migrated across the bridge to Cambridge for the rally. At one o'clock in the afternoon on Cambridge Common, the sprawling park adjacent to the Harvard campus, you could witness the Boston version of the labor movement's ability to unite groups that otherwise would not hang out with one another. On the west side of the park, an enormous, gleaming semitruck with a Teamsters Local 25 logo was parked, its grille dwarfing the shorter college students who passed by. This was Sean O'Brien's home turf. He stood—thick, shiny bald head, in a blue Teamsters polo shirt, with shades—milling about with a swarm of other thick, middle-aged white men with buzz cuts and polo shirts. Teamsters tend to look like cops, but they're good. They were joined on the lawn by army jacket–wearing, twenty-year-old Starbucks baristas/folk singers, nerdy MIT grad students, and a surprising number of tottering old men with white hair and rumpled blazers who looked like the image of Bernie Sanders if he had stayed in New England and become a retired college professor. And just a bunch of other regular folks. It was, in other words, a real cross-section of the community. Nothing channels the old-fashioned civic-mindedness of a town meeting more than a big old labor rally.

Part of the point of these events was to give a public platform to union fights that people should know about, to plug labor as an essential part of community life. So we heard from the Starbucks baristas who were on strike on Commonwealth Avenue, and from an MIT grad student whose newly formed union was locked in a contract fight with the administration, and from a nurse from Saint Vincent Hospital in Worcester, whose union had carried out a grinding nine-month-long strike in 2021, one of the longest of the pandemic era.

When Sara Nelson took the stage, in a blue Teamsters ballcap, the crowd had swelled to 1,500. It was hot. A dehydrated young woman passed out in the front row right next to me. Nelson is usually incapable of not shouting when she addresses a crowd, but she lowered her voice to try to frame the moment at hand. "This rally is not a political rally. This rally is for you," she said. "Yesterday in Philly, when Bernie got up onstage, people were obviously very excited. And somebody yells out, 'It should have been you!' And he said, 'It is me. I'm here with you.' This is about you!"

It did not take long for her to build back up to a crescendo. Within ten minutes, she was thundering, jabbing her finger to punctuate each sentence. "The billionaires will keep going. But even on those dick rockets that they built to go out into space, while they leave the rest of us burning on this earth—even there, there are flight attendants on those rockets who asked us if we could help them unionize!" she said. Then her voice notched up into a full holler. "Get this in your head: we are one. And we are everywhere! We got this handled. They think they're safe on their golf courses and in their boardrooms? Guess what? Who serves them their lunch in their boardrooms, and who serves as the caddy on their golf courses? Working. Fucking. People!"

Sean O'Brien, the Teamsters president and hometown boy, came up, flanked by his son and the local's president and bolstered by the event's heavy Teamster presence. It felt like being surrounded by a gang that probably means you no harm, but you shouldn't push it. O'Brien speaks like a

Boston dad, which he is. He has a charming kind of PG-13–rated stream
of class war zealotry. He kept referring to Howard Schultz as "Sahh-gent
Schultz," a very dad type of joke that harkens back to *Hogan's Heroes*, a show
that ended in 1971. The billionaire union-buster trio of Schultz, Jeff Bezos,
and Elon Musk were O'Brien's favorite targets.

"Let's get back to the Three Stooges," he would say. "Those three nit-
wits," he would say. "These three *bozos*." It was like hearing your muscled
Little League coach harangue some ballplayers who weren't looking out for
the team. Bernie Sanders events sometimes pull crowds that are mocked as
effete, overintellectual weaklings, but the Teamsters are decidedly not that.
Having O'Brien at these events inspires that variety of glee that comes with
the realization that the people who look like the bullies are actually on your
side.

Toward the beginning of his speech, O'Brien casually told a little Pope
joke. "We got a very special opportunity to meet the Pope. And I had a conversation with the Pope. And he even said, 'Corporate America? Corrupt
politicians? God can't even help them!'" This got a chuckle. And it was true,
at least partly. In early August, a delegation of transportation labor leaders
from around the world—including Sean O'Brien and Sara Nelson—were
invited to the Vatican to speak to the Pontifical Academy of Sciences about
the overlap between the church's agenda and labor's on issues like climate
change and fighting poverty. For O'Brien, the Boston Irish guy, accepting
the invite was an easy call. He got a photo of himself shaking Pope Francis's
hand and a headline in *People's World* that read "Teamsters get papal blessing for their UPS contract campaign," which by itself was worth the trip.

For Nelson, the lapsed Christian Scientist turned outspoken feminist, the
invitation required a little mulling over. The Catholic Church, just a month
after *Roe v. Wade* had been overturned? And the guidelines say you're supposed to wear a *veil* to meet this guy? Is this what she stood for? After some
thought, though, she decided to go, for the same reason that she tends to
say yes to every invitation: she wants to be in every room because she thinks
labor should have a voice in venues where it usually doesn't. Deep down, she
believes that she can convince anyone of anything if only she can get some
time to talk to them.

As it turned out, the veil thing was optional. The Pope himself has been a vocal friend to unions since he assumed office. In 2017 he told a group of Italian unionists that "There is no good society without a union," and then warned that "Unions over time have ended up resembling politicians too much, or rather political parties," and encouraged unions to look out for the most oppressed workers even if they weren't members. That puts him to the left of quite a few union leaders in America today. So it is fair to think of the Church under Francis as a potentially valuable ally. It has 1.4 billion people listening to it. In America, there are more than twice as many Catholics as there are union members. Wouldn't hurt if the big boss could cajole some of them into organizing.

In a beautiful Vatican courtyard, over wine, cheese, and crackers, the transportation labor leaders made their remarks, pausing every few sentences to let the translator catch up. When it was Nelson's turn, she spoke of the Delta organizing campaign, and of the need to support the coal miners on strike in Alabama, and of her love for Psalm 23—"The lord is my shepherd. I shall not want. He maketh me to lie down in green pastures. He leadeth me by the still waters. He restoreth my soul." She compared those words to the mission of unions, which help people lead full and dignified lives.

Nelson also, characteristically, recited her favorite Mother Jones quote about how the bosses are always organizing, and pointed a finger at capitalism as the culprit underlying the range of issues that they were all discussing in such lovely environs. "If we are going to fight the climate crisis, we are going to have to fight capitalism. And that will take growing unions," she said. "And the church has an incredible position of encouraging workers—in the United States, seventy million Catholics—who should become union members. So that we can be in partnership together to take on capitalism, and force them to put in place a plan for climate justice that includes good jobs, green pastures, and still waters for all of us."

=

A LOT OF THE INTERACTION BETWEEN UNIONS AND ELECTORAL POLITICS IS purely transactional. Municipal workers' unions back mayoral candidates who will support them at contract time. National unions back candidates for Congress and the White House who will vote to their benefit on issues of international trade and tax policies and prevailing wages, and who will be considerate enough not to back bills that try to eradicate unions from the face of the earth. There is nothing wrong with this sort of directly transactional calculation—where businesses have lobbyists and lawyers, the working class has unions to keep an eye on the same things. But it does mean that if you want to discuss unions and politics at a level of ideology more abstract than "who promised us higher raises," it can help to look outside the ranks of people directly employed by unions to do politics.

To ask, "What material gains does my union want in the next few years, and which politicians will help?" is a straightforward question. It can, like all policies focused on short-term material gains, lead to perverse decisions that are destructive in the long term. Construction unions back environmentally damaging projects that will give them some jobs; union pension funds invest in private equity that turns around and destroys the jobs of other union members for a profit; unions may turn a blind eye to all types of atrocious business practices or social policies in exchange for an agreement of corporate neutrality in an organizing campaign, or of targeted support on an issue from a politician. To see this as the normal order of union politics is to acquiesce to the view that unions are not uniquely democratic institutions with the potential to transform society, but are instead just another special interest, out to get whatever they can.

The more meaningful question is: "How can the labor movement, after dwindling for decades, turn itself into a force strong enough to bend politics in its own direction, rather than being bent?" A politically powerful labor movement is not one that hires the most plugged-in consultants to advise it which candidates to donate money to in order to get their support; it is one that derives its power from the fact that it *has all the people.* Unions should always be building toward a situation in which politicians must ask themselves how they can satisfy this indomitable progressive beast. Organized labor should be able to warp the political landscape like a massive star warps space-time, pulling everything in its own direction. To do that, organized labor must grow—in visibility, in influence, and, most importantly, in membership numbers. Electoral politics can help labor get there, and labor, in turn, can transform the electorate in a way that moves national politics in a more humane direction. How to accomplish that is the relevant conversation.

Activists often come to this realization from a starting point inside of the labor movement. Political operatives can come to it from the outside. Faiz Shakir built a career advising Democratic Senate leader Harry Reid, and he went on to work for other prominent Democrats on Capitol Hill, as well as for stalwarts of the DC nonprofit industrial complex like the Center for American Progress and the ACLU. He advised Bernie Sanders during his 2016 presidential run, and then became Sanders's campaign manager in the 2020 race. The more he came to understand the systemic challenges to the success of a grassroots-powered, left-wing campaign like Bernie's, the more his focus was drawn to the importance—and weakness—of the American labor movement.

The underlying barrier, Shakir concluded, is the pervasive absence of class consciousness in our country. It is a way of understanding the world that has never been allowed to take root here. (It is no accident that labor history is not a class taught in America's public schools.) Part of the problem, he felt, was the unwillingness of the mass media to cover stories of worker struggles. So in 2021, he launched More Perfect Union, an activist media outlet that produces slick video stories about labor issues, focusing on strikes, organizing campaigns, the predations of private equity, and other staple elements of the class war. "People ate that shit up," Shakir says. Its immediate success convinced him of a latent desire for this type of reporting that wasn't being served, a sort of media parallel to the desire for Bernie's own brand of politics that the Democratic Party has long relegated to the fringe.

The most powerful progressive nonprofits, he knew, were tied deeply into the existing power structure, and mostly failed to focus on economic justice. Finally, his gaze turned to organized labor itself. Where were *they* in this battle to instill class consciousness to an embattled nation?

"Obviously it's been crunched. They've had a painful ride over the last fifty years. Compression, compression, compression. Let's say you and I go to a room with a thousand people, right? We're standing in a room with a thousand people. There's power. There's all these people. Now let's imagine that someone comes in and says, 'Nine hundred of you, out of the room.' And we're left with a hundred people, and slowly that starts to sink in. What happens to the psychology in that room is that you're like, 'Oh shit, we're getting smaller and smaller. Do I got your back? Do you got my back? We've got to stick together here.' And what I'm saying happens in that world is just like the national labor leaders. Because there's a shrinkage there, there's more of a protection of what is left. It's not evil intent. These are not people out to do harm. It's really a self-preservation tactic," he says. "It's like, 'What's our power? We got Biden! We got Marty [Walsh]! There's Marty!' And you can see how this is what they lean on to keep themselves relevant. And I think what it misses, obviously, is a really deep connection to going back out and expanding. It's a good tactic for maintaining. But what are you doing to expand, and draw those nine hundred people back into this room? How are you gonna grab them and bring them back?"

From his perch leading the most successful—but not quite successful enough—left-wing presidential campaign in our era, Shakir came to the same conclusion that I did watching the race play out from afar: the path to shattering the ceiling that seems to hold any leftist candidate to a minority share in Democratic primaries runs through the labor movement. After his surprisingly strong performance in 2016, Sanders came into the 2020 race with high expectations. But after the party coalesced around Joe Biden and deflated Bernie's momentum after Super Tuesday, one Brookings Institution analyst dismissively wrote that "Exit polling shows that Mr. Sanders has not changed the Democratic electorate in a significant way."

Political candidates do not change the electorate. Movements and the institutions that they create do that. Polls have shown that Bernie Sanders is the most popular national politician in America, but that popularity reflects voters who *identify* with his hopeful vision, not the number of voters who have been magically transformed by it. The participatory nature of union organizing is the transformational experience that electoral campaigns can only dream of being.

When does the typical American ever experience democracy? As a child, they are told what to do. At school, they are told what to do. When they grow up, they get a job, and are told what to do. If they go to church, they are told what to do. And everyone with any common sense can see that voting, the one activity explicitly branded as participating in democracy, seems to change nothing, as power is concentrated and decisions are made by unknown people in places remote from the everyday experience of a normal person. From this base of nothing, we expect Americans to treasure democracy as their greatest value. That is a hard ask, when it is something they have never seen in the wild.

Unless—unless—they happen to be in a union. In a decent union, their opinion will matter. They can directly participate in discussions that lead to a set of demands. They can decide, collectively, to take direct actions to win their demands. They will be able to see how power is formed from a group of individuals coming together. Being in a union, for millions of Americans, is the one and only experience they have of democracy at work. It is not democracy as a slogan, but democracy as a lived experience. That changes people. It serves as a prism through which the flaws in our national politics can be viewed. And it is a school that teaches people what can be unleashed when they come together for a common goal. In 2019, at a rally in front of the Queensbridge housing projects in New York, Bernie Sanders articulated the basic philosophy underlying social democracy when he said, "Look around you. Find someone that you don't know. Are you willing to fight for that person as much as you're willing to fight for yourself?" It is a beautiful sentiment presented with great moral clarity. Throughout American history, the systemic answer to his question has always been "no." If progressives want to push tens of millions of voters to give up on the cowboy ethic and embrace this view, we must provide them with some way station on the path: a place where people can see collective democracy in action at a manageable scale. That place is a union.

This is the sense in which the growth of unions is intimately connected to any hope of a leftward evolution of the American electorate. Unions are not taskmasters that issue orders for members to blindly follow; rather, they make the ground fertile for an opening of minds. Citizens here are raised in an endless stream of messaging about the need to win the cutthroat, zero-sum Game of Life. Then we wonder why seemingly obvious truths like

"It would be better for everyone if we had public health care" are not universally embraced. People need to see that democracy is not a bullshit game for suckers. People need to see that democracy is not just another scam to rip them off. People need unions. Unions are the proof.

This frame for the union/politics connection has long eluded the Democratic Party. The way Bernie Sanders has staged rallies with union leaders that aren't just hype for elections, has relentlessly promoted labor fights, and has used his own coveted email lists to raise money for various labor groups is bizarre in the view of the conventional wisdom of campaigns. Rather than just recruiting support for himself, Sanders's goal in many of his mass emails "was to recruit people to go to a picket. It was to recruit people for organizing drives, recruit them for various rallies that labor was holding. When you do that, there's a cost to the campaign," Shakir says. "There's a reason why no one else does it. Part of it is ideological, yes. But part of the other reason they don't do it is because you're not raising money. Every text, every email that you send—it's costing you. If you're not doing a fundraising email, you're not doing a text send for money, you're doing it to ask people to go do something. Most elite political consultants would say, 'What the F are you doing? You're screwing with our lists. You're using people the wrong way. We've got an election to win. That's your goal. Stop worrying about what the hell this other thing is about.'" As someone coming into the world of organized labor from the world of politics, he could see how the weaknesses of the national union establishment could parallel those of the Democratic Party establishment: an overreliance on technocratic solutions, and an aversion to genuine populism.

In order to grow (or even maintain) labor power in America, the scale of new union organizing must increase dramatically. A consequence of giving people unions is that those people have power they did not have before. That power exists in their own workplace, but it also exists inside of the labor movement itself. And to the extent that the labor movement, like all institutions, naturally produces in its leaders a sense of inertia borne from the realization that an influx of new voices clamoring for new stuff could be a big pain in the ass, there exists in many large unions an unspoken but very real distaste for the idea of flinging open the doors to a large number of new members. This institutional intransigence, combined with an all-out assault on the very existence of unions from the political right wing, is what has led to the long, slow, steady decline of union density and all that has come with it.

People want unions. There is so much organizing to be done. Who is going to do it?

CHAPTER ELEVEN

THE WORK
ORGANIZING ISN'T EASY

October in New Orleans is still hot. Hotter when you are sitting on a bare metal folding chair propped up on a curb with no shade in the parking lot of the Lowe's Home Improvement store on Elysian Fields Avenue, next to the Mardi Gras Truck Stop and Travel Plaza. Nevertheless, Felix Allen is there. It's his day off, but he's there. Sweating.

Allen, twenty-six, has wispy brown chin hairs, a faded orange T-shirt, and a friendly but serious manner. He squints out from underneath a baseball cap at the store's entrance, looking for coworkers coming in and out. On his lap is a hand-lettered posterboard that reads "ASK ME ABOUT THE LOWE'S UNION VOTE!!!" He carries a sheaf of printed petitions and lists of names in a battered schoolchildren's-style folder with a photo of a kitten printed on it. In his wallet is a small stack of union cards, which he printed up himself. They are as basic as can be: small paper rectangles that read "By signing this petition, you acknowledge that you are requesting the representation of a collective bargaining unit (a union)." Typically, there would be the name of a specific union there, but Allen is trying to organize the first Lowe's union in America on his own, as an independent. The information officer who he spoke to at the NLRB assured him the cards are still legal.

Lowe's, worth well over $100 billion, is the second-biggest home improvement company in America. Neither it, nor its larger competitor, Home Depot, have any unionized stores. In September 2022, workers at a Home Depot in Philadelphia filed for a union election. They had organized the union drive themselves. Allen began getting union cards signed at his Lowe's right around that time as well. Thus, the first serious step for organized labor to enter into the two biggest mega companies in this entire industry came about because a small handful of regular-ass workers just decided to give it a shot themselves. Whatever your definition of centralized strategic planning by the labor movement is, this was the opposite.

Felix Allen did not have any background with unions. He is a musician. He plays the drums. He grew up in North Carolina, went to the University of North Carolina, and then attended Florida State, studying music, and moved to New Orleans during the first year of the pandemic. He got the job at Lowe's in December 2020 and worked it full-time until August 2021. Then he went part-time to have more time to play gigs in a rotating cast of bands down on Frenchmen Street. At his day job he is a merchandising service associate, which means that he wears a blue polo shirt and helps build displays for Valspar paint and Craftsman tools. He often helps Lowe's customers out with their requests too—cutting a piece of wood, or tracking down an appliance in the back—although that is generally frowned upon by management. But the store is understaffed, and Felix is a decent person, so he does what he has to do. For his work, he is paid less than fifteen dollars an hour.

The first union campaign he remembers being conscious of was the Amazon organizing drive in Bessemer, Alabama, in 2020. If they can do it in the deep South, he thought, that means something. After he moved to New Orleans, he made friends who talked to him about the labor movement—DSA people, various young lefties. He saw a local Starbucks unionize. Why not his job? He moved ahead with the combination of tenacity, idealism, and a touch of ignorance that is necessary to accomplish unlikely things.

Allen did not just rush into this with the idea that he was going to do it independently. In fact, he and some coworkers went and met with the local

Teamsters, who have an office right down Elysian Fields Avenue. The union was helpful, answered all their questions, and even bought them food, but ultimately, Allen didn't see the point. "I was saying, 'This is gonna be a really uphill battle. It'll be really hard to win the election.' And the [Teamsters rep], he's like, 'Oh, if y'all can get the cards signed, we're winning that election! We're getting you a contract!'" he says. "And I'm just thinking, 'Yeah, but getting 80 percent of the cards signed is the shit that's impossible.'" He figured if he was going to do the hard work, the workers might as well have control of everything.

Just by asking around quietly, he was able to find three other employees willing to help him get union cards signed. (They didn't want their names known, though, leaving him as the sole public face of the organizing effort.) They cobbled together a spreadsheet of every employee and what department they were in, using educated guesswork and an internal "associate lookup tool." They came up with a figure of 172 employees, total. Then, they started talking to them all.

With a year and a half on the job, Allen had been there long enough that he felt comfortable just going up to coworkers and saying, "Hey, man, do you know what a union is?" He was pretty sure they wouldn't run and snitch to managers, and if they did, well, he wasn't one of the people supporting a family from their meager Lowe's salary. It was not hard to identify the things that employees wanted to change. There was understaffing, and there were workplace injuries, and, most of all, there was just not enough money to live.

"Shit, I can drive three different fucking types of forklifts, and they're paying me $12.88? And I'm training the new employees who get paid fifteen dollars?" Allen says. "I talked to someone, and her exact words were 'I work here every fucking day, and I'm still on subsidized housing. That's just not cool.'"

The first round of talks with coworkers focused on the basics of what a union was, how it worked, and what it could do for them. He asked everyone point blank if they would sign a union card if he asked them to. Most said yes. After that, it took only three weeks to gather signed cards from about 40 percent of the workers—more than enough to legally trigger a union election. As soon as he filed with the NLRB, the store began to fill up with managers from all over the region and from other states, along with hired outside anti-union consultants. All of them were eager to pull employees into meetings and advise them on the terrible pitfalls of a union. Allen was fearless, posting up in front of the store and in the breakroom to try to tell people exactly how management was lying to them. He was ordered to move and to stop repeatedly by various managers, but he persisted, politely, asserting his rights the whole time. He felt confident that this thing was worthwhile, no matter what.

And then, in the last week of October, a wrench in the gears. After challenges from lawyers representing Lowe's, the NLRB told Allen that, actually, the union cards he used without a specific union name on them weren't going to work—he would have to pull his petition and do it all over again. It was a pure paperwork error. A fairly predictable one, given the complexity of the legal process involved in pulling off a contested union election, and the fact that a twenty-six-year-old drummer was navigating the process without a hired attorney, and the fact that he was up against a megacorporation with an entire team of attorneys who were very well-paid for the task of making it as difficult and time-consuming and confusing as possible for employees to hold a free and fair vote for their union. Allen was pissed, but he was not surprised.

One day in early November, when the fate of the organizing drive was still up in the air, a notice was posted in the employee break room at the store, printed on bright yellow paper with a Lowe's logo on top and the headline "NATIONWIDE WAGE INCREASE."

"For the past several months, Lowe's executive leadership team evaluated the market and associates' BEST survey responses. Many of you said you're concerned about pay, and Lowe's heard you," it declared. "The majority of associates here at 2470 will receive a raise from this huge investment in our frontline workers." Lest anyone miss the message, a bullet point on the flier said, "This pay raise is something that Lowe's associates across the country are receiving—all without a union." The company has around three hundred thousand employees, so its announced $170 million wage increase could give the average worker a raise of a whopping forty-seven dollars a month. A few weeks of part-time organizing by a single drummer had prodded the company to give everyone enough to take their family to dinner at McDonald's once a month. Who needs a union when you have a Big Mac value meal?

Two weeks before Christmas, Allen publicly announced that he was withdrawing his union petition from the NLRB. It wasn't fair, but the nitpicky legal objections to the paperwork had proven too difficult to overcome. Employees at the store were growing tired of being surveilled by managers every day. There had been a good deal of turnover since the summer. Still, Allen's hope bubbled on. He nursed plans to form a new, stronger organizing committee in the new year. Union drives are never really over until you give up.

Six months later, in late June 2023, Allen was fired. The company said they fired him for violating safety protocols by momentarily using a forklift that was out of service. Allen says he was clearly fired in retaliation for his organizing. He filed unfair labor practice charges against the company. Meanwhile, Lowes still didn't have a union.

=

THE EXPLOSION OF INDEPENDENT UNION ORGANIZING IN 2022—ALL OF IT driven by workers themselves, not aligned with existing unions—was simultaneously a thrilling sign of how much enthusiasm exists for organized labor among regular people and a galling demonstration of how broken the institutions of organized labor are. For decades, union leaders have been saying that they would spring into action when the masses awoke to the necessity of what they had to offer. Hell, there is an entire doctrine called "Fortress Unionism," coined by the labor writer Richard Yeselson in a much-discussed essay in 2013, that holds that the labor movement should stop trying to launch difficult organizing campaigns and conserve its resources "because the smart union strategists can't compensate for a mostly (though not entirely) uninterested working class." The smart move, Yeselson wrote, would be for unions to just bolster their existing strengths and bide their time "until the day arrives, if it ever does, when the workers themselves militantly signal that they want unions."

Besides being a callous abdication of one of the core moral responsibilities of unions—the responsibility to help as many working people as possible—this doctrine assumes that the labor movement will be able to detect when the wondrous day arrives that the workers "militantly signal" their desire to organize. (Perhaps every worker will emerge from the office and fire guns in the air until the smoke wafts over AFL-CIO headquarters?) If there were any validity to this idea, then 2022 would certainly have been that day. The pandemic radicalized millions of workers. High-profile strikes happened. Successful union drives at Amazon and Starbucks grabbed widespread media attention. All over the country, workers began organizing on their own. In addition to Amazon's Staten Island warehouse, successful independent unions were won at Trader Joe's and New Seasons Market, and independent organizing drives were announced at a diverse array of major companies, ranging from T-Mobile to Geico to Chipotle. For people who had toiled in the union world for the first two decades of the twentieth century, through indifferent-to-hostile White Houses and public disdain and an uninterested media, the post-pandemic labor boom was like emerging from a dark cave into a daytime fireworks show. It was all going down! The party had started! Get on the dance floor or be left behind!

And what happened? Did the institutions of organized labor—the AFL-CIO, the biggest unions in America, the richest nonprofits—spring nimbly into action to guide and nurture and take absolute advantage of this newfound hunger among working people? Not at all. The story of Felix Allen and his Lowe's union drive is more important as an illustration of what *didn't* happen than of what did. When the plucky young man rallied his coworkers and quietly got union cards signed and filed for a union election at a major nonunion company and got national publicity for doing so, was he flooded with support from a grateful union establishment? Did a team of professional organizers parachute into New Orleans to help him? Were union lawyers dispatched to ensure his NLRB paperwork was bulletproof, and to file unfair labor charges against the company for its union busting? No. None of that happened. Because there *is* no real national infrastructure for labor organizing that is able to intelligently respond to opportunities, or take advantage of the newfound demand. At the center of the labor movement lies a black hole.

Getting the first union at a big company is incredibly important. It is a toehold, a base in hostile territory, a foundation from which organized labor can expand. It is, above all, proof of concept to every other worker in the company: this is possible. The successful union vote at the Amazon Staten Island warehouse did not change the mega company overnight, but it showed that unionization could be done. It was a jolt of energy for every other dispirited, overworked, underpaid employee in every soul-crushing, neon-lit big box everywhere. If Felix Allen could win a union election at one Lowe's way down in Louisiana, it would no longer be possible for the company's managers at the other 1,700 Lowe's in America to wave their hands dismissively and say that unions were old, outmoded, not worth trying. Any and all workers willing to risk their own livelihoods and brave the bosses' wrath in order to try to win a company's first union are strategically valuable for organized labor as a whole. They should be treated as VIPs by the labor movement. They should be sought out and encouraged and assisted and protected in every case. That would be the norm, if we had a labor movement that functioned as effectively as the corporations it is up against. But we are a long, long way from that. As it is, companies dispatch union-busting teams to any location where a union drive pops up, but there is no union-assistance team dispatched from the AFL-CIO to even things out.

Consider where Felix Allen *did* get his advice from: He spoke to some local Marxists. He spoke to some people in the DSA. He spoke to people from the International Workers of the World (IWW), the once-mighty "One Big Union" that is now a small, left-wing group with a few scattered union shops around the country. He spoke to the Emergency Workplace Organizing Committee (EWOC), a group that exists to help get people in touch with union organizers—a scrappy, nonprofit joint project of the DSA and UE, a small but radical union that has always been militantly committed to organizing and is not part of the AFL-CIO. Allen did find his local Teamsters willing to talk and offer help (to their credit), but they did not have a pile of resources or personnel to offer. To the extent that Allen got encouragement, inspiration, and consultation, almost all of it came from a

loose network of labor-adjacent, left-wing people motivated by pure ideological belief, not from any major national union group capable of identifying
and assisting important worker activists like him. The true believers did the
work, and the big institutions with all the money did not. The existence of
true believers is always heartwarming, but this ad hoc arrangement is not
one capable of a grand revival of organized labor at a large scale.

The most well-capitalized parts of the organized labor world are, in
effect, still pursuing their own inward-looking version of "Fortress Unionism," even as opportunities reach historic heights. But while the original
theory was that these institutions would be ready to leap into action when
the time was right, what has instead happened is that—predictably—they
have found the walls of their fortress to be too cozy to leave. A 2022 report
by the labor researcher Chris Bohner (aptly titled "Labor's Fortress of
Finance") found that between 2010 and 2021, the total annual revenue of
unions in America grew by a third, to $18 billion per year. During the same
period, union membership declined by more than seven hundred thousand
people; union density fell to barely over 10 percent; and unions employed
nearly twenty-five thousand fewer people. Even as the financial stockpiles of
organized labor grew, unions did not deploy those resources to organize new
workers. Rather than being on a path to revive the power of the working
class, they were on a path toward a day when there would be one remaining
union in America, with a paid staff but no members, sitting atop a huge
investment account, sending out press releases about why unions are still
important.

Some in the union world object to this analysis. They say that unions are
each their own discrete organizations, operating in their own specific areas
on behalf of their own members, and that therefore to expect them to act
as a coordinated national body is unfair. This is true, and it is part of the
problem. There are endless inspiring stories within the labor movement. This
book's chapters are full of them. But if we want to change this country—to
bend the harrowing curve of inequality, to establish some reasonable balance
of power between greed and humanity—we need labor to operate with a
level of organization that is at least as formidable as that of the corporations
on the other side of the equation. A highly paid team of professional union

busters is guaranteed to appear on the scene at any major company that finds itself subjected to a union drive. There is no pro-union Delta Force to balance that out. Some unions organize quite well, some unions organize half-assedly, and some unions organize not at all. This splintered arrangement of individual approaches has for decades wilted in the face of the ceaseless, professionalized assault of business on every pillar of legal and economic strength of workers. In aggregate, the numbers don't lie. Organized labor is everywhere being out-organized by capital.

=

IN DECEMBER 2021, THE FIRST STARBUCKS STORES IN AMERICA VOTED TO unionize in Buffalo, New York. One year later, there were nearly three hundred unionized Starbucks stores, across thirty-six states, all under the banner of Starbucks Workers United. The campaign was remarkable not just for its rapid spread, but for the fact that there has long been a quiet assumption that unionizing fast food outlets (and restaurants in general) was either impossible or not worth the effort since the turnover is so high and the workforce so tenuous. That was false, and Starbucks was the proof.

The union that took on the Starbucks campaign, Workers United, had already had success organizing coffee shops in upstate New York. Beginning in 2019, they ran victorious union drives at several Spot Coffee cafes in the Buffalo area, making them some of the first unionized coffee shops in the country. That caught the attention of baristas across the city—including those at Starbucks, who didn't see why they should be considered any harder to organize than anyone else.

Much of the day-to-day work of spreading the union has been carried out by Starbucks workers themselves. Workers at stores that have unionized become part of the SBWU machine that fields incoming requests from other interested workers, answers their questions, and helps them through the process. It is a wonderful demonstration of how to scale up a national union drive in a cost-effective way. The Workers United organizing guru who has overseen it all from the start is Richard Bensinger, a man whose own career has shown him all of the promise of organized labor, and all of its discouraging institutional failures.

Bensinger has a white mustache and white hair and looks a little bit like an older Paul Newman playing a factory worker. In the mid-1970s, he was working at a tennis racket factory in Colorado, watching his coworkers breathe in fiberglass particles, catch cancer, and have hands ripped off in industrial machinery. He launched a bitter, years-long effort to unionize the plant and got drawn into a career in the labor movement. He spent the next decade knocking around the country as a union organizer, and ended up in Washington, DC, in 1989 as the executive director of the newly created Organizing Institute, an effort by the AFL-CIO to train thousands of new organizers, jumpstart union organizing nationwide, and reverse the decline of union density.

Sound familiar? The same problems that organized labor faces today were perfectly clear in the 1980s. When John Sweeney was elected president of the AFL-CIO in 1995 on a platform of reenergizing new organizing, he appointed Bensinger as his organizing director. It fell to Bensinger to sell to the leaders of all the AFL-CIO's member unions Sweeney's plan for them to massively increase their organizing budgets. When Bensinger gave his first speech touting the plan to a roomful of union presidents at an annual meeting in Florida, they responded with gripes and prickliness. How dare he suggest that the decline of unions was *their fault*? The ambitious strategy was doomed from the start.

"I wasn't trying to be disrespectful. I was trying to be *provocative*," Bensinger recalls. "I didn't say, 'It's your fault.' I said, 'We can't change the Republican Party, or the law.' If we did change the law, it won't make any difference. And that we had to hold a mirror to our face and change our own behavior. Organizing for my whole career has been underfunded, under-prioritized. We're always out there as an adjunct of the Democratic Party." Those words were the hard-won wisdom of someone who actually knew what organizing took from the ground up. Quite a few union presidents, though, saw it as an unforgivable attempt by some upstart at the AFL-CIO to insinuate they weren't doing their jobs, to intrude on their private fiefdoms. And because the AFL-CIO had no real ability to force its member unions to do anything, they proceeded to mostly ignore Sweeney's exhortations for them to each spend 30 percent of their budgets on organizing.

Bensinger, uninterested in the gladhanding of DC union politics, was out of that job a year and a half later. He carried on as an organizing director at a number of different unions, but Sweeney's attempt to reorient the priorities of organized labor itself crashed on the rocks of apathy and independence inside the big unions.

The importance of this piece of history is this: neither the problems nor the solutions to labor's problems have changed much since then. In 1995, when Sweeney took over, about 15 percent of American workers were union members. That was considered a crisis. Now, it's about 10 percent. Unions decided not to invest in organizing for the past quarter century, and union density proceeded to decline. Surprise! At the heart of this slowly unfolding insanity is a structural flaw familiar to Bensinger and every other reformer: union leaders are elected by their current members, not their future members. Dues are paid by current members, not future members. Getting unions to care about members they don't have yet is just hard, for the same reason that it is hard to get taxpayers to care about schools they don't send their own kids to. People tend to prioritize their own interests. Though the fact that the labor movement will eventually collapse and die if we do not increase our new organizing only requires a very small leap of theoretical thought beyond "What is good for the union members who already exist, right now," that is a leap too far for many union leaders. Climate change is a useful parallel for this dynamic. We know the rising seas will eventually swallow our homes if we do not make radical changes but . . . ehh, it's gonna be a while, and we have problems now. Why worry?

Union organizers are tortured souls. Their plight is to be true believers in the power of unions; to have seen firsthand how unions can change lives for the better; to know exactly how to go about giving unions to people who don't have them; and then, at some point, to find that the institutions that should be enabling them to carry out this task just don't care about it as much as they should. It is a career freighted with the knowledge of the gap between the labor movement's potential and its reality. Because of this, most organizers acquire a sort of Zen fatalism about big-picture national labor issues. They focus on what they can do with what they have. Those who think too much about what they *could* do if the leadership of the labor

movement were better tend to leave the profession. It's just too hard to mari-
nate in those frustrations forever.

For Bensinger, the Starbucks campaign is the capstone of a four-decade
career of successful organizing. He knows how to make unions. He knows
how to train other people to make unions. He knows that if you spend
more money to train more organizers to make more unions, you will create more union members, which is what unions need more than anything.
And he has seen the bureaucracy of organized labor continue to fail to do
this straightforward thing in a sustained way, decade after decade. There
is always someone looking for a shortcut, or a brilliant new tactic, or new
technology, or a regulatory tweak that will make the whole thing easier. But
the fact is that there simply aren't enough union organizers in enough places
organizing enough unions.

"The real point was, the lack of being a social movement, where you use
your resources to help the most disadvantaged workers, instead of a special
interest group, where you use your resources to help yourself," Bensinger
says. He, like many others, had harbored hopes that the right person might
turn it all around. "I do think if you had the leadership—that's where Sara
Nelson would have made a difference. She was the first labor leader we had
speak to us up in Buffalo, and she set the room on fire. The AFL doesn't
have leadership like that."

CHAPTER TWELVE

SARA NELSON CARRIES THE FLAG

It was a mid-October morning, and the chill had already crept into the New England air. In New Haven, Connecticut, the haunting gothic campus of Yale was dappled by sunlight filtering down through the branches of maple trees. Sara Nelson was in town to deliver the Gruber Lecture at the Yale Law School, given annually by someone selected as an exemplar of women's rights. Before the afternoon speech, Nelson spent her lunch hours sitting in a church basement with a bunch of Yale grad student workers who were members of Unite Here Local 33. Over pizza, the grad workers shared with Nelson their stories of immigration, struggles to get health care, and long, strenuous organizing efforts. She listened to everyone and offered words of support. A week later, the Yale grad workers would finally file for their union election—the culmination of three decades of organizing in the face of hostility from the school's administration. In January 2023, they would win, bringing four thousand more Yale members into Unite Here. Nelson's visit had the feeling of an NBA superstar dropping into the locker room of a college team to rally them before their big game. When she left, she affixed a "Local 33" pin to her lapel, to wear during her speech later that day.

Students and faculty packed into the airy and ergonomically comfortable tiers of the lecture hall at Yale Law School. Nelson spoke from a table down front, answering gentle prompts from a Yale law professor. She wasted little time twisting the knife into the guts of her host university's union busting. "There are many workplaces where people think, 'Oh yeah, I'd like to have a labor union, but that's not really for my workplace.' Certainly, that has been the message here at Yale for the grad students for years. And the grad students are overcoming that, and they're gonna win now!" Claps broke out across the room from the dozens of Local 33 members who had shown up to the event. That energy, in the rarefied classroom surroundings, spurred Nelson on.

"We have to organize in the tens of millions. This is the only way that we are going to not only save democracy, but actually make democracy fulfill its promise in this country. I stood in Miss Muldoon's classroom when I was in kindergarten with my hand over my heart every single day looking at the flag and ending that pledge with 'indivisible, and liberty and justice for all.' And there can be a lot of criticism about the Pledge of Allegiance to the flag, and when I talk to many students, they don't necessarily have that experience anymore. But I thought that was a *solemn vow* that we were making to each other," she said. "Unchecked capitalism has run amok, and is putting us on the march to fascism. And if we don't give people power, and give people the right to organize—and especially women, who have just been told that not only do we not have equal rights, but we can be controlled forever by a man, through rape or some other action that keeps us in our place. That's what the Dobbs decision was about: it was about lopping off half the power of the working people in this country. And if we don't call that out . . . we will lose any hope of reclaiming our democracy. It's on life support now."

The moderator paused a beat, and then said, "Whew!"

=

SARA NELSON'S FAILURE TO ASCEND TO THE HIGHEST SEAT IN LABOR STILL sat bitterly with her, swallowed with an obligatory smile but hard to digest. It had robbed her and her supporters of a neat narrative arc. Like the double defeats of Bernie Sanders's presidential campaigns, it represented another instance of progressives getting their hopes up for a definitive Overton window shift, only to be dashed on the confounding shoals of reality. Leftists and radicals of all stripes should be used to this by now. Their icons—the ones who didn't get so sick of the struggle that they went ahead and sold out—were always getting steamrolled or assassinated or otherwise frozen out of power. Sometimes, they're just hobbled by inconvenient surgeries. Yet the losses still stung. Hope springs eternal, and so does heartbreak.

On the other hand, little had materially changed for Nelson. She was still one of the only labor leaders sought out by all points of the political compass to serve as the Voice of Labor, when such a thing was called for. Thus, in the waning months of 2022, she gave speeches at both the *New York Times* DealBook Summit, alongside famous power brokers and financiers in Midtown Manhattan, and at the convention of a newly revived Students for a Democratic Society, held at Kent State University in homage to the student protesters shot down by National Guardsmen in 1970 for protesting the Vietnam War. She spoke at the convention of the Teamsters for a Democratic Union, leading the room in a chorus of "Solidarity Forever," and she spoke at the *Fortune* magazine Most Powerful Women summit, surrounded by corporate types with plastic smiles; she spoke at a labor summit at Princeton University, and gave equal time to go speak at the Rockford (Illinois) Labor Council. She continued doing her best to say yes to everything.

All the while, the campaign to organize the flight attendants at Delta was grinding on. Nelson hired Boston mayor Michelle Wu's former chief of staff to run the organizing campaign from Atlanta, Delta's biggest hub. Whipping the densely unionized transportation sector into a showcase for labor power stayed on her mind. When the news broke in November that the White House would be imposing a contract on the railroad unions against the will of members, Nelson was closely involved in the push by progressives in Congress to win sick days for the workers. (Even if they had won the sick days at that time, which they didn't, it would have been a small consolation prize compared to the potential of the moment. When the rail strike looked like a real possibility, Nelson had privately begun planning for the prospect that railroad workers might set up picket lines at airports, which flight attendants would refuse to cross—thereby spreading the power of the strike into the nation's aviation system, a demonstration of sectoral labor power that could have gone down in history.) In November, the AFA announced a "coordinated campaign" with the Teamsters and the Machinists to organize a total of forty-five thousand workers at Delta. That was followed in December by the AFA's announcement that it had formed a "United Airlines Union Coalition" with the Teamsters, the Machinists, and the other unions representing workers at United, to coordinate bargaining demands and strategy for seventy-eight thousand employees of that airline. What all these things had in common was that they were steps toward thinking nationally and industrially. Thinking *bigger*.

The midterm elections came and went, with Democrats retaining control of the Senate but losing the House. Nelson had spent less time than usual out on the campaign trail for Democratic candidates. She didn't have time. Her mind was occupied with the question of how to drag labor to the center of American political life. She was obsessed with doing whatever she could to see to it that the most high-profile union battles in the country, the handful that penetrated the consciousness of the general public—at Amazon, at Starbucks, at Warrior Met Coal in Alabama, where the United Mine Workers strike was stretching into its twentieth month—were resolved in unions' favor, to avoid defeats that could make casual viewers conclude that unions are weak. Nelson had spent the year taking every opportunity to bolster those campaigns. She had flown thousands of miles to speak at multiple rallies for all of them, even traveling to Alabama over the summer with Starbucks union leader Jaz Brisack to speak to UMWA Warrior Met strikers, to draw the threads of those campaigns together. Nelson was sad when health issues stopped her from going to Buffalo on December 9 to celebrate the one-year anniversary of the first successful Starbucks union vote, but she appeared via Zoom to cheer them on anyhow. She prioritized that work because she believed that in the long run, those campaigns would be more important than the midterm political campaigns. Regardless of who was in charge of Congress or the AFL-CIO, the national situation remained the same: people still urgently needed unions, and wanted unions, and stumbled over a thousand obstacles trying to get unions. To let Starbucks's illegal union busting go unchallenged, or allow Amazon to refuse to fairly bargain a contract, or let the Warrior Met strikers lose after they had sacrificed so much, felt like it would be devastating—not only for the workers themselves, but for the labor movement's argument to workers everywhere that it was the tool they needed to gain power. (Alas, the Warrior Met strike ended in March 2023, after nearly two years, when union members returned to work without having won a new contract.)

"I spent the last two months building power for workers, and building power for the working class. Because the election was essentially going to be what it was going to be," Nelson said shortly after the midterms. "What I can do is seed the ground for actually having a fighting working-class movement that makes the parties come to us." Every election cycle would offer a choice between bad Republicans and less-bad Democrats, and Nelson was a committed leftist. But she understood that organizing campaigns like Starbucks, which had managed to penetrate red and blue states alike, had transformational potential that elections never would. "People got so excited about that. It connected mostly young people from all over the country. All these places that supposedly are so divided and impossible to penetrate by labor because labor has become so identified with a political party, rather than with the working class."

The new organization that Nelson wanted to build to fill the gaps in the labor movement was inching toward reality. In the last month of 2022, she hired a former congressional staffer who had been active in the recent formation of the Congressional Staffers Union to start laying the groundwork to build the organization's structure. Nelson had begun combing her mental Rolodex for sympathetic rich people to fundraise from, and thinking about existing alt-labor groups that she might be able to pull in to do pieces of the comprehensive work she envisioned. After kicking around several names for the new entity, she settled on "Go Union"—an open door for any working person to walk through into the labor movement. (Later, she settled on the name "Go Union.") It would have the organizing capacity to help people start unions at their workplace; legal resources to file unfair labor practice charges against union-busting employers and help struggling unions navigate paperwork issues; and it would have communications expertise to elevate individual labor battles in the media, and to raise the profile of the unions as a whole. Much of Nelson's vision for the group came from long hours spent thinking about how, almost a century ago, independent unions propelled by little more than grassroots determination had been the original seeds of organized labor in America. Today's wave of independent organizing, at Lowe's and dozens of places just like it, showed that desire for unions had outpaced the ability of existing unions to grow. She wanted her new organization to be the bridge between what was and what could be, the structure that workers could use to give shape to their own ambitions.

The potential was vast. Nelson's ambitions for unions to change America were too big to fit neatly in the role of AFA president. She had dedicated decades of her life to the flight attendants' union. That dedication was so complete that she had essentially no knowledge of pop culture for the past twenty years, given that she had been concentrating so single-mindedly on union issues. But—and this is an ironic fact for all union presidents—the job of running an individual union demands so much narrow focus on the circumstances of a single industry that it can hobble the ability to think and speak about the bigger picture. When the media wants to talk about education it turns to leaders of teachers' unions, and when it wants to talk about health care it turns to nurses' unions, and when it wants to talk about tips for navigating the holiday travel crunch it turns to the flight attendants' union. What often gets left out in this dynamic is the idea of the union leader as a spokesperson for the working class as a whole—the union leader as a natural voice to decry inequality and agitate for organizing and denounce capitalism. Sara Nelson has done a better job than most of her peers in using the ostensibly limited reach of her office to launch broadsides on systemic issues, but that has been a project sustained by personal passion. Having an organization with a more general focus than AFA would allow her to launch those broadsides more cleanly, to stick and move without having to be rooted in the world of aviation the whole time. The head of a union answers to the union members; the head of the AFL-CIO answers to the affiliate unions. There was tantalizing possibility in something that would give Nelson an additional forum to answer to nobody but the workers of the world.

Leadership is a self-fulfilling prophecy. It is not the same thing as power that is awarded with title or money or position. Those are descriptions of people who are just *in charge*. Leaders, true leaders, arise by embodying something that many other people see in themselves. They put into words and deeds qualities that are widely felt and have been searching for expression. That is why they can arise from anywhere. Sara Nelson, the small-town girl from Oregon, the flight attendant, the head of a relatively small union, is an unlikely candidate for power by traditional metrics, but she has the attribute that movements demand of their leaders: ambition. Not for herself, but for everyone. Ambition for the people. The belief that things can be better, and that we can get there. The labor movement, in its best form, will never be a cult of personality. It is too sprawling, too democratic, too varied. It is us. Millions of us. What it needs are brave and selfless people who will pick up its flag and charge up the hill, expecting everyone to follow. Nelson is running up that hill with as much determination as anyone. Maybe that is enough.

For all of 2022, Nelson's right hip had continued its deterioration. Just before Christmas, she had yet another hip replacement operation, this time on the right side. Thus, the year ended for her as it had begun: in pain, recovering, and plotting what was to come.

At the end of her lecture at Yale in October, Nelson took questions from the audience. One person asked her why, with all of America's failings, did it sound like her belief in unions was motivated by *patriotism*? Nelson paused for a moment in thought and replied that if you love something, you have to be willing to fight for it. Then she pursed her lips and recited, from memory, a quote by Mary Baker Eddy, the founder of Christian Science, who she had studied for so long growing up in Corvallis.

"Love is not something laid upon rose leafs with sugar tongs," she said. "I make strong demands on love, call for active witnesses to prove it, noble sacrifices, and grand achievements as its results."

CHAPTER THIRTEEN

THE PATH

HOW THE LABOR MOVEMENT CAN
SAVE AMERICA AND ITSELF

A union is a great way to meet new people, and argue with them. In a nonunion workplace, you are obligated to blindly accept the boss's decisions about pay and working conditions and every last policy governing life on the job. When you unionize, you earn the right to help decide these things, by arguing. Being active in a union can be thought of as one long period of argument, concluding only when you die. What do you think democracy is, anyhow?

The institutional enemy of the union is the boss, but in practice, most of the arguments you will have as a union member will be with your beloved fellow union members. To suddenly bestow upon a group of people the power to make collective decisions is to let a million arguments bloom. You will argue about what to ask for in the contract. You will argue about what to agree to in the contract. You will argue about when to walk out, when to strike, and when to send a strongly worded letter. You will argue about when the meetings should be held. At the meetings, you will argue. You will argue about the union logo, and the cut of the union T-shirts, and the union movie night selection. You will argue about unionwide policies of great importance, and you will argue about extremely minor matters inside your own workplace that can only be settled one way: argument. Sometimes, in an effort to turn down the temperature, you will temporarily refrain from arguing about something. But inside your head, you will be arguing still.

A democratic union has something of the New England town meeting spirit about it. Everyone will be afforded a voice, and a bunch of those voices will piss you off. The union speaks for all of you. Things must be voted on. If you want to send out a statement in everyone's name, then by god you will listen to everyone's thoughts about how that statement should be edited, long past the point of sanity or usefulness. Absurdly, the union is required to represent the interests of even those foolish members who *disagree* with you. And they will all have their say. Oh, you better believe it.

If you are lucky enough to be part of the founding of a healthy union, you will be able to witness the process whereby paralyzing arguments evolve into a functioning system for getting things done. This is a marvelous thing to see. With the help of experienced organizers, a group of regular working people can slowly come to the realization that perhaps having everyone argue about every single issue is not the most efficient way to operate. Some issues can be walled off into committees, where they can be argued about by a smaller number of people. Some issues can be delegated to elected representatives, who can only be argued with after they've already made their decisions. And, most astonishing of all, the entire group may—with time and bitter experience—stop arguing so much.

Not completely, you understand. But less. This is a democracy, not a utopia. I spent many nights sitting in council meetings at my union, listening to a famous television writer who used to be a journalist thirty years ago argue about what the journalists in our union needed to do. All the people there who actually worked in journalism today would tell him that in fact we needed to do the opposite of what he was saying. That would only make him redouble his efforts with longer and more self-referential speeches. This recurring bit of the democratic union experience often made me consider the virtues of Stalin's methods of governance. I developed a months-long toothache due to the involuntary grinding of my teeth during

these meetings. Still, in calmer moments I could admit that even this excruciating process was better than the alternative. In a dictatorship, the dictator
might turn out to be *that* guy.

The union that began at Gawker Media in 2015 was notable for the fact
that it would be impossible to construct a group of colleagues more prone to
argue about everything. We were one hundred or so people whose careers
consisted of waking up each morning to write strongly argued pieces on
the internet. "Here's why I'm right, and you're wrong, and by the way fuck
you" was the job description. Naturally, we brought this approach to our
early discussions about unionizing. Even in our left-leaning ranks, the urge
to stake out the "this seemingly obvious idea is bad, actually" position was
irresistible because many of us were so used to being professional contrari-
ans. Describing in harsh terms why some popular idea or another was stupid
made up a large portion of my own daily essays at that time. Battering oppo-
nents into submission with rhetoric was the only style of political negotia-
tion that I knew. Attempting to organize a union was the first thing in my
life that forced me to spend an extended period of time genuinely listening
to the positions of people who disagreed with me and pissed me off—not for
the purpose of crushing them, but for the purpose of understanding them.
In other circumstances, their failure to acknowledge the brilliance of my
arguments would have provoked nothing but a determination to bombard
them with even louder arguments. If they still failed to agree with me, I
could write them off as just another of life's idiots. This is one of my own
devastating personality flaws, yes, but it is also an illustration of how unions
can force you to become a better person.

We are all lonely participants in this atomized world. The anomie of
modern life and all that. Isolated by our cars and inhuman urban design
and the collapse of organized religion and the algorithmic encouragement of
tribalistic politics, we despair at the sensation of our nation descending into
warring, alienated factions. All our differences seem to loom larger as time
passes, to grow into unclimbable walls: red versus blue, young versus old,
urban versus rural, affluent versus just scraping by, socialists versus the goddamn fascists. We embed ever deeper into our little categories and assume
that this is the natural order of things. We holler about "elites," who might

be anyone at all other than us. We accept this war of identities because we can imagine nothing more pure that exists to compare it to.

Try this: join a union. If you don't have a union to join, make one. You can. It's your right. I bet you'll be surprised how good it makes you feel, even with all the arguing. There you are, sitting at work every day, griping about this and that. You get pissed at your jerk boss, at your too-low salary, at your paltry health insurance, at the grinding hours, at the incessant and unreasonable demands that commerce places upon your life. Everyone, with the exception of a small number of lottery winners, is annoyed at something about their job. Mostly, we are taught to suck it up. What is reinforced to all of us from a young age is not how to change the stupid decisions your boss makes, but to tolerate them. Stoicism in the face of hard work is fetishized. Your grandaddy and grandmother suffered, and your father and mother suffered, and you will honor them by suffering in the same way. Thankless hours for low pay? Character building! Sexual harassment on the job? We all went through that! Workplace injuries? Makes you strong! Decades of toil that barely allow you to pay the bills while a cabal of mediocre white guys who all seem to be pals with one another are in charge and make a lot more money than you despite exhibiting no real merit? It's the way of the world! Stop your complaining! If you want a friendly ear, go whisper to Jesus. What makes you think that *you* should have it so much better than everyone else did?

The placidity that exists in the absence of a union is not evidence of happy peace; it is evidence of dictatorship. The absolute power of the company and the boss to determine everything about a job's conditions is so common in America that most people never even think about it. It is widely seen as a state of nature. "If you don't like the job, quit," we are told, a sneering rebuke that leaves unspoken the fact that you will then become homeless. The idea that workers deserve to be able to have real power at work is fundamentally un-American. (Could Thomas Jefferson have run his successful plantation that way? Ridiculous.) It is a rejection of the cult of the business genius. We are trained to see our economy as one in which titanically gifted entrepreneurs launch flourishing companies that provide us, the grateful normal citizens, with jobs. Who are you to tell John Rockefeller or

Andrew Carnegie or Henry Ford or Jack Welch or Bill Gates or Jeff Bezos or Elon Musk how to run their businesses? If you were so smart, you'd be as rich as they are, wouldn't you? Stop being greedy for more, and start showing a little gratitude to these gods of capitalism. They are the mighty figures who pull all of society forward into prosperity. Progress, ho!

This mentality has always been drilled deep, deep into the bedrock of the American psyche. It still prevails. Men who love football and drive big trucks and prize nothing more than masculinity and strength will, without a moment's thought, slip meekly into groveling servitude at the mere suggestion of anything that sounds socialist. It is what we are taught. For obvious reasons, unrestrained capitalism prefers that workers accept their place. Any increase in worker power is an interruption to the extraction of wealth from the world and its distillation into ever fewer hands. We all laugh at the sight of North Korean propaganda on the news, of an entire stadium full of people with pasted-on smiles dancing for the dictator. And then we go to work and do the same thing. Americans are still very much a nation of "temporarily embarrassed millionaires," as the apocryphal John Steinbeck quote goes. To suggest that poor people should get more and rich people should get less and nobody really deserves a billion dollars often provokes a bizarre, outraged response in the public mind, driven not by any rational analysis of our common plight but by the unexamined conviction that the balm for our own suffering is for everyone else to suffer as well. I learned this by spending twenty years reading hate mail about stuff I wrote. But really, all you have to do is look around.

=

I WAS BORN IN SEPTEMBER 1979, JUST MONTHS BEFORE THE DAWN OF THE Reagan era. My lifetime is a tidy box containing the modern American age of inequality. From my birth until my forty-third birthday in 2022, the real income of the bottom 50 percent of Americans grew by less than 25 percent, according to data from economists at the University of California, Berkeley. That ain't much. The real incomes of the top 10 percent of Americans grew by more than 150 percent during that time, the incomes of the top 1 percent grew by more than 250 percent, and the incomes of the top .01 percent grew by nearly 500 percent. On top of that, the productivity of the average worker in 2022 was more than 60 percent greater than it was in 1979, but that average worker's wages had grown by less than 20 percent. Those two figures had grown in tandem from the end of World War II until the eve of the Reagan era, and then decoupled to the distinct disadvantage of workers. A Rand Corporation study found that the sharp upward divergence of income inequality beginning in the mid-'70s had, by 2018, cost workers $47 trillion—money they would have had if the historic levels of postwar equality had carried on as usual. That money went, instead, to the top 10 percent of earners. The class war has been fantastically profitable for its beneficiaries.

The rich have spent the past several decades redirecting more and more of the money that used to go to the working class into their own pockets. Federal Reserve data beginning in 1989 shows that that year, the top 1 percent richest Americans controlled less than 23 percent of the nation's wealth; by 2022, they controlled more than 31 percent. The bottom 90 percent started that period with 40 percent of the wealth, and ended with 32 percent. The bottom 50 percent of Americans still have less than 4 percent of all wealth—which is to say, almost nothing, signifying how common a paycheck-to-paycheck existence is.

In 1979, union density sat comfortably over 20 percent. More than one in five American workers were union members. Today, it is less than half of that, barely one in ten; in the private sector, it is even worse at barely 6 percent. This decline, more than any other factor, is the reason why it has become so hard to sustain a middle-class lifestyle today. The sociologists Zachary Parolin and Tom VanHeuvelen studied the past fifty years of earnings data for American men and found that union membership resulted in an average of $1.3 million more in lifetime earnings—"larger than the average gains from completing college."

Because unions raise wages not only for their own members but for nonmembers as well (as nonunion firms are forced to compete with unionized ones for workers), this absolute loss in worker power has been magnified across the entire economy. The Economic Policy Institute estimated that if union density had remained at 1979 levels, the average *nonunion* worker in the mid-2010s would have been earning $2,700 per year more. For workers without a college education, the financial hit was even greater. And that cal-culation doesn't even account for the positive effects that the maintenance of union density would have had on the political power of the working class, during the era of corporate deregulation and anti-labor legislation that fur-ther exacerbated economic inequality's rise.

Taken together, these figures tell a straightforward tale, one so simple that it should be included in America's elementary school books: this coun-try's post–World War II balance of power between capital and labor—which produced, for three decades, the greatest shared prosperity that the world has ever seen—has become wildly tilted in capital's favor. This skew has produced a level of inequality that has eroded faith in American institutions, warped our politics, and drowned the classic version of the American dream in a dirty puddle. After organized labor helped keep American production humming to win World War II, even conservatives accepted the vital role of unions in society. "Today in America unions have a secure place in our industrial life," Dwight Eisenhower said in a 1952 speech to the Ameri-can Federation of Labor. "Only a handful of unreconstructed reactionaries harbor the ugly thought of breaking unions." By the 1970s, that attitude had been replaced with well-organized hostility from business, a hostility granted the full opportunity to flourish within legal and regulatory sys-tems after Reagan assumed office. Today, the majority of American states, including an unbroken Southern front stretching from Texas to West Vir-ginia, have "right to work" laws that make it difficult to build and maintain powerful unions in the private sector. Furthermore, all public sector unions have been rendered "right to work" by our right-wing Supreme Court. Many states severely restrict what public employees can bargain for, and make pub-lic sector strikes illegal or outlaw public collective bargaining entirely. And private companies that violate labor laws and use illegal tactics like firing, lying, and intimidation to stop their workers from organizing face laughably small penalties. The laws protecting workers when they organize are sup-posed to be enforced by the National Labor Relations Board, an agency that is overstretched and underfunded during Democratic administrations and actively weaponized against labor during Republican ones. Corporate power and its allies have quite successfully arranged America's laws and prevailing culture so that, in most places, most of the time, working people are not taught about unions, must face great risk to their livelihoods to organize unions, and, if they do get unions, often find themselves mired in an endless bureaucratic struggle to secure a halfway decent contract from intransigent employers. Companies know very well that they can illegally union bust and refuse to negotiate in good faith. They have worked for many years to knee-cap the government referees capable of preventing these things at a national scale. This sort of implacable determination that unions will not be allowed to exist or function has become the norm in corporate America. Any gains for organized labor must now be extracted with a hammer.

CAPITALISM IS LIKE NUCLEAR POWER. IT IS A MIGHTY FORCE CAPABLE OF producing great energy that can be harnessed for human progress—but if you don't keep it tightly controlled, it will poison everything. The logic of capitalism is simple and relentless, a financial version of the sci-fi nanobots programmed to replicate themselves that end up turning the entire planet into gray goo. That logic pushes companies to maximize profits and, consequently, to push labor costs as close to zero as possible. It is a logic that is intensified with every level of economic abstraction, growing more prominent as you move from employee to business owner to investor to, at its peak, private equity and hedge funds and other investment vehicles that are completely removed from the human reality of what produces their wealth. Left to its own devices, this system will always trend in the direction of its final form, which is a tiny handful of incredibly rich people living in infinitely luxurious bubbles served by equally infinite armies of low-wage labor. A nation in which we have both a $7.25 per hour federal minimum wage and multiple centibillionaires building private space rockets to escape our overheating planet has already progressed a little too far down this dystopian road for comfort.

The project of distilling great wealth and power into few hands is always made harder by organized labor power. No matter how you brand it, the labor movement is fundamentally socialist. It works to empower the many, not the few; it tends to produce greater equality, rather than inequality; and the ability of global capitalism to achieve its preferred state of the world is limited in direct proportion to the ability of workers to reserve power for themselves. It is possible to imagine an enlightened form of capitalism that is happy to subject itself to democratic power-sharing and to spread its material bounty widely in the interest of collective peace. But in practice, though these conditions may flourish more in certain times and places, they will always be at risk from the demands that inexorably flow from shareholder capitalism. The profit motive is a simple killer robot that will never stop trying to take as much money as possible from labor's pockets. It has a fiduciary duty, after all. Any overly optimistic approach to labor organizing that relies on building goodwill with business will, in the long run, fails. Capitalism and labor are cats and dogs. Each will revert to its nature in time.

Power. That is all that works. The hammer, not the handshake. The labor movement has always won things by fighting. It has taken what it has because it got strong enough to do so, and it has lost much of what it once had because it got too weak to keep it. Getting that power back demands, first of all, having the people—the people who are the workers who do the work that produces all the wealth, and who can withhold that work as leverage to get their fair share. Unions today don't have enough of the people. They have been content to huddle on their shrinking islands for far too long. Ten percent of the workforce ain't gonna cut it in a world of trillion-dollar corporations. We will organize more people, or we will anticlimactically wither away.

Union membership is not the same as membership in a self-selecting affinity group. It is not like a political party or a book club or an activist group, in which the only people who join will be those who are predisposed to have the same set of likes and dislikes as the organization itself. Giving people a union is not giving them a mandatory set of beliefs they must buy into; it is giving them *power*. Unions in different places and in different industries will do a lot of different things because a union represents the ability of workers to collectively enact their own will. This natural capacity for variation in what unions are doing can distract the labor movement from thinking about the big picture. It is tempting to focus on the individual battles that different unions are always fighting at any given time. But the big picture is the one that shows you why going to all this trouble is necessary in the first place.

One thing that we can say with absolute certainty is this: increasing union density will change America for the better. It is the single most straightforward adjustment that will begin to reset the skewed balance of power between labor and capital. It will reduce economic and racial and gender inequality. It will reduce workplace injuries and sexual harassment and discrimination, and it will promote humane schedules and higher wages and better health care. It will provide a bulwark against the ravages of the gig economy, the Uber-ization of every job that has deprived millions of Americans of ever achieving long-term career stability. It will meaningfully improve conditions in entire industries, even for nonunion workers. It will represent a concrete, measurable step in the right direction for an entire universe of metrics of social good, which have all been weakened by the flow of capital away from the many and toward the few. Achieving these things will involve dozens, hundreds, thousands of individual battles. But in aggregate, the improvements will be tangible. We can say these things with confidence because what we are describing is the difference between a situation in which most working people have almost no power, and the situation in which they have some. You don't have to know what someone will build when you give them a hammer to know that if you don't give them one, they won't be able to build anything.

The other thing to understand is that organized labor can be its own political power center, one that sits outside of electoral politics. This notion is foreign to most Americans, who have been trained their entire lives to imagine "politics" as a straightforward game of red versus blue, leavened perhaps by some color on the fringes, measured by elections. Politics is presented to the public in the same manner as NFL football: a game between two teams that you can get rabid about, but can't really affect. Labor, unlike traditional political partisanship, comes with a direct form of power—the fact that workers do the work, and can shut the world down if they stop doing the work—and an effective, functional, national labor movement can leverage this power to bring politicians to heel. A model of politics that involves organizing with coworkers and building power on the job and

winning material gains and becoming part of a larger union that is able to
exercise broader economic and political power on behalf of workers just like
you is far more inspiring than one that involves idly yelling at the cable news
hatefest of your choice. Much of the cynicism that the public feels about our
political process, and the accompanying disillusionment with democracy
itself, arises as a rational response to the fact that the average person does not
have any influence at all in politics. You can't fight city hall, and you can't
fight the big corporations, and the rich people control all the politicians. So
why try? This sense of futility, bolstered by a lifelong experience of having
two eyes and living in this country, is too strong to be dissolved by celeb-
rity cheerleading and "Rock the Vote!" campaigns. But show someone their
power in action, and watch that cynicism fall away. Regular people cannot
make big political donations or hire lobbyists or mingle in Davos and DC
with the power brokers. But they can organize a union at their job. Yes they
can. And when they do, these long-ignored people will see the world's most
rich and powerful corporate leaders leap to attention. From the smallest seed
of desire for basic fairness at your crappy job, the labor movement can guide
anyone down a long and fruitful path of political awakening.

This path begins at work and leads progressively to power and consciousness at the city and state and national and, sometimes, global level. Hotel
room cleaners in Las Vegas become serious players in presidential elections.
Longshoremen in South Carolina project their will to ports around the
globe. Forgotten fast food workers in a tiny town in West Virginia carry on a
struggle for dignity that began a century ago in the state's coal mines. Labor
organizing is the *only* thing that offers all these groups of regular people a
democratic path to power. It is a daunting path. It is a path that demands a
lifetime of effort, a path that often leads upward only after a punishing series
of setbacks. But it is a path. It ain't bullshit. It's real.

Giving every working person a chance to plug into this current of latent
power is the first and most important task of the labor movement. It is a
job that the labor movement as it is constructed today does poorly. Regular
people need to know what a union does, know how to start one, and have
access to the trained organizers and lawyers and other resources that are
necessary to do so. They need support to get union cards signed and win

a union election in a hostile workplace and successfully negotiate a union contract. Outside of specific islands of union power in certain industries in certain cities, the infrastructure for this does not really exist. Where it does, it is usually ad hoc. Workers often must rely on the luck of having a family member or friend who can connect them with the right people. That is a prayer, not a system. It is a sad irony that the greatest failure of organized labor as an institution is that it is not very good at organizing.

We know that most unions do not spontaneously organize themselves. It takes a modicum of guidance and expertise. As Felix Allen at Lowe's and countless other enthusiastic workers like him across the country have learned, it is hard to organize an independent union from scratch with nothing but idealism to sustain it. Companies can and will lay out a field of landmines, from intimidation to endless legal challenges, that make success not impossible, but statistically unlikely. Unions know how to navigate these things. They have organizers to keep the process moving and lawyers to handle the paperwork and communications experts to get sympathetic press and a treasury to print up a bunch of T-shirts and stickers and picket signs. Working people are fully capable of organizing and running their own unions once they have learned how to do so. But they need to be given the tools and taught how they work. (The "teach a man to fish" metaphor does require the existence of teachers.) We have to provide access to this basic set of tools to every worker, everywhere. It is a straightforward task that can be accomplished by the smart expenditure of resources. Yet it is so, so far from being done.

In January 2015, the *Washington Post* published its story headlined "Why Internet journalists don't organize." It purported to explain the "generational" and "structural" reasons why unions had never penetrated the online media industry. Five months later, we had unionized Gawker Media. Why was the story's thesis wrong? Because in 2015, for the first time ever, a union organizer sat down and talked to us about unionizing and then helped us do it. Our industry had no unions while no unions were trying to unionize it. Once a union really began to try, our industry got unions. Beware of big theories where simple explanations will suffice.

Public support for unions is higher now than it has been in more than fifty years. Tens of millions of people understand that unions are good and wish that they had one. Most of these people will not get a union, unless the institutions of organized labor get their shit together and create the infrastructure necessary to make it happen. There is an enormous chasm preventing Americans from realizing the opportunity of this moment. That chasm is the amount of work that must be done and the money that must be spent by the labor movement to turn the passing moment into permanent institutions. It would be dishonest not to admit that there is a very strong possibility this grand opportunity will be squandered by a lazy, unimaginative union establishment. That is sad, but it is true.

As I wrote this book, I kept coming back to something that D. Taylor, the hardboiled international president of Unite Here, told me. I was asking him, as I asked everyone, about how the labor movement could scale up organizing—how it could become, in effect, more like Unite Here, a union with a stronger commitment to continuous organizing than many of its peers. Taylor shook his head and admitted that he experienced the same problem in his own union. "Human nature is to be conservative once you have something," he said.

With that, he had put his finger on the structural flaw that has consigned unions to their shrinking island of membership for many decades. A group of working people form a union. They win gains for themselves in contracts. The more they win, the more they take on the characteristics of an institution, with the natural conservatism that plagues all existing institutions. Their direct concern is serving their own members. Those members vote for the union's leaders. Those leaders decide how to expend union resources with an eye toward what will please that constituency. Unions that have been around for long enough to become established have a built-in incentive structure to focus their time, effort, and resources on keeping existing members happy. Where does that leave workers who don't have unions? Nowhere. Thus, in many unions for many years, new organizing—the work of proactively reaching out into the hostile, nonunion world and doing the time-consuming and expensive job of organizing new workers—is viewed as a luxury, as charity work, if not as an outright drag on the union's resources. Union members pay the dues that sustain the union. If those union members are not particularly ideological, and have not been taught to think of themselves as part of a larger movement, they can become like grumpy suburban taxpayers, asking why their hard-earned dollars are going to help some people they don't even know.

This dynamic explains why unions as a whole have failed to react energetically to the existential threat of their own decline in American society. As long as a union president can satisfy his little pool of existing members, it is of no great consequence to his own life if that pool is gradually shrinking. Maybe his union shrank from a million to half a million members. So what? That is still plenty of members to pay the (usually quite healthy!) salaries of the union's leadership team. Despite the fact that new organizing is the most important thing that unions can do to strengthen society, there is little direct short-term incentive for union leaders to work very hard at it. So many of them don't. And here we are. Ideology, it turns out, is a thin reed to rely upon to save us all from inequality's trap. I have sat through meetings in my own union where elected leaders, striking a pose of fiscal responsibility, asked, "Why are we doing all this organizing?" It made me yell, and it made me grind my teeth, and it made me feel sick. But such attitudes are baked into the conventional wisdom of many unions in a way that is not easy to eradicate.

This is true not only within unions, but by extension within larger labor institutions like the AFL-CIO. That vital group's constituency is not "working people as a whole," but rather a group of fifty-five leaders of individual unions, each of whom is accountable to their own members. The tendency to cater to those already inside the unions rather than to anyone outside of them is reinforced by this structure. Thus, the maddening lack of urgency among those charged with taking care of this shrinking island. Organized labor has found itself with too many interior decorators and not enough builders, absorbed with spiffing up a few old houses rather than building more to meet the overwhelming needs of the population.

Of course, there is one group with a powerful incentive to organize: the 90 percent of working Americans who do not have a union. They are being taken advantage of at work, and they know it. They need to work two jobs where one used to suffice; once-stable careers have been turned into "gigs," which offer nothing but an endless hustle until death; and everyone, everywhere watched as "essential workers" were cynically encouraged to risk their lives to maintain America's consumption during Covid, and promptly forgotten as soon as the coast was clear. People know that the situation is fucked up. They want to do something. They just need to know what, and how. The raw demand for some sort of protection from corporate domination constitutes a humongous opportunity for the unions and true believers who do have the will to organize. That is why charismatic leaders like Sara Nelson, who can wave the flag of unions high enough for people to see it, are so important. There are thousands of smart, ideologically driven, committed union leaders and organizers and activist members strewn all over this country, doing the arduous work of helping workers realize and use their power. In order for there to be a real, nationwide labor movement, though—to make us all a unified force, rather than a very lightly connected universe of separate interests—there must be national leaders who have credibility both inside of organized labor, and in the wider world where all those millions of future members must come from. It's not so easy to identify leaders who fit this profile. Union insiders often have no charisma, and charismatic activists often don't have a strong, established union power base, and those who possess both mostly exist in local areas or within specific industries, without a broad public profile. Sara Nelson is not the only good labor leader in America, but she is one of the few who checks all the boxes for becoming a labor *movement* leader.

The unfortunate secret of the labor movement is that it doesn't really exist. I spent years looking for its center before coming to this conclusion. Organized labor is not organized. It is a roiling pot of molten metal that has not yet been shaped into a useful tool. This is partly because organized labor is persecuted by capital and its hired forces, yes, but that is a trivial answer. It will *always* be persecuted. That's the nature of the thing. If you announce your intention to climb Mount Everest, you can't complain about the altitude. It comes with the job. If unions cannot function successfully in an atmosphere of persecution, we might as well give up.

There is so much to be done. The first thing is to simply create the infrastructure for people to have access to labor organizers. Everywhere. That means opening offices with trained organizers in every state, promoting their existence to the general public, and expanding their capacity as needed. Until the average worker in South Carolina knows what a union is and how to start organizing one, this job is not done. How to pull off a project like this is no great mystery—every fast food chain in existence manages to do it, providing a uniform customer experience whether you're in Maine or California. It requires a national level of coordination and an adequate pot of resources to deploy. I refuse to believe that the entirety of organized labor is incapable of matching the organizing prowess of Taco Bell.

It will take some billions of dollars over a number of years to credibly build a national organizing project. In the context of the combined resources of unions in America, which are in the tens of billions, this is not an unreasonable amount of money. Currently, labor organizing is not a major spending priority for do-gooder foundations. Even those that do concern themselves with labor and inequality tend to fund meta-labor nonprofits that produce white papers far more than they produce actual unionized workers. Nor do unions use their government lobbying clout to extract money specifically for organizing, despite the fact that the National Labor Relations Act makes it the policy of the federal government to "encourage collective bargaining." Now is the time to get aggressive on both of these fronts—to think in terms of building a combined private and public revenue stream capable of funding what needs to be done, rather than an unsteadily dripping faucet of internal union money that funds a tiny, inadequate portion of what needs to be done. All this revenue is just seed capital. Unions, once they are established, pay for themselves through member dues. In the long run, organizing is an investment, not an expense. In this case, it is an investment from unions in their own continued existence, and one that will produce an environment that is more and more conducive to its own success, as union density increases and the political and economic balance of power changes. It is a good investment.

In addition to the primary mandate of organizing more new workers, the quickest way to expand labor power is to scale up the things that we already know will work. Unite Here's model of building political influence on city and state levels via the relentless organizing of an economically vital industry and nonstop internal organizing to keep those workers mobilized is a good example of a strategy that could be used to great effect in many, many more places than it is now. So, too, is the type of dogged commitment, statewide planning, and coordination between multiple unions that produced the victorious unionization of child care workers in California. Transforming Republican cities into livable places for the working class, or unifying tens of thousands of far-flung, isolated workers into a coherent industrywide union, are the sort of ambitious goals that the labor movement should have. They are also long-term goals that require long-term planning and long-term investment and long-term commitment. They require thinking big. They require the vision to look at a bunch of unorganized, powerless workers and see the path that runs from labor organizing to political power to a new world.

The promising upsurge in enthusiasm for unions will inevitably recede if it is not able to find any useful outlet. Workers who organize independently of existing unions—whether they are surrounded by press attention like the Amazon Labor Union, or just a determined guy sitting on a folding chair in a parking lot at Lowe's—must be actively sought out and showered with support. There is no asset more valuable to the labor movement than those workers who care enough about this stuff that they are willing to take the first step. They must be treasured, rather than ignored or shunted aside by unions too busy for them. When brave workers like the ones at Tudor's Biscuit World in Elkview do find unions willing to help them, it is vital that those unions not be stretched so thin that they have to give less time to one campaign in order to pick up another. In this sense, unions need to do something that businesses do very well: generate demand for themselves and grow their capacity to meet that demand. Failure to do this is a major reason why unions have been getting their asses kicked by business for so long.

The demand is already there. For those inclined to pay attention, the post-pandemic years have felt like a vibrating hive of newfound labor energy. Cornell University's "strike tracker" tallied an average of a strike somewhere in America every single day in 2022. Successful union drives at Amazon and Starbucks brought the viability of organizing into the consciousness of the general public. The National Labor Relations Board said that petitions for union elections in 2022 were up 53 percent from the previous year. You could take your pick of breathless odes from the many official annual reports across the political spectrum. "Organized labor appears to be having a moment," said the White House Council of Economic Advisers. "We are on the cusp of witnessing what has the potential to be one of the most pro-union eras in modern history," said prominent anti-union law firm Littler Mendelson. Everyone seemed to agree that it felt like a vibe shift had arrived.

The more you zoomed out, though, the harder it was to be impressed. The number of workers who participated in major strikes was still nowhere close to its highs from the 1970s. After being hailed as the most pro-union president of our lifetimes, Joe Biden ended the year by imposing a contract on railroad workers that they didn't want, crushing the possibility of an inordinately consequential strike. Inflation had eaten up much of the modest pandemic-induced wage gains for workers, even as corporations posted record profits. In 2023, major strikes in Hollywood and the auto industry displayed what union power was capable of, but access to strong unions remained out of reach for most. And all the attention that certain high-profile union drives had gotten had not been enough to actually raise union density, which still hovered barely above single digits.

The opportunity of the moment is real. The widespread desire for union is real. The need for unions is real. And yet, and yet, and yet. The labor movement can make you feel crazy. Whenever I think about it too much, I always start to imagine millions of people, powerless and oppressed, trudging out to break rocks with their bare hands. Scattered on the ground around them are the pieces of a hammer. But nobody points them out. Nobody picks them up. And nobody puts them all together.

=

AFTER MANY YEARS OF SLOTH AND EXCUSES, I FINALLY WENT TO THE NEW York City Labor Day Parade. It was a warm September Saturday morning, and the side streets for many blocks north of Bryant Park were jammed with delegations from every union in the city, bristling with floats and restless union members waiting for their chance to start stepping.

My union, the Writers Guild of America, East, was lucky to be near the front of the marching order list. We got an early start. We strode like gods down the middle of blocked-off Fifth Avenue, jeering at Trump Tower as we passed. The sidewalks were not any more crowded than usual, but the street itself was packed. It was the most inclusive parade I've ever been to, in the sense that almost everyone who wanted to come to the Labor Day Parade was free to march in it as a worker.

The finish line was up at Sixty-Fourth Street, where a little tent and a modest viewing stand had been set up. Labor Secretary Marty Walsh stood there robotically shaking hands. After we had finished our official stroll, a few union friends and I loitered on the next block, cheering on each passing group of union members as they rolled by: the American Federation of Musicians, with their full band; the various building trade unions that showed up with a fleet of Harleys and matching biker vests, purposely gunning their engines when they passed the "Quiet, Please" signs erected outside of the fancy Central Park East buildings; and an endless procession of people in matching union T-shirts of every possible description.

"Heyyyyy, carpenters!" we would yell. "Let's go, steelworkers! Alright, pipe fitters! Yeahhhhhhhh!" Many of the marchers were tired by the time they got to us. Our cheers would make them perk up. Hey, flight attendants! Hey, electrical workers! Hey, nurses and teachers! Hotel workers and boilermakers! Bus drivers and painters! Artists and carpenters! Hey, hey, hey! Alright!

We didn't know them, and they didn't know us. But we were all here, together. They would smile, and we would cheer louder. And in response, always, they would raise their fists. It was the purest feeling I'd had all year. Hey, strangers. Hey, friends. Hey, workers of the world. Pick up that hammer, and start smashing.

ACKNOWLEDGMENTS

Neither this book nor anything else I've ever done would be possible without my parents, Becky and David, who taught me to read, write, and think about righteousness. I also owe a lifelong debt of gratitude to my sister Sudie, who has given her little brother many years of encouragement and support, even though she is much busier and harder-working than me by any reasonable standard.

Being a "professional writer" is the kind of ridiculous job that is much easier to pursue if you have the sort of overconfidence that a loving family instills in you. I am lucky enough to have an excellent extended family that is too large to name individually, yet is small enough that I get to see them all on a regular basis. To all my relatives in all of the various winding branches (including all extensions by marriage!) of the Nolan, Hamilton, Cassimatis, and Rigolot families, thank you for everything you have done for me over the years. My aunt and uncle Jennie Skillman and Jim Skillman, two people who lived their lives in dedication to the cause of social justice, especially helped to inspire this book. To my nieces, Lilo, Elena, and Silla: I won't get mad if you don't read the whole book, but I do expect you all to save the world. You have what it takes.

Thank you to my agent, Jud Laghi, who made this book a reality by teaching me how to write a book proposal that would actually sell, and waiting patiently for years to make his first dollar from me. And thank you to my editor, Brant Rumble, who enabled me to write the book that I wanted.

You are both wise men (depending on how the reviews go). Thank you to the entire team at Hachette, who did the work of copy editing, design, layout, printing, distribution, marketing, and promotion of this book. It wouldn't exist without you.

To whatever extent I am a serviceable writer, I must thank all of the colleagues I've had over the course of my career in journalism, at *Folio Weekly*, *PRWeek*, *Gawker*, *Deadspin*, *Splinter*, *In These Times*, and all the other places that have published my stuff. In particular, thank you to the editors and reporters who helped me learn to write, and later indulged me when I whined about how much I hated being edited—a group that includes, but is not limited to, Anne Schindler, Julia Hood, Nick Denton, A. J. Daulerio, Tommy Craggs, John Cook, Max Read, Alex Pareene, Tom Scocca, Aleks Chan, Jack Mirkinson, Jessica Stites, Sarah Lazare, Miles Kampf-Lassin, Amana Fontanella-Khan, Bucky Turco, the Defector idiots, the Giggle Kids, and David Carr.

I became an official, card-carrying union member in 2015, when Gawker Media unionized. For this I thank all my coworkers there who were brave enough to take that leap into what was then the great unknown—and all of the later members of the GMG and G/O Media unions, who fought against an ongoing series of new owners and bad bosses to try to protect the people who do the work at those companies. Thank you to the Writers Guild of America, East, for opening its doors to us. And thank you, especially, to the organizers and other staff members—including Justin Molito, Ursula Lawrence, Megan McRobert, and everyone else—who guided us, helped us through crises, and put up with all of our complaints. One of the greatest privileges of my career has been watching the ongoing wave of unionization in the media industry. To the thousands of people who have done the work of organizing your newsrooms and trying to make this industry better, I credit you for being the one thing powerful enough to overwhelm my considerable cynicism about journalism. Keep kicking ass.

My years as an elected council member at the WGAE taught me more about politics and the reality of how unions function than anything I have ever read. Thank you to all my allies there. And thank you just as much to the people there who made me mad many times about many different things, which forced me to remind myself that we're all on the same side. Getting extremely mad is vital to achieving a true understanding of unions. Please, never stop organizing.

All labor reporting is about people. I extend my heartfelt thanks to every working person who spoke to me during the reporting of this book. Your stories—the small ones contained in this book, and all the parts before and after that didn't make it into these pages—are the most important thing of all. Thank you to the many dedicated union staffers and officials and true believers who spoke to me as well. You build the structures that sustain this movement. If your name appears in this book (or if you spoke to me on background), I thank you for generously taking the time to participate. The most committed people who work in organized labor tend to be the most modest. But I see you, and appreciate you. Special thanks to the communications staffers who helped to facilitate portions of the reporting of this book, including Bethany Khan, Diana Hussein, Kate Moulding, MJ Leira, Denae Ayala, Dan Arel, Taylor Garland, and others.

In my journey as a union member and labor journalist I have been graciously mentored by many fellow labor reporters, activists, academics, and badass people who have passed on their wisdom and commiserated over every battle. Thank you to Kim Kelly, Michelle Miller, the Solidarity Slate, Steven Greenhouse, and the hundreds of other compadres who fit this description. In my journey as a human, I have benefited from the love and friendship of many great people. For the sake of the poor readers I am not going to write all of your names here, but you know who you are. Thank you.

During the time that I was working on this book, I was aided by a number of organizations that provided me with grants and other support. Thank you to the Economic Hardship Reporting Project, the Omidyar Network's Reporters in Residence program, Roy Bahat's worker power storytelling grants, and MacDowell. Your assistance made the past two years of my life much less punishing than they otherwise would have been. You are champs.

The coolest thing about the labor movement is that it offers anyone a chance to be a hero. All you have to do is unionize your workplace, and you will have done something that will help out your coworkers, their families, your community, and, by extension, the whole damn country. That's something to be proud of. If this book inspires one person to do that, it will have been worth it. If that person is you, I thank you in advance.

INDEX